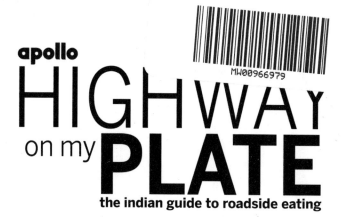

apollo
HIGHWAY
on my PLATE
the indian guide to roadside eating

Based on the television show 'Highway on my Plate',
researched and directed by Small Screen
for NDTV Good Times

apollo
HIGHWAY
on my PLATE
the indian guide to roadside eating

ROCKY SINGH

&

MAYUR SHARMA

RANDOM HOUSE INDIA

First published by Random House India in 2010
Eighth impression in 2011

Text photos by Rocky Singh
Back cover photos by Prashant Sareen

Random House Publishers India Private Limited
Windsor IT Park, 7th Floor, Tower-B,
A-1, Sector-125, Noida-201301 (UP)

Random House Group Limited
20 Vauxhall Bridge Road
London SW1V 2SA
United Kingdom

978 81 8400 136 5

Typeset in PMN Caecilia by InoSoft Systems, Noida
Printed and bound in India by Replika Press

Contents

To the people of India we have met on our travels. Thank you all for sharing yourselves so generously and welcoming rather intimidating looking strangers with so much warmth and such awesome food. To the songs we have sung together, the dances we have danced and to the conversations on the street corner over a cup of 'chai'. Above all, thank you for all the love. There's no place like India in the world, where strangers become family with just one smile.

Acknowledgements

No life is complete without the people we hold close. No task can be done without the support of family and friends. This show could not have been made and consequently this book could not have been written without some such people. Without them the status the show enjoys would have been diminished, or perhaps never attained. We start with our parents.

To our parents who made sure we feasted well through the real journey, the journey of life! In their homes, food is love made visible. And now the ladies. Thank you Rupali Singh and Michelle Sharma. The women behind the men. Thank you for being supportive over those long distance calls month after month. Thank you for holding fort, for running the homes, for filing the tax returns, for getting school admissions for the kids, and for all those things you have had to do on our behalf. Above all thank you for the love. We're lucky and words will never be enough.

At NDTV Good Times, Monica Narula, thank you for taking a chance with us and believing that we could do it. You're our star and may you always shine; and the smile really helps. Stop bullying us now. Thanks to Tanu Ganguly for hanging in there through the hard times, Shibani Khanna for the advice, inputs, always pleasant disposition and encouragement and, last but not the least, Smeeta Chakrabarti for the support and faith. Angels do exist.

The longest journeys begin with just one step. We had been travelling and eating on the highways of this country since the mid-eighties and it was because of this 'expertise' that Abhinandan Sekhri (Niku), our producer/director called us to screen test for this show. It felt right the very first time we did it. We were in and 'Highway On My Plate' began.

Niku, you are crazy (you part Surd and part Tam-Bram maniac)!! Don't let the world fix that. We have had a lot of fun running down the path you showed us. You broke the ground when we needed a trail, you're a star! The show is a testament to the craziness that the three of us create when we are together. Thanks Niku, it cannot be done without you and may the madness prevail.

Prashant Sareen (producer) sat stoically through it all and drove across the country just for the hell of it. Thank you for all the arguments Prashant. Life and the show would have been a little dull without them. Thanks for putting your money where our mouth was and driving while we all slept. We've come a long way together and you're the man, so what if your name is 'Happy'!

We started with some weird angles and shots that people felt were 'not going to work.' We did not address the camera, we ran all over the place, we switched frames constantly and Ajay Arya (Ajju on the camera) followed the action and even led it. His pure Hindi and impure sense of humour has remained a constant source of enlightenment for us.

Giri Raj (GJ, camera) solidly followed us through thick and thin, downhill and across dale, never complaining even if his angle required him to lie down in fine sand or stand up to his neck in fast flowing water, thank you for always getting the shot.

Vaidyanathan (Vaidehi, audio) put up with some of the most insane sounds ever recorded as we sang, screamed, and hammered our way through the series. 'LONG LIVE TAMIL NADU' Vaidehi, and may you never have to climb another snow covered mountain. Thank you for teaching us how to curse in Tamil and for all those screams of 'Kunnu Pudavai' (I will kill you).

Deep Sir, our wise camera assistant, may you continue to write those (terrible) poems, that we are too polite to tell you, are horrible. And stop calling Vaidehi 'BEDI' even though your strong Himachali accent will not allow it. Thank you for always, uncomplainingly staying with the task at hand no matter how hard.

S'tish (driver, Satish) who has been our stout and strong driver taking us through the whole country complaining constantly about what the roads are doing to his beloved car. 'Hariyana mein kehte hain unpad jaat pade likhe barabar' (it is said in Haryana that an un-educated Jaat is as capable as a well educated man). You're that man. Thank you for the safe driving that allowed us to sleep in peace between gruelling shoots on tight schedules.

Subodh Gupta (production controller), who has come a long way himself, has handled things immaculately and done a great job, always. Even when no one has appreciated it. Well done Mr Gupta and all that at the ripe age of 23. Wish you many good things.

It takes a special kind of madness to edit a crazy show like this one, Thank you Vishal Verma, Bishwajeet Singh, and Mehraj Ali for making us look normal! All's good.

To those who came and went and contributed immensely, Sunil Khanna (audio, Season 1), Hitesh Chauhan (camera, Season 1), Shiv Das (audio, Seasons 3, 6, and 8).

Thank you all, many times over.

To Priyanka Sarkar, our able editor, for her untiring work and endless patience, Rachel Tanzer who always goes the extra mile and always with a smile, and Chiki Sarkar for the idea in the first place, thank you all at Random House.

How to use the book

Travelling in India? Want to eat fresh, hot, and delicious food? Then read on.

This book is for times when you're on the open road, highway, or in another city/town, or state and you suffer sudden hunger pangs. Need to grab a bite? Then open the book, and:

1. Pick a state. All states have been organized alphabetically.
2. Open the first page and ta daaa there's a map, before every section.
3. Orient yourself and move on to the town closest to you. Towns have also been organized alphabetically.
4. Under every town are the dhabas or the most famous street foods in or around it.
5. The first paragraph is a bit about the dhaba. We also have something on the side, bit of juicy tidbit about the place to bite on.
6. Specialities have been listed and, very important, the prices along with contact details.
7. Ratings:

   Taste:
   9/10: Unique and/or exceptional. A must have!
   7/8: Very good, well worth a visit
   5/6: Indifferent
   3/4: Barely edible
   1/2: Avoid it at all costs

   Ambience:
   9/10: Amazing location/setting, a must-visit.
   7/8: Good feel, pleasant. (Remember the rating is for a dhaba-style place).
   5/6: Average
   3/4: Avoidable setting
   1/2: Terrible, you will not be able to eat here.

Service:
9/10: Speedy, fast, accurate, and very attentive.
7/8: Good service. Friendly
5/6: Indifferent.
3/4: Inefficient or rough.
1/2: Rude or no service.

Value for Money:
9/10: A great price for the taste. Very worth the money.
7/8: Well priced, suits the pocket.
5/6: Average for the kind of food.
3/4: Overpriced and not worth it.
1/2: Ridiculously overpriced for what you get.

Wishing you smooth and happy highways!

ANDHRA PRADESH

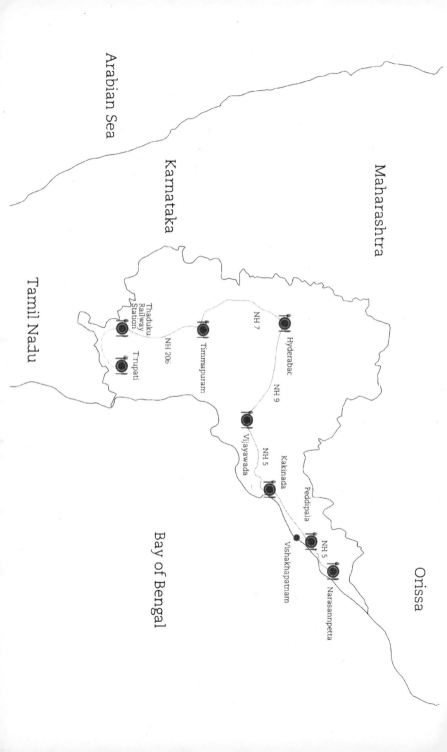

Hyderabad

EAT STREET Eat Street is an ideal evening spot built along the lines of a food court. Along the bank of Hussain Sagar Lake, this place offers a great view while you stuff yourself with everything ranging from dosa to gelato. Hyderabad is a buzzing city full of young people in the BPO industry and techies from all over the country. At Eat Street they find whatever their taste buds desire. Even the multinational fast food chains have set up branches here.

The shops are arranged in a long row facing the lake and there is ample seating for everyone. The atmosphere is one of a party in full swing. Hundreds of young people gather here every evening to eat, watch the action, or simply 'hang out'. Come here for your pizzas, burgers, kathi rolls, Italian dishes, dosas, and a variety of desserts.

SOMETHING ON THE SIDE The city of 'Cyberabad' attracts people from all over the country and the food choices in Hyderabad reflect this. Today, you can get almost any type of food in the city that was once famed only for its biryani.

Rocky's Verdict: A nice place to bring the kids, hang out, and eat some fast food.
Rating: Taste: 6, Ambience: 9, Service: 6, Value for Money: 4, Total: 25
Specialities: Multinational pizza chains, fast food, and ice creams
Veg/Non-veg: Non-veg
Contact Details/Timings: Necklace Road, Hussain Sagar Lake, Hyderabad.
Prices: Pizza chains sell pizzas from ₹ 150 all the way up to ₹ 1000 depending on size and toppings. Ice creams are for ₹ 75 and gelatos can even go to as high as ₹ 100 per scoop

GOKUL CHAAT Located adjacent the Women's College, this place is famous for its amazing chaat. The mirchi bhaji is a delightful batter fried green chilli. The ragada (crushed) samosa and kachori are delicious and are served with piping hot chana (chickpeas) from a giant cauldron which lies bang in the middle of screaming staff, yelling customers, and fast moving waiters. Almost all items are less than ₹ 20 and are served hot and spicy. Make sure you grab some kulfi or an ice cream softy before you leave.

SOMETHING ON THE SIDE The shop is guarded by shutters and has tight security after the bomb blasts of August 2007 but it remains as popular as ever. This place is always crowded and being asked to wait is not unusual. The shop itself is mainly used to store all the chaat items for sale although a few things are prepared inside the shop itself. The staff communicate vocally and scream at the top of their voices to be heard, adding to the high decibel levels in the place.

Rocky's Verdict: A nice place for chaat and snacks. If you're in the vicinity you should pop in.
Rating: Taste: 7, Ambience: 6, Service: 3, Value for Money: 8, Total: 24
Specialities: Mirchi bhaji, ragada samosa, kachori, and kulfi
Veg/Non-veg: Veg
Contact Details/Timings: Gokul Chaat, Women's College Road, Hyderabad. Phone: 0-9849206521
Prices: Almost all items are for less than ₹ 20

MEDINA HOTEL Medina Hotel is a Hyderabadi landmark. This is possibly the best known place in Andhra Pradesh for haleem. Most of the clientele is here for their breakfast and you can tell that they are regulars. Nihari, the ever popular breakfast favourite, is available most mornings. This delicacy is prepared by boiling the paya (hooves) and zabaan (tongue) overnight and then removing them, leaving the stock which is prepared using a traditional secret recipe to yield the soupy, delicious nihari. All you need to do is go to the counter and choose your hoof or tongue which is then dipped in a generous portion of the steaming, soupy stock and served to you. The nihari is so nourishing that they say that once you eat it in the morning you will sleep till the afternoon! In the afternoons and evenings you can expect the usual meat specialities.

SOMETHING ON THE SIDE Remember that haleem is only served during the holy month of Ramzan. If you go there at any other time you will find a slightly run-down place that has seen better days.

> **Rocky's Verdict:** No visit to Hyderabad is complete without the haleem breakfast. First-timers must note that paya and zabaan are acquired tastes and may not be for everyone.
> **Rating:** Taste: 6, Ambience: 9, Service: 6, Value for Money: 4, Total: 25
> **Specialities:** Nihari and haleem
> **Veg/Non-veg:** Non-veg
> **Contact Details/Timings:** Nihari is available only in mornings. Medina Hotel, Medina Building, Hyderabad.
> Phone: 0-9391966528
> **Prices:** Paya and zabaan ₹ 25 and chicken curry ₹ 35

Kakinada

KAKINADA BEACH If you are feeling really adventurous then wake up at 5 am and head out to Kakinada port. Boats of all shapes and sizes pull up to the beach carrying fresh catch. The fish is laid out in areas on the beach and soon a crowd of people surrounds the sellers with everyone gesticulating and talking at the top of their voices. As a stranger you could be forgiven for expecting a fight to break out at any moment but strangely enough it never does. Fish of all types such as cod, grouper, tuna, and even large sharks and rays are on sale along with crabs, prawns, and anything else edible that was snared in the nets. Rates are decided depending on the size and type of fish and a large seven feet long shark can be bought for as little as ₹ 20,000.

SOMETHING ON THE SIDE   If you are hungry there are little carts and shacks on the beach selling fried food, hot tea, and little packets of the local cigars, which may be small in size but pack a punch like an angry boxer.

Mayur's Verdict: All the freshly caught seafood and the early hour may not leave you feeling hungry and yet it's a fantastic experience to see and learn where your food comes from. A good way to spend an early morning if you like your seafood and want to wake up to hot tea and cigars!
Specialities: Fresh seafood which does not get fresher than this.
Veg/Non-veg: Non-veg
Contact Details/Timings: Dawn at the beach
Prices: Whatever you can bargain for

KOTAIAH SWEETS   This open-sided sweet shop is the home of the kaja sweet. The kaja aka Kotaiah kaja aka Gottam kaja, is a cylindrical sweetmeat with a firm crisp exterior and a syrupy centre. Deep fried in ghee this is essentially a cylindrical version of the jalebi. The shop has been around since 1900 and the sweet was first made by Ponugumati Kotaiah in Guntur before he moved to Kakinada to set up this sweet stall.

The shop, now run by the fourth generation of Kotaiahs, has diversified its offerings and you can now order sweets like kaju burfi, Bournvita burfi, balaji laddus, dry fruit laddus, chegodis, etc. These range in price from around ₹ 180 per kg for the kaja to over ₹ 400 per kg for the dry fruit halwas, all of which can be bought at the shop or even ordered online.

SOMETHING ON THE SIDE   Popularly called gottam kaja for its tubular shape, Kotaiah's kaja proudly advertises its range of customers such as former chief minister (N.T. Ramarao), diplomats, politicians, NRIs, foreigners, high-ranking officials, film artists, producers and directors, middle class, and the lower rung of society.

Mayur's Verdict: If you are in the area, and you like Indian sweets, and want to take home a piece of Kakinada with you, then go to Kotaiah Sweets and get your happiness over the counter.
Rating: Taste: 7, Ambience: 6, Service: 8, Value for Money: 7, Total: 28
Specialities: Kaja
Veg/Non-veg: Veg
Contact Details/Timings: Kotaiah Sweets, Pallamraju Nagar, Kakinada. Phone: 0-9848659599
Prices: Kaja ₹ 180 per kg, dry fruit halwa ₹ 400 per kg

SUBBAYA HOTEL On a street in Kakinada is an interesting restaurant that looks like a house on the outside and a school on the inside. Sri Krishna Vilas, or Subbaya Hotel as it is popularly known, has been serving authentic Andhra food to passionate foodies in Kakinada and beyond since 1947.

Food is served on large green plantain leaves out of many containers carried as a set of four, and served to you. The thali costs ₹ 38 and for this sum you get more than ten items of food including three types of rice (plain, tomato, and lemon) along with dahi vada, dal, and a host of vegetables besides dahi and rasam. The pessarapullu and thondakaaya are unique both in appearance and taste. This being a meal you can ask for umpteen refills and need leave only when you are full.

The inside is a large, long hall with rows of wooden tables and chairs laid out to form a U, leaving space in the middle for the servers. The walls have beautiful tiles painted with images of Hindu deities and a large ornate statue with a garland of fresh flowers in the centre.

Meals are classified as set meals, tiffins, and parcels depending on whether you have them there, or they are being packed and delivered. Parcels are packed in woven cane baskets for up to three people and cost ₹ 65.

SOMETHING ON THE SIDE What we found unusual was that the food storage and kitchen area at the back are three times the size of the eating room and so large that they have a loudspeaker and microphone for coordination. Subbaya Hotel is so successful they send food out to cities and towns up to 150 km away!

Mayur's Verdict: Subtle flavours, incredible taste, and bright colours make for a meal that is brilliant visually and in taste. Almost makes you wish you were back in school, being served this kind of food! The owner, a kind and gentle old man, sits in the kitchen area every day to ensure that the quality of food served to guests is maintained.
Rating: Taste: 9, Ambience: 8, Service: 8, Value for Money: 10, Total: 35
Certified: Rocky and Mayur rating of excellence
Specialities: Thali, pessarapullu, and thondakaaya
Veg/Non-veg: Veg
Contact Details/Timings: Subbaya Hotel, Nageshwar Rao Street, Kakinada.
Prices: Thali ₹ 38 and parcels for up to three people ₹ 65

Narasannpetta

VAIRA MODERN HOTEL This is a no-frills eating place serving food made in the rustic Andhra style. The thalis being 'All You Can Eat', with plenty of pickles, onions, and even a glass of buttermilk thrown in, makes this the best value-for-money place we have come across in our travels. The staple in the thali is a puffy short-grained wild rice. The main course is vankai (brinjal), dal, sambar, yogurt, and a beetroot preparation. For the non-vegetarians there's egg and chicken curry.

The Vaira is set amidst stunning green fields and looks like a large hut with a thick thatched roof and no walls. It has rows of immovable stone tables and benches arranged in a rectangular pattern with the serving area in the middle. As you walk in, you will find pattals (leaf plates) and a glass of water laid out for all comers. Carry a bottle of water as there is none available here and the strong spices in the food will soon have you trying to douse the fire in your mouth.

Be warned, they work on a very punctual time system and lunch is from noon to 3 pm. YOU WILL NOT BE SERVED if you are even five minutes late, so make sure you're on time. After a meal lie down and enjoy the scenery.

SOMETHING ON THE SIDE The spread on offer is an incredible value for money and it is surprising as to how the owners can make a profit at the rates they charge. The only limitation they seem to insist on with the thali is that just one piece of chicken is allowed!

Rocky's Verdict: Surprisingly tasty food. This was a very enjoyable meal.
Rating: Taste: 8, Ambience: 3, Service: 6, Value for Money: 10, Total: 27
Specialities: Thali
Veg/Non-veg: Non-veg
Contact Details/Timings: Vaira Modern Hotel, Narasannpetta, NH5.
Prices: Non-veg ₹ 25, veg thali ₹ 25

Peddipala

AMAN PUNJAB DHABA This is a rustic and real Punjabi dhaba catering to all the Punjabi truck drivers who pass this way. Since this is the rice belt and most Punjabi drivers are not satisfied without their rotis all the Punjabi drivers seem to know about this place. Spicy tadka dal and Punjabi-style chana masala make this a worthwhile stop if you feel the urge for Punjabi food. Tasty aloo parathas in the morning and strong dhaba tea are the highlights here.

Other than the style of cooking the place is rather unremarkable. It does have the essential manjis and you are welcome to sleep the night here for the price of a meal.

SOMETHING ON THE SIDE Punjabi drivers starved for some thick rotis and ghee-laden dals are the regulars here. It is also a great place to get information about obscure roads from the visiting drivers.

Rocky's Verdict: Average Punjabi food.
Rating: Taste: 5, Ambience: 5, Service: 6, Value for Money: 7, Total: 23
Specialities: Aloo paratha and tea
Veg/Non-veg: Veg
Contact Details/Timings: About 30 km short of Visakhapatnam as you approach from the Peddipalam side on NH5. Aman Punjab Dhaba, Peddipalam, NH5. Phone: 0-9949946376
Prices: ₹ 30–50 per person. Dal ₹ 15 and the chana masala ₹ 20

Thaduku Railway Station

VENKATESH DHABA This truck drivers' stop is bang on the highway and is a basic open-sided dhaba with a thatched roof held up by wooden poles. The floor is simply packed mud and the open kitchen shares a room with the diners enjoying lunch sitting at plastic tables.

Meals are served on fresh green banana leaves and you are given some water to clean your leaf. You can order a vegetarian thali and add chicken curry if desired. Large helpings of rice are ladled out from a big bowl and dollops of different vegetables and dal are added alongside. The dal, called pappu, is a meal by itself and is thickened by cooking it with vegetables. Chicken curry or egg curry is served separately and can be added as desired. There are staples like cabbage, carrots, and brinjal. This being a thali you can ask for multiple refills of everything. There is an astonishing amount of chilli added to the food so do not be surprised to find yourself sweating as you eat.

SOMETHING ON THE SIDE   The language of choice is Telugu with the waiters only being able to understand a few words of Hindi and English, so be prepared to play some sign language games to order your meal.

Mayur's Verdict: This is a very basic dhaba and there was no evidence of people travelling by car stopping here. Rather it's a stop for those who are ravenous and are looking for good quantities of local food without any fuss or fanfare.
Rating: Taste: 6, Ambience: 5, Service: 7, Value for Money: 6, Total: 24
Specialities: Thali
Veg/Non-veg: Non-veg
Contact Details/Timings: Venkatesh Dhaba, Thaduku Railway Station, NH205.
Prices: Thali ₹ 30, chicken curry ₹ 30, and egg curry ₹ 7

Timmapuram

DOLPHIN DHABA   Almost all the dhabas along the highway in Andhra Pradesh have set mealtimes and you must not expect to get lunch past 3 pm. The Dolphin, however, does not adhere to these dhaba standards and is more relaxed with its timings. It offers indoor seating, but for those who like eating outdoors there are little huts where you can eat in privacy while enjoying a great view of the highway and the paddy fields.

This dhaba offers food from both the north and the south of India as well as the obligatory Chinese selection. The paneer butter masala and the dal fry are oily, heavily spiced, and not too tasty. The chicken biryani and mutton curry suffer from the same fate though the prawn curry served with rice is well cooked and flavourful. Free rasam is served along with the food and chilled buttermilk is available for ₹ 7 a glass.

SOMETHING ON THE SIDE   They have a little store selling packaged food, soft drinks, ice creams, perfumes, and deodorants!

Mayur's Verdict: Stop at the Dolphin for some packaged goodies to snack on as you continue down the highway or have a cup of tea and enjoy the amazing views of the sun setting over the paddy fields. If you want good food you might want to get here before 3 pm and eat at the Muskan which is across the road from the Dolphin and serves fresh, traditional fare.

Rating: Taste: 5, Ambience: 8, Service: 6, Value for Money: 6, Total: 25

Specialities: Prawn curry and rice

Veg/Non-veg: Non-veg

Contact Details/Timings: Dolphin Dhaba, Timmapuram, NH5. Phone: 0-9866122299

Prices: Paneer butter masala ₹ 40, chicken biryani ₹ 50, mutton curry ₹ 50, buttermilk ₹ 7

Tirupati

SRI VIJAYA VENKATESHWARA BHAWAN Bang opposite a row of five cinemas in the very busy TP Area, there are a couple of restaurants catering to hungry cinemagoers and other diners. You can eat standing at high tables put out just by the road and enjoy the view, the noise, and the traffic as you munch, or you can sit indoors and enjoy your meal at leisure. There is a separate room for families to eat in and though poorly lit, the area is clean and hygienic.

Multiple food options are available and you can eat a meal ordering items you prefer, a tiffin, which is a set course thali, or a parcel where you carry away packed food for consumption when and where you desire. The menu is huge with a choice of dosas, idlis, vadas, rice, sambar, dals, parathas, chole puri, and assorted vegetable dishes served on traditional banana leaves with chilli chutney, fried onions, and spicy gunpowder with ghee served on the side. The masala dosa and the perugu vada (₹ 15) are a must-try as are the thin golden layered parathas which feel really light while you eat them but later feel as light as bricks in your stomach!

The full meals are for ₹ 25, and considering you can ask for countless refills this is fantastic value for money. Parcels for take away are ₹ 35 and a la carte items range in price from ₹ 10 to ₹ 20 making this restaurant a gourmand's delight.

SOMETHING ON THE SIDE Try to eat here before the evening movie shows end and hordes of viewers descend on the eatery.

Mayur's Verdict: If you're watching a Telugu or a Bollywood film in this area and get hungry then this is the place to go to for truly fresh and tasty food. The service is excellent and the food comes quickly and steaming hot. The Tamil equivalent of popcorn maybe?
Rating: Taste: 7, Ambience: 5, Service: 8, Value for Money: 8, Total: 28
Specialities: Thali, masala dosa, perugu vada, and thin paratha
Veg/Non-veg: Veg
Contact Details/Timings: Sri Vijaya Venkateshwara Bhawan, TP Area, Tirupati. Phone: 0-9966050893
Prices: Full meals ₹ 25, parcels for takeaway ₹ 35, a la carte items ₹ 10 to ₹ 20, and perugu vada ₹ 15

SRI DAMODAR FAST FOODS This place really lives up to its name in that it is all about fast food. Most people either have their food parcelled for takeaway or eat it at standing tables. There are a couple of small tables and some chairs for about six people to sit down and eat.

The onion dosa is served with sambar and coconut chutney, while the paratha is served with a spicy dal–sambar mix. The lemon rice is hot, the rice fresh and fluffy.

SOMETHING ON THE SIDE You have to get tokens and then present them before your order is taken and cooked.

Mayur's Verdict: Nothing spectacular about the food but
nothing wrong with it either. Basic, fresh food served to eat
on the go.
Rating: Taste: 6, Ambience: 6, Service: 6, Value for Money: 7,
Total: 25
Specialities: Lemon rice and onion dosa
Veg/Non-veg: Veg
Contact Details/Timings: Sri Damodar Fast Foods, TP Area,
Tirupati. Phone: 08574-6574768
Prices: Onion dosa ₹ 15 and lemon rice ₹ 10

Vijayawada

SWAGRUHA FOODS   Don't let the nondescript exterior fool
you. This place has a range of sweets, some of which we had
never heard of nor seen before. Here is where you can find the
unique pootharekulu which is also known as the pothraiku,
pootharaiku, or poothurekulu among other names. 'Pothrai'
means flower and this delicate sweet is made with rice, ghee,
and sugar and costs ₹ 6 per piece. It is made of a tissue-thin
plastic-like sheet wrapped over and over again to create a roll-
like shape. It's texture is one of a kind that we have never had
before or since.

In addition to these there are the bandar laddus which
at ₹ 160 a kg are the most popular with the locals. There are
also delicious pickles of which the prawn pickle was most
memorable. At ₹ 700 a kg it was a touch expensive but well
worth it. People here love their sweets and there is a constant
stream of customers coming in to get theirs. Most will walk in
and order a sweet by the plate and eat it right there.

SOMETHING ON THE SIDE   The Vijayawada traffic police is active
and committed; they are polite and firm with the people and
well respected. It's a pleasure to see well-behaved traffic and
smiling policemen.

Rocky's Verdict: Get in here and have some fun eating the goodies. The pootharekulu is a must-have simply because it's so much fun to play with.
Rating: Taste: 7, Ambience: 6, Service: 6, Value for Money: 8, Total: 27
Specialities: Pootharekulu, prawn pickle
Veg/Non-veg: Non-veg
Contact Details/Timings: Swagruha Foods, PWD Grounds, Vijayawada. Phone: 0866-2475763
Prices: Bandar laddus ₹ 160 per kg, and prawn pickle ₹ 700 per kg

ARUNACHAL PRADESH

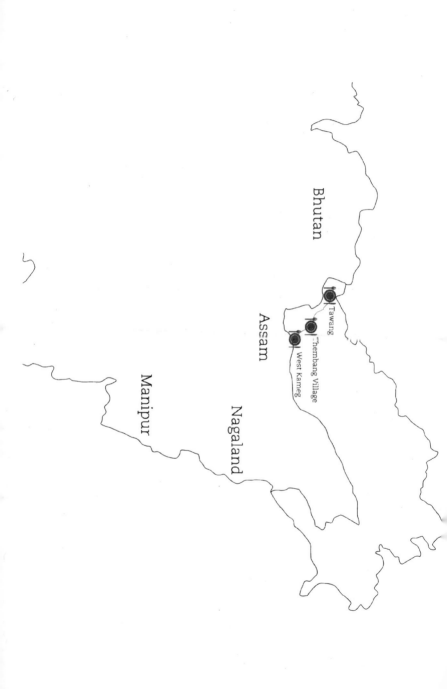

Tawang

TAWANG MONASTERY The largest monastery in India and the second largest in the world after the Potala Palace in Tibet, the Tawang Monastery is counted as one of the Seven Wonders of India. Morning prayers at the crack of dawn are accompanied by servings of hot salted butter tea to keep the monks warm in the freezing, snow-laden environment of the monastery. Besides morning tea the monastery also has to feed the 450 monks residing there. The kitchen is a large, spacious dimly lit room, which is very warm thanks to the fires burning high in the clay ovens.

Extremely thick and large maida rotis called kiptong and tasty and spicy cabbage subzi make for an extremely simple yet filling meal. The subzi called pa is ladled on to the kiptong itself and accompanied by a bowl of steaming butter tea. The main focus seems to be more on providing a hearty meal, high in fat and carbohydrates, necessary for survival in this cold climate.

SOMETHING ON THE SIDE As you shiver, even though warmly clad, you admire the very young monks who saunter through the snowy slush in their slippers. They are off for the dawn prayer and the hot butter tea to warm them through the chilly day ahead.

Mayur's Verdict: Fill the stomach and the soul at one go when you visit this imposing monastery. Once you have permission to eat, the meals are free though a small (or large) donation to help in the monastery's upkeep is sure to be welcome.

Rating: Taste: 6, Ambience: 10, Service: 10, Value for Money: 10, Total: 36

Certified: Rocky and Mayur rating of excellence

Specialities: Hot salted butter tea and morning prayers for the soul.

> **Veg/Non-veg:** Veg
> **Contact Details/Timings:** Tamang Monastery, Tawang.
> Phone: 03794-2222430. Buddha is available 24×7
> **Prices:** Free

Thembang Village

HOME OF MR SATYAM JORME, THE HEADMAN OF THEMBANG This is a small village by any standard and has about twenty houses. Dominated by a small wooden fort at the highest point, Thembang belongs to a tribe called the Monpas. We stayed at the home of Mr Satyam Jorme, the quiet headman of Thembang. Due to the extreme cold all members of the family spend their time in the kitchen which has a fire going. The atmosphere is bright and cheery, the food hearty.

Dinner starts with the local blood sausage called juma. It is made by collecting blood and mixing it with flour, ginger, garlic, salt, and chilli powder before being packed into the cleaned yak intestine and rolled like a sausage. It is fried in churpi or yak butter cheese and is addictive after you get over the initial strange metallic taste. This is washed down with arak or maize liquor which is a strong distilled alcohol which is heated and served with yak ghee and packs quite a punch. The main course always has a yak preparation and we got the yaksha kamtang, which is yak meat and vegetables. Prepared using generous amounts of fat, this is a nutritious broth with leafy vegetables and glass noodles called phing. The broken rice is called kut. It is difficult to provide vegetarian items but they can make a tasty and basic dal and dry cabbage called gobhi mom.

Breakfast is usually pokpui or ragi flour boiled and served hot. It is served along with frum or cow cheese. The frum is very pungent and the older it gets the more it is prized. It is also known as churpi and after storing for a few years it turns red. This is when the churpi is at its finest. Be prepared as it smells very strongly of a chicken shop or very pungent blue cheese (bleu cheese). It is not an easy thing to eat unless you already have a taste for it. Needless to say, be brave. The locals though have grown up on this diet and prize the taste. The breakfast is a very nourishing one and gets you ready for the cold hard day ahead.

The Monpas are a warrior tribe and a large number of them now live across the Chinese border. These are people who are quick to smile and will take good care of you in case you ever happen to be their guest. It's an experience everyone must try at least once in their lifetime.

Rocky's Verdict: The food is designed to fatten you up, to be able to survive the harsh temperature; there are no frills in this cuisine. It will make you strong.
Rating: Taste: 5, Ambience: 10, Service: 10, Value for Money: 10, Total: 35
Specialities: Yaksha kamtany, churpi, gobhi mom
Veg/Non-veg: Non-veg
Prices: Everything is included in the price of the room which is ₹ 750 per head

---

West Kameg

PADMA HOTEL   Hotels and dhabas are few and far between on the road to Tawang, and the Padma is a welcome break. A long, single-storey building, with an adjoining thatch kitchen, it is perched on a steep hillside with a roaring river below. The kitchen stove, and tables are all fashioned out of earth and clay while the furniture in the hotel is wooden and very basic.

Piping hot parathas with a dollop of some unidentifiable, but tasty, green subzi, hot masala noodles in different sizes and colours, and scrambled eggs with lots of turmeric and sliced green chillies make for a filling and reasonably tasty meal.

SOMETHING ON THE SIDE   Hot drinking water is served to fight the chill and the hot, sweet masala tea tastes even better when you have the fourth cup while enjoying the view.

Mayur's Verdict: The food is not spectacular but do tuck in and fill your stomach, as the next hotel/dhaba is a long way off. Make sure to sit in the beautiful wooden balcony at the back and enjoy the sound of birdsong and the roaring river as you eat.

Rating: Taste: 6, Ambience: 9, Service: 7, Value for Money: 8, Total: 30

Specialities: Tea

Veg/Non-veg: Veg

Contact Details/Timings: Padma Hotel, Nikmedhu, West Kameng.

Prices: Parathas with subzi ₹ 40, for all you can eat and hot masala noodles ₹ 30

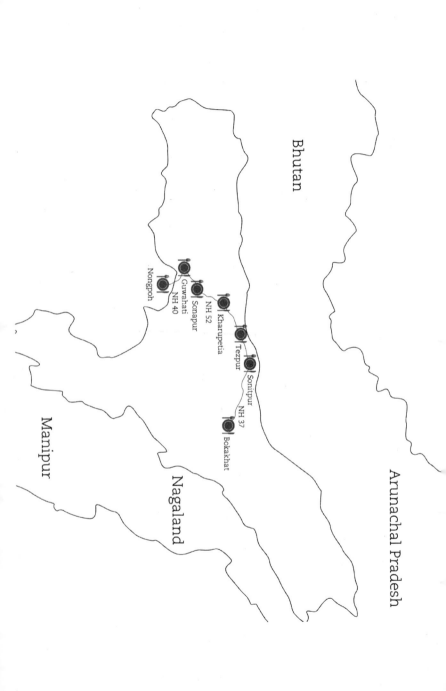

Bokakhat

KRISHNA GOPAL HOTEL   This little hotel is famous for its aloo-puri and pedas. One of the many brightly lit shops selling a range of fresh food, tea, fresh and packaged snacks, this shop is open twenty hours and has no doors or shutters to close. Aloo subzi, with chunks of potatoes cooked in their jackets, is served along with piping hot, golden brown, fluffy puris on banana leaves. Unlike most Assamese dishes the aloo subzi is not spicy at all and in fact is so bland it is hard to even taste any salt. Do not despair if you like it hot because the accompanying side of mashed and pickled red chilli will burn a hole in your mouth and your stomach for free! Follow the spicy with the sweet as you tuck into delicious pedas made from khoya, sugar, and ghee. Gopal offers 'low sugar more khoya' pedas with a slightly caramelized flavour if you are diabetic or prefer a less sweet taste. Be adventurous and try eating some pedas wrapped in a hot puri and if you like it then try a few more.

SOMETHING ON THE SIDE   The shop is open twenty hours and has no doors or shutters to close so you can come in anytime for a hot meal.

Mayur's Verdict: Visit Gopal if you are missing the taste of north Indian food in Assam and want to tuck into a hot meal at any time of the day or night. The aroma of fresh pedas being prepared at the back of the hotel is an added bonus.
Rating: Taste: 7, Ambience: 6, Service: 7, Value for Money: 10, Total: 30
Specialities: Aloo-puri and pedas
Veg/Non-veg: Veg
Contact Details/Timings: Situated off the highway about 20 km from the Kaziranga National Park. Krishna Gopal Hotel, Bokakhat, Assam.
Prices: Aloo subzi ₹ 10 and pedas ₹ 120 per kg

Guwahati

GAMS DELICACY RESTAURANT GAMS serves traditional tribal cuisine on banana leaves and copper plates. The selection it offers is so vast that it confuses the customer!

Start with the duck curry with gourd if you are non-vegetarian, followed by the pork and bamboo shoot curry. Smoked fish is also popular here, and is served with lemon and ginger juice. It is incredibly flavourful and tastes like a fish roasted in barbeque sauce. The other unique item here is the outenga or elephant apple and it is a large lemon-like fruit. The pigeon pepper curry is unusual.

The akhaj or the vegetarian thalihas khar is a raw papaya gravy. This bitter starter to the meal is popular but should not be eaten with the tenga. A mashed potato dish called pitika is a pleasant and delicately flavoured potato dish made with mustard oil, chillies, and onions. Fried herbs are common as is yellow dal. Rice abounds and many varieties are available.

SOMETHING ON THE SIDE The fish is smoked by putting the whole fish above the cooking area. Salt is the only thing that is applied to it. The smoke continues to cook the fish over days and finally you have a dried, smoked, and delicious fish ready to eat even without cooking, if you should so please. Most homes will have a wooden rack over the fire in the kitchen for smoking fish and meats.

Rocky's Verdict: If you are a foodie you will love GAMS.
Rating: Taste: 7, Ambience: 8, Service: 9, Value for Money: 8, Total: 32
Specialities: Tribal Assamese food
Veg/Non-veg: Veg and non-veg
Contact Details/Timings: Ganeshguri, Guwahati.
Phone: 0361-2233402.
Prices: ₹ 250 per person

PARADISE Paradise is a speciality food restaurant serving all kinds of Assamese specialities from amla soup to pigeon curry. The décor is creative and highlights the culture and colours of Assam. Run by a family who are patrons of the arts, it has a homely and comfortable feel to it. The best choice here is to have the thalis. The non-vegetarian thali called the 'Parampara Thali' starts with the amla soup and features the tenga fish curry which is sour, tangy, and incredibly tasty. The ilish or hilsa fish is also well loved in Assam and available in certain seasons. Also unique are mustard seeds cooked into little balls to be eaten as an accompaniment. Rice is the staple here and the pigeon curry is always present. The vegetarian thali has the vegetable tenga or maharpode, saag (mashed mustard leaves), paneer, potatoes, and dal. The dominant taste is of mustard and there is a similarity to Bengali cuisine. However, unlike Bengali cooking, the use of oil is marginal in traditional Assamese cooking.

Be warned that all Assamese food is spicier than that of almost any other state in India with the possible exception of Andhra Pradesh. The chillies called jalokia are plentiful and used generously. You can wash down your meal with a chilled beer as they do serve alcohol as well.

SOMETHING ON THE SIDE The family that owns Paradise is committed to the arts and culture of Assam. Little touches of local arts and crafts can be seen throughout the restaurant. The practice of ringing the bell if you enjoyed the meal has been here for ages.

Rocky's Verdict: Go to Paradise and grab a heavenly meal.
It is hugely recommended, for a change, by both of us. We
rated it as one of the best lunche places you will find in this
country.
Certified: Rocky and Mayur rating of excellence
Rating: Taste: 9, Ambience: 8, Service: 9, Value for Money: 9,
Total: 35
Specialities: Thalis
Veg/Non-veg: Non-veg
Contact Details/Timings: Paradise, Silpukhri.
Phone: 0361-2666904.
Prices: Veg thali ₹ 100 and non-veg thali ₹ 300

Kharupetia

LOVELY HOTEL AND RESTAURANT Owned by a Marwari
family from Rajasthan, this is the best place to eat the gurka,
an Assamese sweet, which is made by dipping a rasgulla in
date palm jaggery. The resulting delicacy is a firm, dark, juice-
filled rasgulla with a strong flavour. Traditional juicy rasgullas
dripping with sugar syrup are equally popular.

Another famous treat at this restaurant is the onion
kachori, which is made of flattened balls of dough stuffed with
a mixture of cooked onion masala. This one is a bit different
as they also add saunf (fennel seeds) which leaves a pleasant
aftertaste. The restaurant also offers a range of sweets such as
gulab jamuns, laddus, burfis, etc. but the main attractions are
the kachori and the gurka.

SOMETHING ON THE SIDE Check out the little paan shop right
outside because the man there can twist paan leaves into some
pretty exotic shapes.

> **Mayur's Verdict:** It is well worth stopping at Lovely Hotel to snack on a few plates of kachoris and gurkas, even though the hotel is poorly lit and not very clean.
> **Rating:** Taste: 8, Ambience: 6, Service: 7, Value for Money: 10, Total: 33
> **Specialities:** Gurka and kachori
> **Veg/Non-veg:** Veg
> **Contact Details/Timings:** Lovely Hotel and Restaurant, NH 52.
> **Prices:** Gurka ₹ 7 per plate, pyaaz kachoris ₹ 5

Nongpoh

LC WOODLAND DHABA   The dhaba is a popular midway stopover place between Siliguri and Darjeeling. This has been a favourite stop of travellers for a long time and has slowly grown into a large, slick, glass-fronted place with a little pond, and a few shops selling everything from pickles to papier mâché products. The place is famous for its, surprise surprise, chola bhaturas which are fairly good. In addition you will also find dosas, noodles, momos, and sandwiches. This is predominantly a snack place. The fried momos were the highlight though, bear in mind, the taste is mediocre at best. Most things though are easy on the palate.

Kids can run around and there are even a couple of swings for them. The dhaba has recently been beautified and is pretty clean.

SOMETHING ON THE SIDE   Worth a mention here is that the hill people in and round Nongpoh grow some great fruits and vegetables in the fertile foothills. The fresh pineapples are a must-have as are the chilli pickles. Try out all the seasonal fresh produce from roadside stalls set up along the road all the way up to Darjeeling. There are a few fruits and vegetables you may never have eaten before and they are certainly worth trying.

Rocky's Verdict: Get off and stretch your legs but beware of
the pet geese.
Rating: Taste: 5, Ambience: 6, Service: 6, Value for Money: 5,
Total: 22
Specialities: Chola bhatura and fried momos
Veg/Non-veg: Non-veg
Contact Details/Timings: LC Woodland Dhaba, Nongpoh,
NH 40.
Prices: Chola bhatura ₹ 25

Sonapur

TRISHNA DHABA   It is one of those places where you can be
assured your meat is fresh, as the ducks are taken from the
compound of the dhaba, the pigeons are in bamboo cages, and
the fish is caught from just behind the dhaba. This is unique as
far as I know and the fish are plentiful. Sadly they are all hard
to catch. You're better off ordering from the menu.

The dhaba has a main hall made of bamboo and smaller rooms
raised on stilts which are brightly coloured and are nice and
shady with a cool breeze blowing through them. Rui fish (green
carp) is a favourite in these parts. The fish is cooked along with
lots of potatoes in a spicy coriander gravy. The other favourite
is duck, which is fried Chinese-style with chillies, capsicum,
and loads of onion. The other option is the masala duck but
you will get the Chinese style fried duck with lots of garlic and
ginger, no matter what you ask for. Beware of all the jalokias
in Assam. They are all dangerously spicy and OH SO GOOD!!!

For the vegetarians they have potato and butter paneer,
which are average. The vegetarian food is not the food of
choice here and is prepared in whichever fastest style the
chef knows. Usually the vegetables are boiled, and then fried
along with lots of garlic, ginger, and mustard seeds, and chilli
is added.

Most highway dhabas in Assam will have a very limited
menu so make the most of it. Also, the bigger the place the
better the food, seems to be the rule of thumb across Assam.

SOMETHING ON THE SIDE   Most dhabas in this area will have a little room raised on stilts which serves as a 'family area'. These little outhouse sort of rooms with thatched roofs, are clean, well ventilated and cool even in the summer. They also are away from the noise of the main halls. Grab one of these when you get here.

Rocky's Verdict: Nothing to write home about. The food is reasonable, though a little expensive for a roadside dhaba.
Rating: Taste: 6, Ambience: 7, Service: 8, Value for Money: 7, Total: 28
Specialities: Chinese style fried duck
Veg/Non-veg: Non-veg
Contact Details/Timings: Trishna Dhaba, Sonapur, NH 37.
Prices: Fish ₹ 60, duck ₹ 130, potatoes ₹ 30, and paneer butter masala ₹ 90

Sonitpur

SAMAROH EN DEES DHABA   This invitingly named dhaba owned by Nitul Das (hence the 'En Dees' in the name) right by the highway is a refreshing and inviting sight for travel-weary eyes.

The menu is very extensive with over 150 items available and, amazingly, every item mentioned on the menu is actually available. The pigeon curry has potato chunks along with the meat floating in a sea of oil. It is a tangy, spicy dish cooked with lots of turmeric, coriander, and garlic and the meat is somewhere between chicken and mutton in taste and consistency. The duck cooked with heaps of black pepper and green chilli, is a gamey dish, very strong in flavour. The joha rice has a strong, characteristic aroma and lends to the taste of the yellow dal fry, which is a basic, unremarkable dish here. The boiled vegetables are nothing like boiled food because they are strong with the flavour of ginger, garlic, and chilli, making for a pretty exotic taste. The real winners are the side dishes accompanying each meal. The aloo pithika made by mixing mashed potatoes with freshly ground mustard and sprinkled with finely diced onions and coriander is a delicious, pungent eye-watering taste. The pudi maas, a fish paste chutney with lots of garlic and red chilli, adds a charred, spicy taste to your meal and needs a strong stomach to really appreciate its flavour.

SOMETHING ON THE SIDE   Set among the paddy fields, the entire dhaba is constructed from brightly painted bamboo and cane set up high on wooden stilts as is customary in the tribe that Nitul belongs to. There is a main section, which houses the kitchen and dining area that has private booths behind curtains should you require privacy. If you want even more privacy then walk across a small, swaying bridge to an open space surrounded by small brightly coloured cane huts (also on stilts) each meant for seating six to eight customers.

Mayur's Verdict: This is a highly recommended stop not for the food, which is average in taste, but for the wonderfully relaxing experience of eating high above the ground with views of green paddy fields and forests. Kids will love running around on shaky but safe cane pathways and bridges and they might even get to see some wildlife that has wandered off the Kaziranga National Park area.
Rating: Taste: 7, Ambience: 9, Service: 8, Value for Money: 6, Total: 30
Specialities: Aloo pithika and pudi maas
Veg/Non-veg: Non-veg
Contact Details/Timings: Samaroh En Dees Dhaba, Bhomoraguri, Sonitpur.
Prices: Pigeon curry ₹ 110, duck ₹ 120, yellow dal fry ₹ 30, and boiled vegetables ₹ 60

Tezpur

KF HOTEL   At the intersection of NH37 and the highway leading to Kaziranga you can see this modern glass-and-steel boutique hotel. It offers the cleanest bathrooms seen on a highway and a little shop selling all manner of groceries, household fripperies, and snacks. On the ground floor, easily seen from the road, is a small counter selling pastries, snacks, chaat, and ice cream, which can be savoured right there. You can also buy packaged snacks like chips, potato puffs, and namkeens to carry away with you, to munch on the way.

Mayur's Verdict: The pastries are fresh though the chaat is nothing special. It is a quick, clean, tasty snack break.
Rating: Taste: 7, Ambience: 7, Service: 8, Value for money: 7, Total: 29
Specialities: Fresh pastries and ice cream.
Veg/Non-veg: Veg
Contact Details/Timings: KF Hotel, Mission Chairali, Tezpur, Assam. Phone: 03712-255203.
Prices: Range from ₹ 20 to 45

Bhaturi

SANJAY BIHARI DHABA   This busy dhaba run by a Bihari named Mithilesh is a concrete and whitewash affair built a bit off the highway. It serves all the usual fare of different types of paneer, dal, vegetables, etc. but also offers chicken curry, egg curry, and fish. Keep in mind that fish is available only in the evenings so during the day you have the chicken or the vegetarian options.

A plate of salad with onion, tomato, cucumber, chillies, and lime accompanies the food and soft drinks are available though not very chilled. This dhaba is pretty popular with truck drivers, perhaps because dhabas are quite rare on this section of the highway. The kitchen is a half-open area where two or three cooks are busy frying and cooking up a sizzling storm. The food served is fresh, hot, and heavily spiced, not to mention quite oily, to fit the bill of a hungry truck driver perfectly.

SOMETHING ON THE SIDE   The large long hall has rows of manjis or rope cots with a wooden slat across them, that serves as a table. After your meal the slat gets taken off and you can stretch out to digest the meal at leisure.

Mayur's Verdict: The food is filling though more on the rough-and-ready side. The clientele were all truck drivers and we saw no families stopping to eat here though there is a separate room provided for them. It's a long way to the next food stop so you might want to stop here.
Rating: Taste: 6, Ambience: 6, Service: 6, Value for Money: 6, Total: 24
Specialities: Fish
Veg/Non-veg: Non-veg
Contact Details/Timings: 30 km short of the Orissa border. Sanjay Bihari Dhaba, Bhaturi, Chhattisgarh.
Phone: 0-9425228914
Prices: Egg curry ₹ 15, dal fry ₹ 20, gobhi aloo ₹ 20, palak paneer ₹ 40, chicken curry ₹ 70

DAMAN & DIU

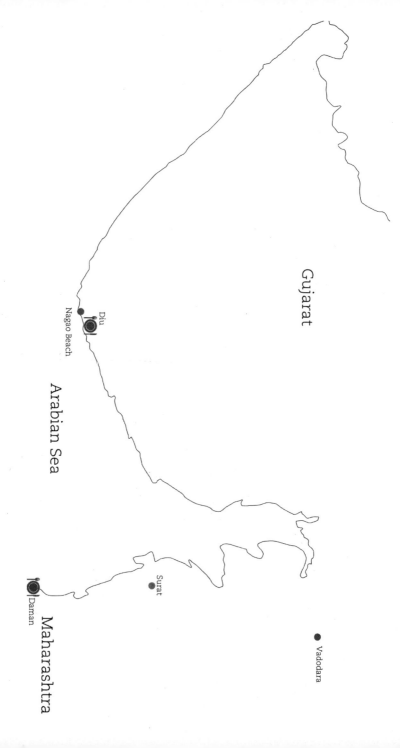

Daman

VEERA DA DHABA   Veera da Dhaba is famous all over Daman for its Punjabi cuisine. Eating here is experiencing a wholesome, clean Punjabi meal with an assortment of dishes to choose from, both vegetarian and non-vegetarian.

Daman being on the coast, you can order fresh seafood preparations such as fish lazeez and even a fish 'n' chips dish. The prawn kolivada, seekh kebabs, and mutton roganjosh are rich in taste, as are the different paneer dishes and the dal, which can be eaten with hot tandoori rotis and naans. For vegetarians a dish called 'vegetable garden' is highly recommended for its fresh, light, and tasty flavour. You are offered chaach or buttermilk as soon as you settle down, but you can also choose from their range of exotically named mocktails like daman delight, white negro, shirdi temple, and coco loco that arrive in cocktail glasses complete with a cherry and colourful paper umbrella!

This restaurant tries hard to build an atmosphere reminiscent of Punjabi life for its primarily Gujarati diners. Besides the regular seating there is a section of manjis or traditional wood and coir cots to lounge on as you eat, on which you can later stretch out for a well-deserved nap. Lanterns are suspended from the thatched roof, and traditional hookahs which you can smoke can be found around the room. There is a modern touch to it though, as the cots are covered with bedsheets, the lanterns are electric, and there are fans to deal with the heat.

SOMETHING ON THE SIDE   'Veera' translates to 'elder brother' in English and it's easy to understand what elder brothers are about when you see the giant hoardings advertising beer!

> **Mayur's Verdict:** A real taste of Punjab with good food
> to follow up on the drinks that a lot of visitors from 'dry'
> Gujarat come to Daman to consume. Comfortable, clean
> surroundings, and a sense of innovation added to the
> experience make this dhaba a must-visit if you are in Daman.

Rating: Taste: 7, Ambience: 8, Service: 8, Value for Money: 8 ,
Total: 31
Specialities: Fish lazeez, prawn kolivada, seekh kebabs,
mutton roganjosh, and mocktails
Veg/Non-veg: Non-veg
Contact Details/Timings: Veera da Dhaba, Daman.
Phone: 09824111535
Prices: Prawn kolivadi ₹ 100, mutton rogan josh ₹ 60, paneer
amritsar ₹ 50, vegetable garden ₹ 95, Golden Temple ₹ 110,
Shirdi Temple ₹ 95, mutton seekanda ₹ 300 per handi, dal
makhani ₹ 45

Diu

APANA FOODLANDS   Apana Foodlands boasts a lovely view
of the water and some faraway lights as you dine. It offers
South Indian, Chinese, Gujarati, Punjabi, Kathiawadi, and even
continental dishes! In reality though, it has a few items of each
of the above and they all taste, well, similar. So stick to what
we tell you as you negotiate this place. Have the cold coffee for
starters, it is great. Seafood is the best and the pomfret of Diu
is famous. The vegetarian fare is prepared according to your
cultural specification and is quite tasty.

SOMETHING ON THE SIDE   Diu is teeming with tourists during
season (October–March) but is lush, green and quiet during the
monsoons. End-August and September is when the effects of
the monsoon can really be enjoyed.

Rocky's Verdict: Tasty and simple; enjoy your drink here as
the sun sets.
Rating: Taste: 8, Ambience: 6, Service: 7, Value for Money: 7,
Total: 28
Specialities: Seafood and cold coffee
Veg/Non-veg: Non-veg

Contact Details/Timings: Apana Foodlands, Fort Road, Diu
Phone: 02875-253650.
Prices: Non veg ₹ 90 per person, veg ₹ 40 per person, chilly
chicken ₹ 99, fish fry ₹ 90, dal fry ₹ 35, and jeera rice ₹ 40

Nagao Beach

DUB CHICK BAR AND RESTAURANT This restaurant is
situated on the beach at Nagao and the bracing sea breeze
and salty air really help the appetite. The specialities of the
restaurant are chicken fry and fish fry though you can choose
from a truly extensive menu. Dub Chick proudly advertises
its 'Punjabi Chinese' food so don't be surprised if the chicken
manchurian dry and chilli chicken dry taste like gobhi masala
with some sweet chilli sauce added to it. The fried pomfret is
very fresh, tender, and cooked Punjabi style with lots of spice.

SOMETHING ON THE SIDE When you sit down to a meal at Dub
Chick you can order fresh and healthy starters like peanuts,
boiled chana, green chillies, onions, and tomatoes with a
sprinkling of red chilli powder and lemon juice.

Mayur's Verdict: The view of the beach and the ocean is
great and the food is quite tasty.
Rating: Taste: 7, Ambience: 7, Service: 5, Value for Money: 5,
Total: 24
Specialities: Peanut and onion salad, fish fry, and chicken fry
Veg/Non-veg: Non-veg
Contact Details/Timings: Dub Chick Bar and Restaurant,
Nagao Beach, Diu.
Prices: Chicken manchurian dry ₹ 80, chilli chicken dry
₹ 80, pomfret ₹ 145

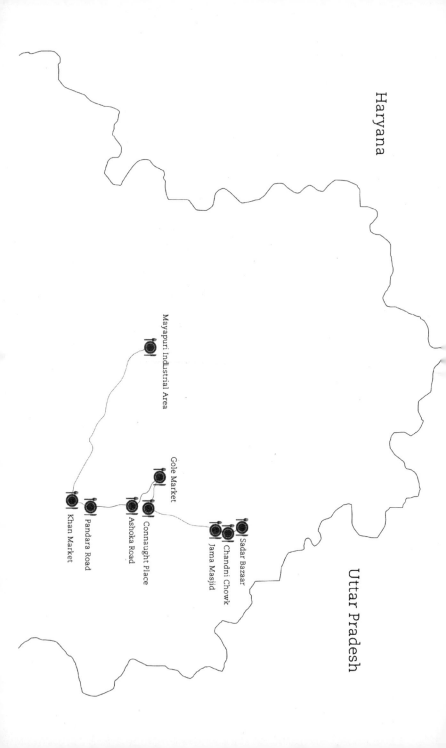

Ashoka Road

ANDHRA BHAWAN You can opt for a vegetarian or non-vegetarian thali and they are both very good. The seating is on a first come, first served basis and works on a 'one man one seat' system. If you are two people on a table for four, soon two more people will be seated there, like it or not. Everyone is here for the serious business of eating and it is done very fast. Thalis are put in front of you as soon as you walk in and the service begins immediately. The vegetarian thali has dal, snake gourd, boiled banana subzi, yogurt, rasam and you can have unlimited helpings. The prawn coconut curry is highly recommended, as is the mutton fry. There is halwa and 'double ka meetha', or bread pudding, for dessert.

SOMETHING ON THE SIDE This place is a hotbed of political intrigue and for spotting the occasional political superstar. Rahul Gandhi visits often.

Rocky's Verdict: The meal is affordable and, outside Andhra Pradesh, this is the best Andhra food you will find.
Certified: Rocky and Mayur rating of excellence
Rating: Taste: 9, Ambience: 9, Service: 10, Value for Money: 10, Total: 38
Specialities: Thalis, prawn coconut curry, and mutton fry
Veg/Non-veg: Non-veg
Contact Details/Timings: No.1 Ashoka Road, New Delhi, 110001.
Prices: Veg thali ₹ 80, chicken ₹ 80 coconut curry ₹ 100, mutton fry ₹ 80

Chandni Chowk

NATRAJ DAHI BHALLA CORNER Natraj Dahi Bhalla Corner is now located at the entrance of the Chandni Chowk metro station. The alley is about five feet wide and about 500 people go past every minute making it hard to get your food, but the trouble is well worth it. The dahi bhalla is surprisingly light and served with lip-smacking spices and sweet yogurt making it almost like a tasty chaat. A fantastic dahi bhalla. Another good thing to order is the aloo tikki.

Rocky/Mayur's Verdict: Well worth a visit and a delicious dahi bhalla. Enjoy the energy of the crowd.
Rating: Taste: 8, Ambience: 6, Service: 6, Value for Money: 10, Total: 30
Speciality: Dahi bhalla
Veg/Non-veg: Veg
Contact Details/Timings: Chandni Chowk
Prices: ₹ 15 per plate

NEM CHAND JALEBI WALA This guy is so famous that his sign says OLD FAMOUS JALEBI WALA. Started about a hundred years ago this shop opened and started serving terrific jalebi, thicker than most and served piping hot. The jalebi is not overly sweet and that is what makes it perfect. Even if you get it packed it tastes just as good after a couple of hours. This is possibly the most written about jalebi in India.

Rocky/Mayur's Verdict: The best jalebi that money can buy in Delhi.
Rating: Taste: 8, Ambience: 5, Service: 5, Value for Money: 10, Total: 28
Speciality: Jalebi
Veg/Non-veg: Veg

> **Contact Details/Timings:** Chandni Chowk
> **Prices:** ₹ 250 per kg

PRINCE PAAN Here one gets the quintessential paan experience of Delhi. Selling everything from paan to cigarettes and candies, this is a famous old place and has been the last stop on the Old Delhi food trail for ages. These days it has come up with some funky new paans like the chocolate paan (weird) and the pineapple paan (yuck!). It does serve a nice nimbu masala soda which is a must-have. As for the paans, stick with the meetha, a slightly modern version of the old favourite. Other standard paans are also available.

> **Rocky's Verdict:** Get on the crowded streets and see what makes Delhiites tick. Eat all of the above.
> **Rating:** Taste: 8, Ambience: 7, Service: 8, Value for Money: 8, Total: 31
> **Specialities:** Meetha paan and nimbu masala soda
> **Veg/Non-veg:** Veg
> **Contact Details/Timings:** Opposite Paranthe Wali Gali, near metro station entrance, Chandni Chowk.
> **Prices:** ₹ 5–₹ 150

Connaught Place

ANAND BIRYANI Tucked away in a little lane between KG Marg and Janpath in Connaught Place, is a restaurant famed for its biryanis. The menu is painted on the glass doors of the restaurant to attract passers-by and slow them down long enough for the delicious aroma to tempt them in.

The meat biryanis are served hot, redolent with spices, and extremely tender pieces of mutton or chicken while the vegetable biryani has chunks of paneer and diced vegetables added to spice-laden rice. Both are served with a topping of fresh coriander leaves and an accompanying salad of onion rings topped with spicy green chutney and red chilli powder.

Besides biryani, Anand also serves dal makhani, kadahi paneer, mattar paneer, rajma-chawal, and butter chicken accompanied by tandoori rotis, naans, or parathas.

SOMETHING ON THE SIDE This eatery is very popular with the CP office crowd so make sure you get there before peak lunch hour if possible.

Mayur's Verdict: While the biryani is great, the restaurant is cramped. It is advisable therefore to have your biryani packed and then eat it elsewhere. However, if that option is not available, don't be put off! The biryani is well worth a try even in the cramped space of the restaurant.
Rating: Taste: 8, Ambience: 4, Service: 7, Value for Money: 7, Total: 26
Specialities: Biryani
Veg/Non-veg: Non-veg
Contact Details/Timings: Connaught Place
Prices: Meat biryani ₹ 82, veg biryani ₹ 51

WENGERS Wengers is a landmark Delhi bakery that has been around since 1926. It has an incredibly tasty shammi kebab made of fluffy, delicious mutton. The other favourites are the chicken patty, paneer roll, rum and raisin chocolates, and chocolate eclair. The bakery items available at Wengers range from a host of chocolates to things like the almond Danish. They also do an old-style tasty cold coffee.

Rocky's Verdict: Very, very good!
Rating: Taste: 8, Ambience: 8, Service: 7, Value for Money: 7, Total: 30
Specialities: Shammi kebab
Veg/Non-veg: Non-veg

Contact Details/Timings: Wengers, A Block, Connaught Place, Delhi.
Prices: Pastries, kebabs, and rolls ₹ 40 per piece

Gole Market

GALINA   Located in a colonial building at the Gole Market traffic circle, this place is a meat lover's paradise. Right by the entrance a glass-fronted display carries trays upon trays of chicken legs, seekh kebabs, mutton tikkas, chicken balls, and chicken nuggets in a range of spice bases ready for cooking. In a mild concession to the odd vegetarian client, there is tandoori paneer tikka and dal makhani on offer as well.

The chicken legs, served Lebanese style, are a must-try here. Boiled chicken leg pieces are roasted over a revolving grill after being dipped in a mixture of spices. This cooking method ensures that the meat is evenly cooked while its juicy texture is maintained.

All dishes are served with the obligatory salad of onion rings drizzled with fresh lime and spicy green chutney. Butter naans or tandoori rotis are also available.

SOMETHING ON THE SIDE   Post your meal step out and cross the road to feed grain to the hundreds of pigeons that flock to the pavements. Share the love for food and food for love.

Mayur's Verdict: Though it does serve the token vegetarian options Galina is primarily a non-vegetarian destination. Eat in to enjoy hot, freshly cooked, aromatic dishes, or take away fresh tikkas, seekh kebabs, and even paneer to be cooked and enjoyed at home.
Rating: Taste: 7, Ambience: 6, Service: 7, Value for Money: 10, Total: 30
Specialities: Chicken legs Lebanese style
Veg/Non-veg: Non-veg

> **Contact Details/Timings:** Gole Market
> **Prices:** Absolutely no idea!! We do not have them listed. The
> fan paid.

Jama Masjid

KARIM HOTEL (KARIM'S) Karim's is probably the most
famous and best known eatery in Delhi. Almost every food
critic and chef worth his salt has been here to pay homage to
this great of greats.

When you get to Karim Hotel, we strongly recommend that
you start with the seekh. Tender and juicy, the seekh must
be eaten hot to be enjoyed. In fact order everything one at a
time and eat it hot else the oil in the food might congeal thus
changing the taste. (They cook with Dalda—another reason
to eat it hot). The place is almost always packed and it's best
to visit during the holy month of Ramzan when many special
preparations appear on the menu. Any day is a good day to
go to Karim's though, and you will get a real taste of Delhi's
Muslim quarter while you are at it. Saunter down the market
place around Karim's to get your hands on a variety of delicious
foods and some unique shopping. Vegetarians, this place is as
good as anywhere else, but choices are a little limited for you.

SOMETHINGONTHESIDE Patienceisavirtuewheneatingthiskindof
food, and Habib, a waiter here since 1970, will tell you that it is
the best way to go. The style of cooking is an ancient one. They
have not altered recipes to suit modern tastes but retained the
old recipes that made them famous all those years ago.

This little complex of restaurants started as one single place
in 1930 and was started by the current owner Zaibuddin's
ancestor, who was the chef of Bahadur Shah Zafar, the last
Mughal emperor of India. The place puts out food fit for a king.
They have now expanded and taken over all the restaurants
in the immediate area and have separate places for families
and singles.

> **Rocky's Verdict:** You have to try this. Your culinary
> education is incomplete without having eaten here.
> **Rating:** Taste: 9, Ambience: 10, Service: 10, Value for
> Money: 9, Total: 38
> **Certified:** Rocky and Mayur rating of excellence
> **Specialities:** Seekh
> **Veg/Non-veg:** Non-veg
> **Contact Details/Timings:** Located close to the Jama Masjid
> (Gate 1) it lies in a small lane known as Gali Kababian.
> Karim's, Jama Masjid, New Delhi. Phone: 0-9899558555
> **Prices:** Mutton burra ₹ 160, mutton korma ₹ 110, mutton
> stew ₹ 110, Paneer tikka ₹ 110, Sheermal ₹ 28, Kheer ₹ 13

Khan Market

SALIM KEBAB CORNER   Situated in a back lane amidst several big retail stores and restaurants, this tiny eatery is nevertheless the busiest in the area. The owner of this tiny hole-in-the-wall eatery is Javed, a large, hospitable, heavily bearded man who enjoys the cluster of happy clients milling around his shop. Pre-marinated chicken and mutton seekh kebabs impaled on the seekh are slathered with Salim's secret mix of spices before they are roasted on an open bed of glowing coals and served to customers.

Vegetarians can enjoy tandoori paneer tikkas or the haryali kebab made from a mix of vegetables and lentils. These meat or vegetarian kebabs can be had standing in the street, or carried away wrapped in aluminium foil.

SOMETHING ON THE SIDE   Salim is not as well known as his competitor Khan Chacha but his kebabs and rolls are as good if not better. He also has a restaurant in Old Delhi, that he claims offers better food than Karim's.

Mayur's Verdict: Lovers of meat claim that the kebabs are fresh, juicy, and deliciously spiced while vegetarian visitors are not disappointed either. This is street food at its best.
Rating: Taste: 9, Ambience: 8, Service: 8, Value for Money: 8, Total: 33
Certified: Rocky and Mayur rating of excellence
Specialities: Chicken and mutton seekh kebab rolls, tandoori paneer tikka, and haryali kebab rolls
Veg/Non-veg: Non-veg
Contact Details/Timings: Khan Market
Prices: Chicken seekh roll ₹ 75, mutton seekh kebab ₹ 60, paneer tikka roll ₹ 65, haryali seekh kebab ₹ 70

Mayapuri Industrial Area

KHALSA RESTAURANT   Situated right by a noisy, smoky road, this restaurant is famous for its brain curry and mutton burras. The menu boasts of a wide range of dishes including staples such as dal makhani, mutton biryani, vegetable pulao, butter paneer, mixed vegetables, hot, buttered tandoori rotis, and naans, and attracts large, noisy groups of people at mealtimes.

The succulent 'liver dana', a dry roasted preparation has a slightly chewy texture and is coated with drippings of fat. The brain curry is mashed and blended with spices before preparation, and is a tasty and unusually textured dish.

SOMETHING ON THE SIDE   The restaurant is situated bang in the centre of an industrial area and so if you stand around outside you will be the smoked meat!

Mayur's Verdict: Khalsa serves a whole range of dishes but is primarily a destination for lovers of non-vegetarian food. Be prepared to submerge yourself in the whole experience as it is very crowded and noisy with groups of people enjoying their cross-table conversations as much as their meal.

Rating: Taste: 8, Ambience: 7, Service: 6, Value for Money: 7, Total: 28
Specialities: Brain curry and mutton burra
Veg/Non-veg: Non-veg
Contact Details/Timings: Mayapuri Industrial Area
Prices: Brain curry and liver dana ₹ 100 per plate, mutton burra ₹ 320 per kg

Pandara Road

PANDARA ROAD FOOD MARKET Starting out as wooden carts and small shacks serving simple food, restaurants like 'Havemore' and 'Chicken Inn' have grown into air-conditioned, plush eateries catering to the hungry Delhiite. Regulars here include families that have been eating here for decades and groups that have the food delivered to their parked cars along with generous measures of their favourite tipple.

The menu reflects the North West Frontier origins of the owners. Delicacies like tandoori chicken, dal makhani, butter chicken, boti kebabs, dum aloo, and hot tandoori naans vie for your attention. Each bite is a sensory delight: from the spicy smell of the mouth-watering spices, to the piping hot naan that burns your fingers.

SOMETHING ON THE SIDE Be sure to try the delicious kulfi-falooda served by a corner sweet shop as the perfect ending to a wonderful meal.

Mayur's Verdict: Pandara Road restaurants are a must-visit both for their atmosphere of bonhomie and for the rich medley of tastes they offer. Parking can be a challenge with cars often lining the main road for a good 50 metres on each side.

Rating: Taste: 7, Ambience: 8, Service: 8, Value for Money: 7,
Total: 30
Specialities: Fish and mutton tikkas, butter chicken, and
naan for the non-vegetarians, while the vegetarians can try
the dum aloo and dal makhani.
Veg/Non-veg: Non-veg
Contact Details/Timings: Pandara Road
Prices: Chicken dishes ₹ 175–₹ 350, mutton platter ₹ 450,
paneer tikka tandoori ₹ 275, pomfret fish ₹ 450, dal makhani
₹ 190, rotis ₹ 25–₹ 100(keema naan)

Sadar Bazar

NAND DI HATTI Lala Nand Lal came across into India
sometime in the 1940s and started this place, which serves
the most famous chole bhature in north India, now known
famously as 'Nand Bhature'. The secret of the delectable taste
of the chole is slow cooking over coals. The chole are cooked
from 3 am to 9 am every morning before they are served to
customers! The bhaturas are tender, fried with a moong dal
paste filling. Fried green chilli is optional as is a tangy raw
mango pickle. They serve very good rajma-chawal as well.

SOMETHING ON THE SIDE Sit by the street covered by a canopy and
brothers Bharat and Arun Makkar will serve you the delicious
chola bhaturas personally. They have now developed their own
chana masala and packeted it. It's available at the shop.

Rocky's Verdict: The place is hard to get to, but the chole
bhature are delicious.
Rating: Taste: 8, Ambience: 5, Service: 9, Value for Money: 8,
Total: 30
Specialities: Chole bhature
Veg/Non-veg: Veg
Contact Details/Timings: Sadar Bazaar. Phone: 9990330476.
Prices: Chole bhature ₹ 45 per plate

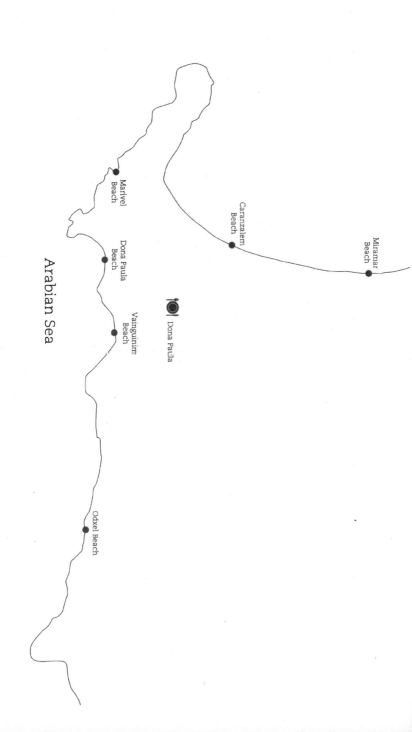

Dona Paula

SEA PEBBLES FAMILY BAR AND RESTAURANT Tucked in a cosy nook formed by an overhanging rock cliff, Sea Pebbles has all you could want from a Goan restaurant. An open kitchen, tons of fresh seafood, a good menu, and a gorgeous setting. You dine on a shell-covered beach amidst palm trees, the spray from the ocean hitting your face as the waves crash off the barnacle-covered rocks just off the beach. The prawn balchao, stuffed crab, and the mushroom xacuti (pronounced 'shacuti') are all freshly cooked, piping hot, and extremely tasty. Served with the standard hot white rice, each dish skilfully blends the sweet taste of the meat and the grated fresh coconut with the spices and chilli. Enjoy chilled sweet Goan port wine along with the food.

SOMETHING ON THE SIDE After your meal take a walk along the beach collecting seashells or starfish.

Mayur's Verdict: Yes, you must definitely eat here if you are in the neighbourhood. A great eating experience.
Rating: Taste: 9, Ambience: 9, Service: 8, Value for Money: 8, Total: 34
Certified: Rocky and Mayur rating of excellence
Specialities: Prawn balchao, stuffed crab, and mushroom xacuti
Veg/Non-veg: Non-veg
Contact Details/Timing: Get to Dona Paula and the main strip and go down a steep flight of wooden steps. Sea Pebble Restaurant, Dona Paula, Panjim. Phone: 0-9890353684
Prices: Prawn balchao ₹ 125, mushroom xacuti ₹ 80, stuffed crab ₹ 125 for 2 pieces

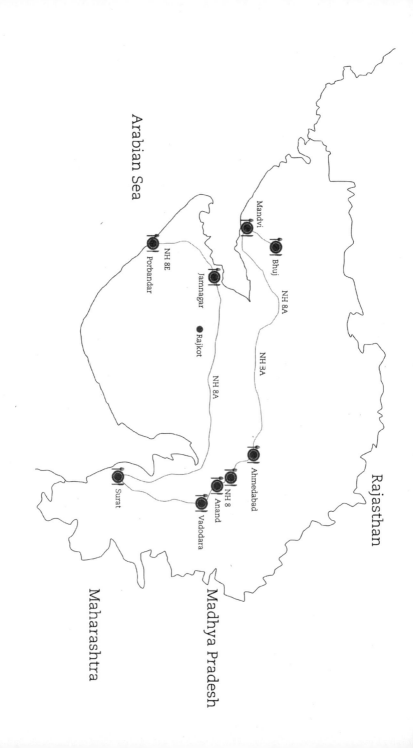

Ahmedabad

ASHARFI KULFI   Asharfi Kulfi is one of those rare places where families and tourists can come to relax, unwind, and eat till about 2 am. Don't expect Gujarati food at this hawkers' market. You can get pizzas, burgers, dosas, pav bhaji, golgappas, etc. and the zest and joie de vivre of the Gujaratis makes this a great experience. The kulfi is really good and you have a choice of some unusual flavours like chocolate, kesar, fig, strawberry, and maha badam. Asharfi prides itself on using quality ingredients and is happy to give a little taste of the varieties to all customers. Families come here for a taste of nightlife and the prohibition in the state means there are no drunks to spoil the fun. Get down here if you have kids with you. They will love it. One can also find many jewellery shops in the area. The party is on at Manek Chowk after the sun sets, and this 'Khani Peeni Bazaar' gets livelier as the day progresses.

SOMETHING ON THE SIDE   Ahmedabad has a wonderful mix of the modern and the traditional. The family unit is of primary importance for most Gujaratis and it is wonderful to see how many families, members of all different ages, have such a good time together.

Rocky's Verdict: A nightlife hotspot, a visit here helps you understand so much more about the people of Gujarat. The kulfi alone is well worth the visit.
Rating: Taste: 7, Ambience: 10, Service: 8, Value for Money: 10, Total: 35
Specialities: Varieties of kulfi.
Veg/Non-veg: Veg
Contact Details/Timings: Open till 2 am. Kulfi Asharfi, Manek Chowk, Ahmedabad.
Prices: ₹ 150 per head for snacks and kulfi

DAS SURTI KHAMAN WALA This place proves that good things come in small packages. A long line of customers and bright colourful boards welcome you to this little gem of a place. Open for breakfast, the place serves khaman and khandvi throughout the day. Here's the inside scoop: if it's made out of rice it's called dhokla and if it's made out of chane ki dal (lentils) it's called khaman. So now you know.

The patra, made from seasonal leaves, is highly recommended as are the little samosas they make. The khaman 'tamtam' is a spicy little bombshell; the plain khaman prepared in the traditional way is also delicious. The khandvi, sandwich dhokla, and just about anything else you can get in this little shop is sure to be delicious. These snacks together are called farsan and any time is farsan time in Ahmedabad.

SOMETHING ON THE SIDE This was truly a revelation, so many tastes and so many textures, all different and all amazingly delicious. Gujaratis eat all through the day and after eating here I understand why.

Rocky's Verdict: Life can be divided into the period before and after you ate at Das Surti . Make the trip to Ahmedabad just to dig your teeth into this. One of the best breakfasts we have ever had!!!
Rating: Taste: 10, Ambience: 10, Service: 9, Value for Money: 8, Total: 37
Certified: Rocky and Mayur rating of excellence
Specialities: Khaman, patra, and sandwich dhokla
Veg/Non-veg: Veg
Contact Details/Timings: Das Surti Khaman Wala, Trade Centre, Naurang road, Ahmedabad. Phone: 0-9898406576
Prices: ₹ 75 per head

Anand

HOTEL UMMIYA ANNAPURNA KATHIYAWAD   This was once a popular stop along the highway. It has now been bypassed with the new expressway. Technically it is still on NH8 in the Anand district, which is the home of Amul Dairy.

Kathiyawad cuisine is spicy, rich, and prepared in a distinctly different manner.

Most of the food is cooked over wood fires, and the rustic flavour mixes well with the delicate combination of spices. The rotis called bhakris have a distinct flavour after they are cooked on clay 'tavdi'. This is one powerhouse of a cuisine and **UMMIYA KATHIYAWADI** represents it with distinction.

The must-haves would be the delicious lassan aloo, sev tamatar, besan gatta, and the ever-present rotla (local bread). This is served with white jaggery and ghee. The accompaniments are equally good and include papads, fried green chillies, onions, and some tasty achaars (pickles).

As you enter the **UMMIYA ANNAPURNA** the tempting smell from the several wood fires burning in the open-air kitchen greet you, preparing you for the meal you are soon to enjoy.

SOMETHING ON THE SIDE   As modern kitchens mushroom all over our highways, places like this stand out like little gems. Traditional methods of cooking traditional foods, which may be time consuming and labour intensive, are still in practice here. We all need to support these places lest we lose our culinary heritage to 'fast food'.

Rocky's Verdict: Must stop for lunch or dinner. A traditional Indian dining experience. Be ready for some serious spice and remember this is NOT the sweet Gujarati cuisine. This one bites right back.
Rating: Taste: 8, Ambience: 9, Service: 9, Value for Money: 8, Total: 34
Specialities: Lassan aloo, sev tamatar, besan gatta, and rotla
Veg/Non-veg: Veg

> **Contact Details/Timings:** Hotel Ummiya Annapurna, Anand, NH 8.
> **Prices:** ₹ 75 per head

Bhuj

ANNAPURNA LODGE The Annapurna Lodge serves Kutchi cuisine which includes the staple rotla, a heavy bread made with bajra, ringda, sev tamatar, and mixed vegetables. It also serves a great thali which consists of six items which change daily and three that are fixed. The fixed items are khichdi (a rice and dal mix), kadhi (prepared using sour yogurt), and chane ki dal. The meal ends with cooling chaach (buttermilk) and gur (jaggery) with ghee.

SOMETHING ON THE SIDE If you're in the mood for some meat, pop in to Noorani Mahal next door for some passable kebabs and tandoori meats.

> **Rocky's Verdict:** Places like these are keeping our food traditions alive. The rates are remarkably low as well.
> **Rating:** Taste: 8, Ambience: 6, Service: 8, Value for Money: 9, Total: 31
> **Specialities:** Thali
> **Veg/Non-veg:** Veg
> **Contact Details/Timings:** Annapurna Lodge, Bhid Gate, Bhuj. Phone: Mr Vinod 0-9725470017.
> **Prices:** All items are under ₹ 10 per portion

KANDOI VELJI KARA The pakwan at this restaurant was invented by the great-grandfather of the present owner and is made with refined flour swilled around in vegetable oil. The result is a fluffy and crisp breakfast dish best had with sweetened milk tea. The pakwan is available in many sizes and flavours including pepper, cumin, and so on. Another unique breakfast dish is the saata, a sweet bread with rose petals.

SOMETHING ON THE SIDE   We saw a number of NRIs (non resident Indians) come and buy the pakwan in large quantities. This is carried abroad as it requires a certain skill to make this dish. Possibly one of the best-travelled Indian preparations.

Rocky's Verdict: A pleasant enough breakfast. The tea is a must.
Rating: Taste: 7, Ambience: 5, Service: 10, Value for Money: 10, Total: 32
Specialities: Pakwan and saata
Veg/Non-veg: Veg
Contact Details/Timings: Saraf Bazaar, Bhuj. Phone: Mr Chetan 0-9825901266
Prices: Saata ₹ 80 per kg and pakwan ₹ 100 per kg

KISAN LODGE   Any local you ask in Bhuj will recommend this eatery as the place to go for home food away from home. The restaurant is a very basic one with a small room that has wooden benches and tables clustered together and a small, dark kitchen. The unique thing here is that all the food is cooked using firewood, lending a nice smoky flavour to the food. Kisan is famous for its thali of traditional Kutchi food including rotlas made of millet, khari bhath, ringda subzi, sev tamatar, and a dry potato bhaji. Fresh buttermilk is served chilled with the thali.

SOMETHING ON THE SIDE   The locals love the Kisan Lodge for its basic and unpretentious food. It is a fabulous place to come to share stories and rotla with them.

Mayur's Verdict: Honest, fresh, basic and tasty food served in modest surroundings with care and attention explains why the Kisan Lodge is highly recommended by the locals. We join in with the crowd in recommending this eatery for a taste of Kutchi food.
Rating: Taste: 7, Ambience: 5, Service: 8, Value for Money: 9,

Total: 29
Specialities: Kutchi food
Veg/Non-veg: Veg
Contact Details/Timings: Kisan Lodge, Bhid Gate, Bhuj.
Phone: Mr Bharat 0-9879842993.
Prices: The dishes are all under ₹ 10 per portion.

Jamnagar

SHIKHAND SAMRAT Shikhand is a tart, tangy, and creamy
yogurt-based delight and you can pick from the twenty-three
flavours that the Shikhand Samrat offers. The shop is very
clean and brightly lit, with a range of sweets and savouries
displayed in glass counters and on glass-fronted wall shelves.
There are trays full of freshly made breakfast goodies like the
juicy khandvi, tasty khaman, and flaky patoda. The golf ball-
sized pharali kachori filled with dried fruits and nuts, coated
with chickpea flour and deep fried to golden perfection, is
eaten when you are fasting.

Delicious tangy green chutney, a speciality of Jamnagar, is
made from ground peanuts and green chillies with a hint of
lemon, and lasts up to a month without spoiling.

SOMETHING ON THE SIDE The brothers who run this place are
just as colourful as the food they serve so make sure you, ask
them for some stories of the food they grew up on.

Mayur's Verdict: If you are in Jamnagar do not miss out on
a visit to the Shikhand Samrat to start your day on a great
note. Fill up on fresh, light, and tasty breakfast snacks and
carry away some kachori and chutney to keep you going
through the day, month and year.
Rating: Taste: 8, Ambience: 7, Service: 9, Value for Money: 9,
Total: 33
Specialities: Plain shikhand
Veg/Non-veg: Veg

Contact Details/Timings: Shikhand Samrat, Central Bank Road, Jamnagar. Phone: 0-9824602351.
Prices: Shikhand upwards of ₹ 80 per kg and other snack items around ₹ 100 per kg

Mandvi

GAABA DABELI   Gaaba arrives at his designated street corner every day at 11 am wheeling his wooden cart, and with a dexterity born of years of practise he splits a pav bun into half, scoops in a mashed potato masala mixture, some chilli, and a bit of vegetable broth. The final product redolent with the aroma of spices, is then served on pieces of old newspaper, which also serve as wrapping for the many parcels of dabeli that are ordered and carried away. The dabeli tastes sweet and spicy and is amazingly addictive. Gaaba's dabeli is so popular that people line up to wait for Gaaba's arrival every day.

SOMETHING ON THE SIDE   He makes and serves only 600 dabelis a day and many regulars will pack as many as twenty dabelis to carry away and enjoy with their families. Make sure you get there early.

Mayur's Verdict: The dabeli is an example of the best, most delicious street food.
Rating: Taste: 10, Ambience: 7, Service: 7, Value for Money: 10, Total: 34
Certified: Rocky and Mayur rating of excellence
Specialities: Dabeli
Veg/Non-veg: Veg
Contact Details/Timings: Gaaba Bhai Dabeli Wala, Subzi Market, Mandvi.
Prices: Dabeli ₹ 4 per piece

Porbandar

HOTEL ANAND   This hotel specializes in khajli (not to be confused with khujli—the skin irritation), a dry crisp biscuit-like savoury which is best had with tea. It also comes in different flavours with mustard seeds, pepper, and so on.

SOMETHING ON THE SIDE   Porbandar is proud of its most famous son, Mahatma Gandhi. His images are all over the city and he is just as revered and respected today as he was when he got our country its independence.

Rocky's Verdict: Try it once!
Rating: Taste: 5, Ambience: 5, Service: 5, Value for Money: 5, Total: 20
Specialities: Khajli
Veg/Non-veg: Veg
Contact Details/Timings: Hotel Anand, Ravi Bagh Chowk, MG Road, Porbandar. Phone: Mr Vipul 0-9426944445.
Prices: Masala khajli ₹ 100 per kg and mori khajli ₹ 90 per kg

---

SHREE GAYATRI PAROTHA HOUSE   As you enter this long and narrow shop run by the portly Girish Bhai, you are greeted by a Gujarati rate list. The speciality of this restaurant is that the food is prepared in the spicy Kathiyawadi style. Popular items include the ringda, ondeo (vegetable stew), besan ki vadi, and sev tamatar. Each dish has its own unique flavour and many are made without using onions. Accompaniments are the rotli (thin flour roti), thepla (delicious paratha made with wheat flour and fenugreek), and the mighty rotla.

SOMETHING ON THE SIDE   Kitchens in Gujarat employ traditional cooking methods but have now started using modern storage methods to keep the food piping hot. Most common is a stainless steel apparatus with deep containers which uses a gas flame to keep the food hot. Most places are also extremely clean.

> **Rocky's Verdict:** Incredibly tasty and well-made food. Each
> preparation tastes unique. A must-stop if you're ever in
> Porbandar.
> **Rating:** Taste: 9, Ambience: 7, Service: 10, Value for
> Money: 10, Total: 36
> **Certified:** Rocky and Mayur rating of excellence
> **Specialities:** Ondeo and ringda
> **Veg/Non-veg:** Veg
> **Contact Details/Timings:** Shree Gayatri Parotha House,
> State Transport Road, Porbandar.
> **Prices:** Most preparations are ₹ 15 per portion

Surat

BOMBAY WALE BABU BHAI TAWA FRY   It is a blink-and-miss
little place with a bright red sign in Gujarati above. This place
has a lot of people who returned from Burma and brought back
the delicious khaosouey and a whole lot of recipes including
the 'Rangooni paratha'. This is a no-frills place that primarily
serves chaamp or a well-mashed and highly spiced mixture of
goat kidney, liver, and rib meat. It is cooked on a large flat metal
plate with oil and continuously ground finer as it gets cooked.
The end-product is one step away from a meat paste and is
delicious. The Irani paratha is a date-stuffed bread flattened
and fried in oil. The other favourites are the seekh kebabs,
mutton keema, and nawabi paratha. The seekhs are tender and
juicy and very spicy, the keema is well cooked and tender, and
the chaamp is undoubtedly the star of the meal and it is tawa
fried. This array is served with shredded onions and fresh mint
leaves eaten whole and the combination is delightful. Carry
lots of water as everything is super spicy.

In case you are a vegetarian you can get a few titbits around
in shops close by but this is predominantly a meat place.
Vegetarians will be hard pressed in this area.

SOMETHING ON THE SIDE   The place is in the Muslim quarter and
there is a tradition to step out in the evenings for a snack of
boti or chaamp over animated conversations before returning

home for a meal. It makes for plenty of company and some great chats on the history of the area if you go there early evening.

Rocky's Verdict: Sit out under the open sky and eat a hearty meal with the locals. Plenty of good stories about the old Burmese connections can be listened to.
Rating: Taste: 7, Ambience: 7, Service: 8, Value for Money: 9, Total: 31
Specialities: Chaamp
Veg/Non-veg: Non-veg
Contact Details/Timings: Bombay Wale Babu Bhai Tawa Fry, Near Randher bus stand, Surat. Phone: 0-9824101318.
Prices: Keema and chaamp ₹ 30 each, seekhs two for ₹ 15, and nawabi paratha ₹ 7 per piece

---

JANI FARSAN It is one of the better known khaman and farsan places in Surat. Young Amit Anantrai Jani tells us that they prepare 'Surti' khaman which is made using chane ki dal and is cooked for up to eight hours. The resulting khaman is dry and very flavourful. They also make the famous ponkh locha where ponkh is crushed into a paste and served with boiled chickpea flour and onions, tomatoes, chopped green chillies, red chilli powder, and lime juice making it a delicious breakfast. The steamed rice idra is also quite good. There are small samosas stuffed with Bengal gram, the bitter leafy patra is another old Gujarati favourite.

Rocky's Verdict: The best way to transport your soul straight to heaven, they say, is to have 'Surat ko khaman aur Kashi ko maran' which means the khaman of Surat and death in Kashi. We can't vouch for the dying bit but we can honestly tell you that the part about the khaman is true.
Rating: Taste: 8, Ambience: 7, Service: 9, Value for Money: 10, Total: 34

Certified: Rocky and Mayur rating of excellence
Specialities: Khaman, dhokla, and locha
Veg/Non-veg: Veg
Contact Details/Timings: Jani Farsan, Parle Point, Surat.
Phone: 0-9898050107.
Prices: Surti khaman ₹ 80 per kg, rice idra ₹ 80 per kg, and
patra 120 per kg

PONKH MARKET It is an annual market dedicated to the humble ponkh. Ponkh comes close to jowar (sorghum) in its raw form but has a fresh and tasty green juicy seed. The market consists of a number of large shack stalls set up for the two months when ponkh is available. They sell a wide array of ponkh products from ponkh chutney, ponkh vadas, and fresh ponkh itself. This humble grain attracts many to this out-of-the-way place and justly so. It can be eaten by itself (it has a tasty freshly boiled lentil sort of taste) but is best had with sev which is available here in many flavours like spinach, pepper, and plain. Add the ponkh to the sev, throw in freshly chopped onions, green chillies, and some masalas and you have a ready-to-eat, great, and healthy snack.

The ponkh spills out into the markets and is mostly seen as ponkh chutney in most shops. It is also famous as the ponkh locha where it is crushed into a paste and served with boiled chickpea flour and onions, tomatoes, chopped green chillies, red chilli powder, and lime juice and it is a delicious breakfast.

SOMETHING ON THE SIDE There are a number of men beating the ponkh seed out of its shell to loud Gujarati music. Young women separate the ponkh from the chaff right next to their men and it is sold over a counter right there.

Rating: Taste: 8, Ambience: 2, Service: 9, Value for Money: 9,
Total: 28
Specialities: Ponkh chutney and ponkh locha

Veg/Non-veg: Veg
Contact Details/Timings: Ponkh Market, under Sardar Bridge, Surat. Usually it lasts from mid-November to mid-January.
Prices: Raw ponkh is ₹ 80 per kg, ponkh vada from ₹ 40 to ₹ 110 per kg

SRI BALAJI JANTA ICE CREAM   There are many by the same name all across Surat but the Parle Point one is special. Pratik Patel, the owner, claims to have customers from all over the country who come to try the strange flavours offered here. It has unique ice cream flavours which could possibly only have been invented in India, by Indians and for the Indian palate. The most popular weird flavours in this otherwise swanky, clean and regular ice cream parlour are (hold your breath!)... garlic, green chilli, lemon, mint, ginger, coriander, whisky, and many other such flavours which are rare in the regular world of ice creams. The mint and ginger are not bad. The coriander and whisky are pretty edible. The green chilli (which tastes like, surprise surprise, fresh green chilli) is a little hard to eat but garlic was never meant to be combined with ice cream and is so bad that you need to taste it to believe it. It's not going to do any wonders for your breath so carry chewing gum or be prepared to eat some mint ice cream after eating the garlic one. Take a scoop and the whole family can try a bite each and compare this rare taste. Have fun!

Rocky's Verdict: It's so weird that it has to be tried.
Rating: Don't ask me
Specialities: Garlic and green chilli ice cream
Veg/Non-veg: Veg
Contact Details/Timings: Sri Balaji Janta Ice cream, Parle Point, Surat. Phone: 0-9904400678.
Prices: ₹ 30 to ₹ 35 for various ice creams

Vadodara

FOOD STREET The whole street comes alive at night as hundreds of students, student lovers, and lovers of street food throng the street enjoying meals served by the row of mobile shacks selling Chinese wok-fried noodles, burgers, sandwiches, biryani, and local fizzy drinks in a range of flavours. Hundreds of scooters and motorcycles are parked by the roadside and the pavement has so many plastic tables and chairs set up that there is no place to walk. The food is served quick, hot, and cheap catering mostly to students, though a fair number of families and young dating couples can also be seen chatting, laughing, and tucking into their food.

SOMETHING ON THE SIDE Somewhere among the stands is a place that does local fizzy drinks. Try the cola soda and decide whether it is the predecessor or successor to its more famous multinational cousin.

Mayur's Verdict: The food is obviously very popular judging by the crowds who are not expecting gourmet meals. A good, relaxed way to spend an evening laughing and joking with your friends or watching other people do the same as you munch on food dedicated to salt, deep frying, and potential heart attacks.
Rating: Taste: 6, Ambience: 8, Service: 6, Value for Money: 7, Total: 27
Specialities: Everything is a speciality there.
Veg/Non-veg: Non-veg
Contact Details/Timings: Food Street, Right by the University on Fatehganj Road, Vadodara.
Prices: Fill your belly for less than ₹ 50 per person

MAHAKALI SEV USAL This hidden treasure is one of the many makeshift shacks and mobile carts selling roadside snacks near the bus station. However, Mahakali is the busiest with high tables and a long counter providing standing room to streams of customers that appear, eat, and depart continuously.

Bowls are filled with thick gravy from a giant pateela and some sweet and spicy chutneys are swirled in. The crisp deep-fried sev is sprinkled on top and a garnish of fresh coriander leaves is added before you are handed the plate, complete with two pieces of fresh pav. This sacred ritual is complete when you break off a piece of pav, use it to scoop out some usal and bite into it. The instantly addictive usal, a thick gravy made from potatoes and dried peas, has a tantalizing mix of sweet and super spicy tastes. Onion and garlic are evident in every pungent bite and many a pav are broken apart, dipped into the usal and consumed as your eyes water with the bite of chillies made tantalizing thanks to the sweet aftertaste. The sev adds a crisp punch to every mouthful and there will be many mouthfuls before you can stagger away with a groan and a big smile.

SOMETHING ON THE SIDE   If you feel like sitting down to eat then check out the new hotel the Mahakali people have built just round the corner.

Mayur's Verdict: This is Indian roadside food at its best and we would recommend a trip to Vadodara just to enjoy a few trips to Mahakali Sev Usal. We really would...really.
Rating: Taste: 10, Ambience: 5, Service: 9, Value for Money: 10, Total: 34
Certified: Rocky and Mayur rating of excellence
Specialities: Usal pav
Veg/Non-veg: Veg
Contact Details/Timings: Mahakali Sev Usal, near Kirti Stambh, Vadodara.
Prices: Usal ₹ 15 and Re 1 for each additional pav

PURAN SINGH'S KHANA KHAZANA Run by a 'retired' chef, Khana Khazana is a gem for lovers of all things meat in mostly vegetarian Vadodara, although the sign does inform you that it is 'Veg & Non Veg'. Puran Singh, the owner, churns out interesting new recipes like the anari kebab made by marinating boneless chicken pieces in fresh pomegranate juice before grilling in the tandoor. It is extremely soft and has an intriguingly different taste. The chicken malai kebab is a really juicy, succulent, tender kebab bursting with the slightly smoky taste of the tandoor.

Vegetarians have plenty to eat too. The cheese and garnish stuffed cheese aloo roasted in its jacket is a savoury delight as is the filling cheese naan full of melted cheese, spring onions, and capsicum chunks. The tandoori paneer tikka has a tasty tomato marinade though the paneer itself is a bit dry. Make sure you ask for extra helpings of the onion ring salad sprinkled with a really tangy, spicy masala. Gravy items such as butter chicken and dal makhani are creamy delights and best had with the tandoori rotis.

SOMETHING ON THE SIDE Order your food and sit outside on a stone slab looking out on to the street or enjoy a conversation with the customers of the café next door as they enjoy their coffee.

Mayur's Verdict: Each bite here is savoury and easily explains why Puran Singh was able to move up from selling his tandoor snacks off a lorry (wheeled food cart) outside the tax office. This smiling man loves to chat whether it is tips on cooking tender meat or stories of important customers past and present. Do visit here for a delicious meal cooked and served with love. You can have your order packed to take away and enjoy at your leisure in more scenic surroundings.

Rating: Taste: 8, Ambience: 5, Service: 8, Value for Money: 7, Total: 28

Specialities: Anari chicken kebab and cheese naan

Veg/Non-veg: Non-veg

Contact Details/Timings: Off Post Office Road

Prices: Chicken malai kebab ₹ 120, anari kebab ₹ 140, and tandoori paneer tikka ₹ 85

RAJU OMELETTE CENTRE This eatery has a menu board on which all twelve out of fourteen items listed start with the word 'butter'. If you want to be 'healthy' then there are four to five options with groundnut oil! Eggs in various forms are moved about on the skillet with deft hands as a mix of chopped onions, tomatoes, green chillies, coriander, and a whole bunch of spices are added. Almost 250 gm (that's a chunk about the size of a closed fist!!) of butter is then added and the mix is quickly fried and ladled on to a plate to eat with fresh soft buns (also soaked in hot butter!).

The butter boiled tikka, essentially a scrambled egg mixture, is a greasy but delicious concoction while the butter crush omelette stuffed into buns is a milder taste though no less buttery. The huge amounts of butter used, really bring out the flavour of the other ingredients and if it is not spicy enough you can always add the spicy green chutney available at tables where crowds of people are standing and eating.

SOMETHING ON THE SIDE Raju, the owner of the place, creates his magic at a giant flat skillet just behind the counter. Five people form the back-up team, boiling, and peeling eggs, chopping the ingredients, and slicing open buns to keep up with the fast moving Raju who will sometimes have up to twenty-five eggs cooking simultaneously in various forms.

Mayur's Verdict: Anything you order from the list is sure to be delicious. Each bite not only tastes heavenly, but also brings you a step or few closer to heaven as this is anything but a heart-healthy meal. It's well worth putting your diet plans aside and tucking into one though.
Rating: Taste: 9, Ambience: 7, Service: 9, Value for Money: 10, Total: 35
Certified: Rocky and Mayur rating of excellence
Specialities: Butter boiled tikka
Veg/Non-veg: Non-veg
Contact Details/Timings: Raju Omelette Centre, Kareilbaug. 4 pm to 10:30 pm
Prices: Butter boiled tikka ₹ 40 and butter crush omelette ₹ 40

SHREE RAJASTHAN KULFI HOUSE Heaven sometimes has interesting addresses! Come evening time and you will find crowds of people clustered around this brightly lit tin shack. Welcome to a place where happiness is a sweet affair. From behind a counter top composed of freezers, a bunch of busy men cut and dole out chunks of kulfi to an ever-appreciative audience.

Kulfi here comes in a range of flavours both traditional such as pista and anjeer (fig), and exotic such as malai, orange, and raspberry. If you want to be adventurous then order the mix kulfi which has slices of a number of flavours. Each helping is of 100 gm or multiples and is sliced off from long tubes of kulfi that look rather like giant candles that set your heart aflame and your taste buds tingling. Each mouthful is a sweet delight and the quality of ingredients and the care that goes into making the kulfis is clearly evident. The flavour of fresh fruit combines with a slightly chewy texture to leave a cool, fresh feeling after each mouthful and the sugar high just makes you happier.

SOMETHING ON THE SIDE If you like your food to be 'good looking' as well as delicious then opt for the mixed plate and enjoy the rainbow colours on your plate.

Mayur's Verdict: Swing by the Race Course Circle in the evening and join in the fun. For some strange reason everyone seems to be in a good mood and the conversations flow quick and loud. A highly recommended place to 'be cool'.
Rating: Taste: 8, Ambience: 6, Service: 7, Value for Money: 6, Total: 27
Specialities: Kulfiii!!!
Veg/Non-veg: Veg
Contact Details/Timings: Corner of R.C. Dutt Road and Race Course Road.
Prices: ₹ 12 to ₹ 17 per plate

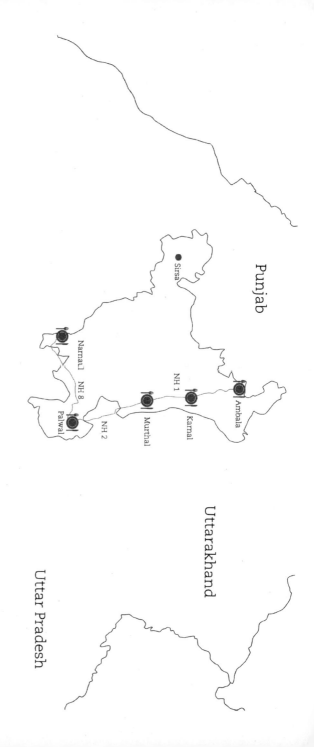

Ambala

PURAN SINGH KA DHABA The town of Ambala has been made famous by Puran Singh's dhaba. The mutton curry has a status and the chicken curry too is very good. But be warned—the hygiene in the place has slipped to dismal standards. The plates are filthy and there are bones and curry on the floor. Risk this if you can handle the filth. Packing your lunch and eating it in a shady spot on the highway might be a better idea.

SOMETHING ON THE SIDE Started sometime in the 1950s, the dhaba was sold in 1995 along with the chefs, the name, and the location to a man named Vijender Nagar, whose family used to supply meat and chicken to the original Puran Singh Dhaba. There is now a violent dispute over the name and rights of the dhaba between Puran Singh's wife and son, and Vijender Nagar and family. This has given rise to at least five different dhabas with the name 'asli' (real) and Puran Singh in them. As far as we can tell, the real one is the (get ready for it)…Puran Singh ka Mashoor Registered Vishal Dhaba.

Rocky's Verdict: Great lunch. Be prepared for the filth.
Rating: Taste: 10, Ambience: 2, Service: 6, Value for Money: 8, Total: 26
Specialities: Mutton curry
Veg/Non-veg: Non-veg
Contact Details/Timings: GT Road, Ambala.
Prices: ₹ 80–100 per head

Karnal

ZHILMIL DHABA COMPLEX   This rather unremarkable stop serves the usual tandoori chicken, dal, and subzi. It is better located to capitalize on hungry highway travellers than Murthal and has stores where you can buy shoes, T-shirts, and even multinational ice cream. But that does not take away from the disappointing food.

SOMETHING ON THE SIDE   The Zhilmil Dhaba belongs to two rather large and loud gentlemen called Mr Saini and Mr Saini who sit and control the entire complex with the power of their booming voices, quivering large moustaches, and a horde of helpers. These brothers started with just one dhaba and now have more than five, some even with the option of air conditioning!

Just across the road is Savoy Greens, a new place boasting poor air conditioning, McDonald's, Domino's, and other such delights for those who like that kind of stuff.

If you ever feel like stopping in Karnal, the Karna Lake Complex run by Haryana Tourism is your best bet. The dosas are the hot-selling item and are rather good. The lake offers clichéd boating and an opportunity to sit in the shade as hoopoes root for worms and treepies hop around expectantly hoping for a morsel or two.

Rocky's Verdict: Avoidable!
Rating: Taste: 5, Ambience: 3, Service: 7, Value for Money: 6, Total: 21
Specialities: Dal, mixed vegetables
Veg/Non-veg: Non-veg
Contact Details/Timings: About 3 hours away from Delhi. Zhilmil Dhaba, Karnal, NH 1. Phone: 0184-2267862
Prices: ₹ 100 per head

Murthal

GULSHAN KA DHABA   Gulshan ka Dhaba lies in the famous highway stop of Murthal. The first meal we ever ate on the show consisted of their paratha and kali mah ki sabut dal, along with some delicious Pachranga achaar and delicious home-made dahi. The Gulshan aloo-pyaaz (potato and onion) paratha remains one of the best that money can buy on the Indian highway. Tandoor roasted and surprisingly light, you could go on eating them but for the large dollops of home-made white butter that they serve on top of each paratha—a must if you want the authentic flavour. We recommend breakfast with Gulshan chai (tea)—sweet, milky, and tasting the way only dhaba chais can. Coffee drinkers can find a new Barista Lavazza a little further on. Gulshan's new menu includes popular Indian Chinese snacks, pizzas, and burgers.

SOMETHING ON THE SIDE   The original Gulshan Dhaba, demolished in 2007 is a small, makeshift set-up under the Murthal flyover. There is now a newer, swankier Gulshan Dhaba about 400 metres past the flyover. There is also a small stall just outside the old dhaba in which a portly, moustachioed gent sits, selling home remedies for the thirty-four ailments listed on the wall outside. These range from the ever popular 'Gas' to the miracle cure for 'All tipe of Canser'. When asked about the cancer cure, we were told it is a 'Top Secret Mix' and involved consuming the ash made from burning certain herbs and minerals over six months. We suggest you stick with the parathas.

Rocky's Verdict: Must have breakfast here.
Rating: Taste: 9, Ambience: 5, Service: 7, Value for Money: 9, Total: 30
Specialities: The aloo-pyaaz paratha
Veg/Non-veg: Veg
Contact Details Timing: About 50 km from Delhi
Gulshan Dhaba, Murthal. Phone: 0130-2482139
Prices: ₹ 50–80 per head

Narnaul

CHANDNI MIDWAY MOTEL Started eleven years ago, Chandni Midway has a lovely backyard which turns lush green after the rains. Lots of gentle green hills in the back, partridges calling, and fresh air are the highlights. The place itself caters predominantly to foreigners going towards Rajasthan. For lunch and dinner the usual fare is an Indian buffet. Catering to the foreign palate, the food is mildly spiced and you will need lots of chilli pickle in case you like spice in your meal.

SOMETHING ON THE SIDE   There is a small shop selling souveniers and snacks like potato chips.

Rocky's Verdict: The food is not very tasty though the place is nice. Stop and stretch your legs.
Rating: Taste: 5, Ambience: 8, Service: 4, Value for Money: 6, Total: 23
Specialities: Stick to the buffet
Veg/Non-veg: Non-veg
Contact Details/Timings: Singhana Road, Narnaul-123001, Haryana. Phone: +91-01282-250114
Prices: Buffet ₹ 190

Palwal

HARI KRISHNA DHABA This section of NH 2 has many dhabas clustered together on both sides of the highway. Each has a young man outside gesticulating and waving in, what they hope, is an inviting manner to try and attract hungry motorists to their dhaba.

Hari Krishna is your basic dhaba with four walls, a roof, a smoky kitchen, and a brick-and-mud wall displaying large containers of pre-prepared food. The names of some of the dishes offered are painted on the wall and include your standard fare of gobhi aloo, parathas, and dal. You could also listen to a young man rattle off the entire menu from memory before ordering. There is a delightfully appropriate sign promising you respect if you make your requests in a polite manner.

The food is cooked fresh every morning and on order it is ladled out into a frying pan where spices are added to it before being served to you piping hot. The hot and tasty parathas are served with the obligatory gobs of butter, fresh yogurt, Pachranga pickle, and fresh and spicy green chilli and coriander chutney. The dhaba keeps it own cows, so you can look forward to fresh dahi, paneer, and white butter.

The speciality of the house is the Hari Krishna Special—a rich, calorie-laden concoction with paneer, coconut, tons of cream, cashew nuts, raisins, tomatoes, and coriander all bound together with a paste made of blended cashews. To add to this, it is cooked in copious amounts of ghee, or clarified butter. It is a very tasty dish though and you will find yourself smiling even while your arteries cringe inside.

SOMETHING ON THE SIDE If you are in need of some retail therapy there are a couple of stores which sell Pachranga pickle and bootlegged DVDs of some pretty shady movies.

Mayur's Verdict: Good, hot, tasty food is on offer for all ye that halt here. The masala chai is an option if you want just a quick break from driving and are not too keen on eating a month's worth of calories at one sitting
Rating: Taste: 7, Ambience: 7, Service: 7, Value for Money: 7, Total: 28
Specialities: Hari Krishna Special
Veg/Non-veg: Veg
Contact Details/Timings: On NH 2 not a long way out of Delhi. Hari Krishna Dhaba, NH 2, Palwal.
Phone: 0-9416103345
Prices: Aloo pyaaz paratha ₹ 15, paneer malai (Hari krishna Special) ₹ 110

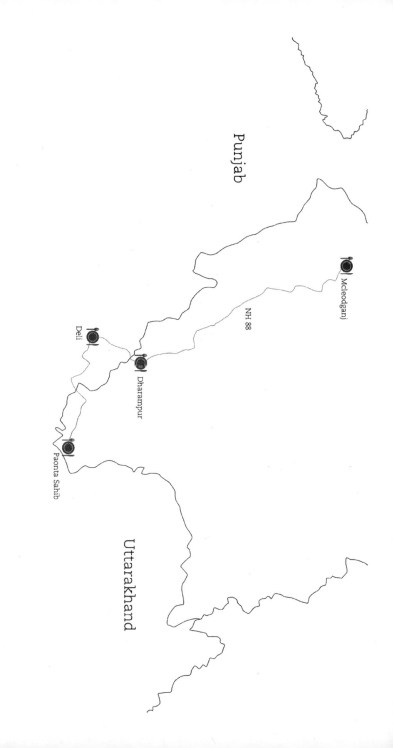

Deli

SHAKTI PICKLES   This is the famous stop on the Chandigarh–Shimla route where meat pickles are available. Deli was made famous by Mr Walia who started a small shop selling meat and chicken pickles to people going to or coming from the hills. What started as one shop many years ago has now turned into many. As the family grows, so do the number of shops. As you turn along an inconspicuous curve of the road you come right into the middle of a dozen or more shops all owned by persons with the same last name (Walia) and all selling the same thing, pickles. The variety too has increased over the years and now you can get mutton, chicken, garlic, mango, mushroom, carrot, turnip, and cauliflower pickle among others.

The meats are boiled and then fried before being pickled and the pickle can last up to two months.

SOMETHING ON THE SIDE   A new addition to the pickles is the apple cider and fruit wines which some of the pickle shops have started stocking as well. They seem to be very popular but try one before buying a case.

Rocky's Verdict: The vegetarian pickles are nice but nothing to write home about, so stick with the meat pickles.
Rating: Taste: 8, Ambience: 4, Service: 4, Value for Money: 7, Total: 23
Specialities: Meat and chicken pickles
Veg/Non-veg: Non-veg
Contact Details/Timings: 20 km from Dharampur, Himachal Pradesh. Shakti Pickles, Deli, NH 22.
Prices: Mutton ₹ 240 per kg, chicken ₹ 240 per kg, garlic, mango, mushroom all for ₹ 120 per kg

Dharampur

GIANI DA DHABA   This landmark roadside eatery offers a
large menu of items including different types of chicken, rice,
rotis, dal, and salads. The aloo paratha and the paneer paratha
covered with melting butter and served with fresh dahi are
made on the tandoor and are truly a treat. Their lemon chicken
is flavourful and cooked to just the right degree. Vegetables and
chicken are available both tandoori style or served in curries.
The food is neither too oily nor too spicy and the salad is fresh
and very tasty.

The whole room is divided into sections by cement columns
and tables are filled with diners enjoying their food. Tiled walls,
fans, and swept floors make this a very popular, clean, and safe
option for travelling families.

SOMETHING ON THE SIDE   Run by the Bhatia family since 1976
this place is so popular that a whole market has grown around
it with other eateries, fruit wine outlets, stores, and even a café
belonging to a well-known coffee chain.

The owner and his sons (and sometimes the sweet
grandmother) run the whole operation from behind a long
counter from where you can also buy all sorts of snacks and
chocolates for the road. Shelves on the wall are lined with soft
drinks and the fruit wines for which Himachal is famous.

Mayur's Verdict: It's not just the perfect location on a busy
highway that makes Giani so popular. It's the personal touch
that the family puts by being there and the comfortable
surroundings that they have created. It's mostly about
basic, clean, fresh food that loyal customers swear has not
changed in taste for the last three decades.
Rating: Taste: 7, Ambience: 7, Service: 8, Value for Money: 8,
Total: 30
Specialities: Lemon chicken, aloo paratha, and paneer
paratha

Veg/Non-veg: Non-veg
Contact Details/Timings: On the winding hilly section of NH 22 at Dharampur, somewhere between Shimla and Chandigarh.
Giani Da Dhaba, Dharampur, NH 22. Phone: 01792-264066
Prices: Lemon chicken ₹ 200, aloo paratha ₹ 10, aloo pyaaz paratha ₹ 12

Mcleodganj

FIRST CUP CAFÉ Walk down the descending and winding Jogi Para Road in the morning and you will encounter people enjoying their breakfast by the road.

First Cup Café is a great place to stroll down to and enjoy a cup of steaming hot cappuccino as you deliberate over your choices. It's a pretty and sparkling clean place with modern wood and steel furniture and you can feast outdoors or indoors. There is a glass-fronted display with the yummies of the day ordered in delicious lines on the shelves. You can get cakes, freshly baked pies, and croissants or you can feel healthy as you munch on a bowl of muesli, yogurt, fresh fruit, and honey which at ₹ 30, is a bargain. Eggs in their many forms are served with some delicious local bakery bread and bowls of jam and butter range from ₹ 40 to ₹ 60. Depending on the filling, crêpes at about the same price are best enjoyed with honey or syrup dripping over them, but you can also opt for chopped fresh fruit instead.

SOMETHING ON THE SIDE Get here early to snag the morning papers to read as you wait for it to get warm and for your 'first cup' to arrive.

Mayur's Verdict: Eat delicious food and watch the world stroll by at an unhurried pace. The best way to ensure that you start your day with a smile. Be warned though that the service is quite slow so expect to wait a while for your food.

Rating: Taste: 10, Ambience: 10, Service: 6, Value for
Money: 9, Total: 35
Certified: Rocky and Mayur rating of excellence
Specialities: Local bread and crêpes
Veg/Non-veg: Non-veg
Contact Details/Timings: First Cup Café, Jogi Para Road,
Mcleodganj.
Prices: Eggs to order ₹ 40–60, cappucino ₹ 40, banana mango
shake ₹ 40, Tibetan toast ₹ 70, muesli ₹ 30

NORLING RESTAURANT   McLeodganj lies at the base of the
Himalayas at an elevation of just over 2,000 metres. The cool
climate is perfect for the steaming hot momos and noodle soup
which this town is famous for.

Momos are steamed or fried with choices of filling including
minced meat, vegetables, cheese, or potatoes. There are momo
vendors at every corner and you can enjoy a plate of five
steaming hot momos with fiery red chilli sauce for ₹ 10 as you
take a break from shopping at the hundreds of stalls selling
cheap clothes and expensive curios. You can also go to the
Norling Restaurant and sit down to plates of momos and bowls
of thukpa or noodle soup. Sit at wooden tables in a dimly lit
room made bright with giant colourful paintings and tuck into
your choice of delicious, steaming hot noodle soup with oodles
of chopped vegetables and/or chicken and of course, noodles.
Each table has three little bowls containing chilli sauce, vinegar,
and soya sauce so enjoy making your combination to dip your
momos in.

Momos are a delicious appetizer to the healthy and
nourishing thukpa, both eaten using chopsticks. You can ask
for soft drinks or go with hot plain tea.

SOMETHING ON THE SIDE   Norling sits bang on the intersection
of two roads so keep a lookout to see if you can spot famous
Buddhists like Richard Gere strolling by.

Mayur's Verdict: Every bite at Norling will leave you smiling, and conversations with monks at nearby tables are always enjoyable. A must-visit.
Rating: Taste: 10, Ambience: 10, Service: 6, Value for Money: 9, Total: 35
Certified: Rocky and Mayur rating of excellence
Specialities: Thukpa and momos
Veg/Non-veg: Non-veg
Contact Details/Timings: Norling Restaurant, Jogi Para Road, McLeodganj. Phone: 0-9418105108
Prices: Veg momos ₹ 30 , chicken momos ₹ 55, thukpa ₹ 30 (veg) and ₹ 40 (chicken)

Paonta Sahib

GURDWARA SHRI PAONTA SAHIB Situated on the banks of the Yamuna River separating the states of Himachal Pradesh and Uttarakhand is this gurdwara built in memory of Sri Guru Gobind Singh. In keeping with the tradition at every gurdwara this one too offers a langar or free kitchen for community eating. The seating is a large open space with long coir mats set out on the floor. People sit in rows on the floor and are served food in metal plates from large buckets by volunteers who move up down the line replenishing empty dishes. The dal, rice, roti, and subzi are cooked in bulk but you would never guess this since the food is so tasty.

SOMETHING ON THE SIDE The gurdwara sits right by the riverbank so stop a while and enjoy the view and the cool breeze coming in from the river.

Mayur's Verdict: Eat at the gurdwara for a filling, tasty, basic meal that is obviously cooked and served with a lot of love. Remember to keep your head covered as you are in a place of worship and do not forget to rinse out and wash your own dishes after your meal.

Rating: Taste: 10, Ambience: 10, Service: 10, Value for Money: 10, Total: 40
Certified: Rocky and Mayur hope for a certificate of excellence from the powers that be!!
Specialities: Langar
Veg/Non-veg: Veg
Contact Details/Timings: God is available 24×7.
Prices: Free

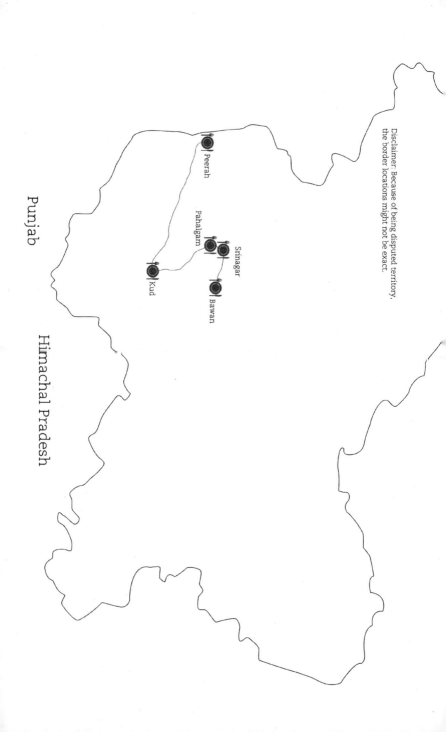

Punjab

Himachal Pradesh

Peerah

Pahalgam

Srinagar

Kud

Bawan

Disclaimer: Because of being disputed territory,
the border locations might not be exact.

Bawan

VAISHNO PUNJABI DHABA   Vaishno Punjabi Dhaba is a simple little place. A few steps away from the dust of the highway, this small establishment has just a kitchen and a few chairs and tables for customers. It may sound rough but this is Kashmir.

The dhaba will serve you Punjabi-style aloo gobhi with Kashmiri mirch, which really packs a punch. Also recommended are the chana masala and the rajma. The flavours are pungent and delicious. Rice is the staple food available but rotis are equally enjoyable and in true dhaba style, served piping hot. The water served is always fresh and ice cold as it comes out from a small spring behind the dhaba, ideal for the summer months. A bright yellow cloth marks the dhaba, but blink and you might miss the place.

SOMETHING ON THE SIDE   Make sure you stop here as next to the dhaba there is a cricket bat factory. Bats made of the famous Kashmiri willow are available here for around ₹ 350. Also next door is a zafran (saffron) trader who sells the best saffron in the world for ₹ 150 per gm. It's not cheap but it goes a long way in cooking. The Indian variety is the very best, followed by Spanish and finally Iranian saffron. The Spanish have very recently (in 2010) developed a saffron spray which is fast cornering the market, but Kashmiri saffron is still the best.

Rocky's Verdict: Eat some good Punjabi-style food here, and buy a good cricket bat!
Rating: Taste: 6.5, Ambience: 3, Service: 6.5, Value for Money: 6.5, Total: 22.5
Specialities: Aloo gobhi, chana masala, and the water!
Veg/Non-veg: Veg
Contact Details/Timings: Vaishno Punjabi Dhaba, NH1A, Bawan.
Prices: Chana masala ₹ 25, rajma ₹ 20. Cost per head ₹ 50

Kud

PREM SWEET SHOP   This town owes its fame to its delicious patisa or sohan papri. This exceptional patisa is made with desi ghee, gram flour, and plain flour. It is heavy due to the liberal amounts of ghee it contains, and served in thick sheets. At ₹ 120 per kg it is fairly priced. You must also try the rather nice milk cake.

SOMETHING ON THE SIDE   Some shops here have been making and selling this delicious sweet since 1925! Most shopkeepers believe it is the air and the water of Kud that makes the patisa as delicious as it is. Who are we to argue? We ate over 2 kg of the patisa while we stood at the shop and bought 10 kg each. Yes, it is that good.

Rocky's Verdict: It's the best patisa in the world! Stop and buy as much as you can carry.
Rating: Taste: 10, Ambience: 5, Service: 5, Value for Money: 9, Total: 29
Certified: Rocky and Mayur rating of excellence
Specialities: Patisa
Veg/Non-veg: Veg
Contact Details/Timings: Prem Sweet Shop, Kud.
Phone: 0-9419161914
Prices: Patisa ₹ 120 per kg

Pahalgam

GLACIER RESTAURANT   Glacier Restaurant serves fairly good Kashmiri wazwaan. The very essence of Kashmiri cuisine, the wazwaan consists of a variety of dishes which are served over many courses. Some popular dishes are methi korma, safed murg, zafrani murg, tabak maaz, daniwal korma, paneer, aab gosht, goshtaba, and finally the yakhni.

We managed to get our hands on seekh, mutton yakhni, rista, roganjosh, mirchi korma, daniya korma, and chicken curry. All dishes are eaten with rice. For the vegetarians there is mattar and palak, and tomato paneer. Liberal use of oil, large amounts of spices, and slow cooking make this a fabulous meal. The prices were a little steep at ₹ 120 for a plate of mutton and ₹ 130 for chicken but it was well worth the price.

The place itself is a little rundown but is cosy and warm on a freezing day, which more than makes up for the old décor and furniture. It's a family place and a popular venue.

SOMETHING ON THE SIDE Weddings are an opportunity to dig your teeth into some real wazwaan as a number of dishes are served. The wazwaan can have up to forty-five to fifty dishes at a grand wedding.

Rocky's Verdict: You must stop here and eat. Great food.
Certified: Rocky and Mayur rating of excellence
Rating: Taste: 9, Ambience: 5, Service: 5, Value for Money: 6, Total: 25
Specialities: Yakhni
Veg/Non-veg: Non-veg
Contact Details/Timings: Glacier Restaurant, Main Market, Pahalgam. Phone: 0-9419045128
Prices: Mutton ₹ 120 and chicken ₹ 130, cost per person ₹ 250

NOORMAHAL RESTAURANT This place can be found a little way away from the hustle and bustle of the heart of the main market. The walk to get there is well worth it as, in Pahalgam you will be hard pressed to find a place with a better view. Across the road from Noormahal lie the roaring white waters of the Lidder River. Behind the river are snow-capped mountains kissed by the clouds. In short, it is a stunning view. Take a morning walk and come here to indulge in a robust Kashmiri breakfast.

Start with a nunchai, or salty Kashmiri butter tea. The butter fortifies you for the cold day ahead and pumps some carbohydrates into your system. Try the lawas or the basic Kashmiri bread topped with butter. The kahwa they make is delightful and a must-have. It's topped with lots of dry fruits, cardamom, and even a touch of saffron. You could also get a simple egg-and-toast sort of breakfast but whatev_r you choose you must sit out in the garden and eat it. The temperature is cold, the sun is warm, and the tea a little strange, but you adapt to it fast. It may not be very dignified but lying on the grass and taking in the view early in the morning was indeed a treat!

SOMETHING ON THE SIDE Lots of butter in everything to help combat the extremely cold weather. A rustic and robust start to the day.

Rocky's Verdict. Enjoy your tea and the view. They will also make you a wazwaan for lunch or dinner but only if you pre-order it a couple of hours earlier.
Rating: Taste: 5, Ambience: 10, Service: 7, Value for Money: 10, Total: 32
Specialities: Nunchai and lawas
Veg/Non-veg: Non-veg
Contact Details/Timings: Noormahal, Main Road Pahalgam, Pahalgam.
Prices: Nunchai ₹ 10 and butter lawas ₹ 20, cost per person ₹ 35

Peerah

KHAJURIAH HOTEL This hotel is located in the area that many believe is the capital of rajma and chawal in India. This humble dish, which is still the staple Sunday lunch of many a family in north India, reaches new heights here. Testaments to it are the several dhabas or 'hotels' which serve only this combination to all comers.

Khajurial. Hotel is forty years old and serves basmati chawal which comes from Uttar Pradesh. The rajma though is the pièce-de-résistance and the famous local Bhadravahi rajma which many believe to be the best in the world, is served here. We tried it and were not disappointed. The rice is aromatic and long grained, and the rajma is perfect. Mildly spiced with a thick curry it is best eaten with anaar (pomegranate) chutney and onions. The options are either with or without desi ghee but either way it costs ₹ 40 a plate. Choose to eat it without ghee to really enjoy the flavour though some believe that the 50 ml of home-made ghee they add to each plate really brings out the taste. We felt it dominated all the flavours and made it too heavy to eat. Ask for the onions and green chillies on the side to get the complete effect.

SOMETHING ON THE SIDE   Sit in the balcony at the back of the dhaba on a pleasant day and you will be treated to the stunning view of water pouring out of the spanking new Bhaglihar dam, a majestic sight. This is the dam on the Chenab or the Chandrabhaga River.

Rocky's Verdict: A must-have, just like home-made rajma.
Rating: Taste: 7, Ambience: 4, Service: 7, Value for Money: 7, Total: 25
Specialities: Bhadravahi rajma and rice with anaar chutney
Veg/Non-veg: Veg
Contact Details/Timings: Khajuriah Vaishno Dhaba, Khajuriah Hotel, NH1, Peerah. Phone: 0-9419339680
Prices: Rajma chawal ₹ 40 per plate

Srinagar

HAT TRICK   Down the road from Hazratbal and perfectly positioned to attract hungry students from the University of Kashmir across the road is the Hat Trick restaurant. The new face of street food, it is a brightly lit, modern shop with well-lit displays.

Chicken and vegetable rolls, pizzas, southern fried chicken, chicken drumsticks, chicken lollipops, fish fries, fish fingers, and seekh rolls all lie prepared waiting to be heated up and served to hungry students. The bakery section inside has an assortment of cookies, biscuits, and patties. The coconut cookie (₹ 5) is chewy, sweet, and delicious especially when fresh out of the oven.

The meat dishes are all served hot in disposable Styrofoam plates with a side of mint yogurt, sliced onions, and carrots. The taste is satisfying, though at an average ranging from ₹ 70 to ₹ 90 a plate, this is not a cheap street food option.

SOMETHING ON THE SIDE   What a great alternative to the standard college canteen!

Mayur's Verdict: If you are tired of old-fashioned, cooked-right-there street food and want to visit somewhere more in keeping with modern times then this place is for you.
Rating: Taste: 7, Ambience: 7, Service: 7, Value for Money: 6, Total: 27
Specialities: Coconut cookie and seekh rolls
Veg/Non-veg: Non-veg
Contact Details/Timings: Opposite Sir Syed Gate, University of Kashmir. Hat Trick, In front of University of Kashmir, Srinagar. Phone: 0-9906740141
Prices: Meat dishes an average of ₹ 70–₹ 90 per plate

KRISHNA VAISHNO DHABA   In the Durganag Mandir area right by the road you will find this pure vegetarian restaurant famous for its rajma chawal and kadhi-chawal dishes. A full, large plate of rajma chawal tastes just like home-cooked rajma though they seem to use a whole lot more oil. Depending on the level of spice you like there is butter rajma, plain rajma, and very spicy rajma fry. The kadhi is also served with a whole lot of fresh, hot rice. It is made with fresh yogurt and is not as sour as it can often be. It has freshly fried pakoras in it and a healthy serving of red chillies. The menu also has other options listed such as bharta, paneer bhurji, different types of rice pulao, and chana, which many diners tuck into with gusto. For dessert the popular choice is rice kheer, which is not too sweet but also not too special.

The restaurant is basically a large room with tile walls. The owner controls the action from his little podium by the entrance. Right behind him there are many large containers with prepared food, which are available for takeaway. Formica-topped metal tables and chairs are laid out in neat rows and columns to maximize space. This is needed because the restaurant is packed with people happily enjoying the food.

SOMETHING ON THE SIDE Feel safe and secure thanks to the numerous policemen and army personnel patrolling the area on foot.

Mayur's Verdict: Good, clean, hot food served in clean, busy surroundings make for a good value-for-money meal with the taste of home-cooked food.
Rating: Taste: 6, Ambience: 6, Service: 7, Value for Money: 6, Total: 25
Specialities: Rajma chawal and kadhi chawal
Veg/Non-veg: Veg
Contact Details/Timings: Krishna Vaishno Dhaba, Durga Nag Mandir, Srinagar.
Prices: ₹ 24 to ₹ 30 for most dishes

MIR BAKERY In an old area of Srinagar where the houses are made of ancient brick, is a small market where shops form the ground floor of apartment houses. You can find your way to the bakeries with your eyes closed guided by the delicious smell of freshly baked bread that wafts across the whole area.

Like most other bakeries here the Mir Bakery serves different types of bread, both sweet and salty. There are breads that are eaten at different times of the day and those that are eaten along with different types of tea, sweet or salty. The lawas, which is usually eaten in the morning with the buttery, salty, red-tinged nunchai tastes best when thickly buttered. The bakarkhani which is usually served at weddings and other celebrations is crisp, layered, and flaky with sesame seeds. The sheermal at this bakery is a uniquely small, thick disc with a sweet touch. Besides the eight to ten different types of bread they also have cookies, cakes, and biscuits such as almond and walnut cookies, cashew claspers, and salty twists. Look out for the tsochvoru, thick, yeasty bagel-like bread with a golden brown crisp outside and soft and moist inside. Covered with sesame and poppy seeds this bread tastes better than any bagel you might find on the streets of New York. Most varieties of bread cost ₹ 2 to ₹ 4 per piece and can be eaten there or taken away to enjoy later with a cup of tea.

SOMETHING ON THE SIDE   What makes your experience really special is Sajjad Lone, the cheerful young man who smiles at everyone he is serving.

Mayur's Verdict: Get to the Mir Bakery first thing in the morning and gorge on some delicious smelling and tasting breads, both salty and sweet.
Rating: Taste: 10, Ambience: 7, Service: 10, Value for Money: 10, Total: 37
Certified: Rocky and Mayur rating of excellence
Specialities: The different types of bread—lawas, bakarkhani, sheermal, tsochvoru, and others
Veg/Non-veg: Veg
Contact Details/Timings: Mir Bakery, Khayyam Chowk (Nanpura Gawsia Bridge), Srinagar. Phone: 0-9419015755
Prices: Most varieties of bread cost ₹ 2 to ₹ 4 per piece

SHER BIBI   The place is run by Nain Singh, a lean and hard-working man who is very proud of his dhaba's reputation. The place is small, crowded, and old but Nain Singh can whip up an omelette, mathis, and some delicious poodas (sweetened, oily, flat wheat bread).

This area is rumoured to have the sweetest water in the world. This sweet water makes for a really nice cup of dhaba masala chai. Making the most of this fact, this small nondescript little shack has been here for years serving hot cups of tea to streams of visitors. It sits by the side of the road above a lovely gurgling stream and jagged rocks, set amidst dense forest. Across the dhaba are three to ten, depending on the season, chashmas (streams) falling on to the road. This almost magical, sweet water has a great taste—fresh, clean, and pure. It is obviously fresh ice melt and possibly the best you will find anywhere. Either way, it's a good excuse to stretch your legs, so make the most of it.

SOMETHING ON THE SIDE   Great taste is often attributed to the 'hawa paani' (air and water) of a place in India. This seems to work, don't ask me how but it just does. The same cup of tea made by the same person tastes a little different elsewhere than it does here. I have no idea why, but it's true.

Rocky's Verdict: We promise that you will not be able to stop at one cup of tea. Try it!
Rating: Taste: 8, Ambience: 5, Service: 6, Value for Money: 8, Total: 27
Specialities: Poodas, mathis, and the water!
Veg/Non-veg: Veg
Contact Details/Timings: 12 km from Banihal, NH1A, Srinagar side. Sher Bibi, Srinagar, NH1, Srinagar.
Prices: Omelette ₹ 20, poodas ₹ 10

SHERA CAFETERIA   Come evening time and the whole of Khayyam Chowk comes alive. The streets get all smoky and the air is filled with the aroma of spices and roasting meat. Every second shop on this particular street is a restaurant or cafeteria serving a range of tandoori meat and fish. The grills are put out on the sidewalk so passers-by can be more easily tempted by the smell and sight of fresh seekhs and tikkas roasting over red-hot coals.

Shera Cafeteria has a cramped inside sitting area with four wooden tables and some vinyl sofas. Before the food arrives you are served a plate full of pickles, two different types of sliced onions, radishes, and cucumbers mixed into yogurt, and some chutney. Freshly grilled, sprinkled with spices, kebabs are served on a plate or on bits of newspaper accompanied by a tandoori roti. Tender, soft, and laden with dripping fat, the kebabs are delicious and are a daily must-eat for many Kashmiris. At ₹ 90 to ₹ 100 a plate this is not a cheap meal and yet it is well worth it.

SOMETHING ON THE SIDE Friendly people are very happy to suggest what you eat but once you mention that you are a vegetarian the looks turn to smiling disbelief ☺

Mayur's Verdict: Come down to this area any time between dusk and 9 pm and enjoy the best tikkas, botis, and kebabs you might ever eat. The meat is fresh, deliciously spiced, and goes down beautifully.
Rating: Taste: 10, Ambience: 7, Service: 7, Value for Money: 8, Total: 32
Specialities: Kebabs
Veg/Non-veg: Non-veg
Contact Details/Timings: Shera Cafeteria, Khayyam Chowk, Srinagar. Phone: 0-9419522592
Prices: ₹ 90–₹ 100 per plate

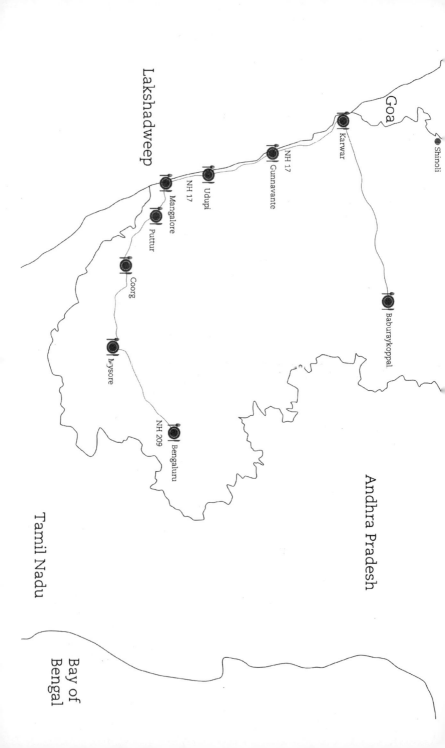

Baburaykoppal

JAI BHUVANESHWARI MILITARY HOTEL   The staple in this area are giant balls of cooked ragi, which are dark reddish brown in colour and dough-like in consistency, requiring a lot of hard chewing before every bite goes down. The mutton chops and the chicken are served separately from the gravy which is very, very spicy. Flavoured with cinnamon, cardamom, and cloves, the meat is a blend of sweet and spicy, cooked to just the right level of tenderness.

SOMETHING ON THE SIDE   Jai Bhuvaneshwari Hotel with its small eating room painted in pastel shades serves only non-vegetarian food but if you go in there and order vegetarian food someone will run out and bring back a thali of vegetarian delicacies from a hotel across the road. The vegetarian thali has dal, sambar, bhindi, rasam, yogurt, and buttermilk all served with a lot of rice. It is also very spicy and if you are not careful you might find yourself shedding some tears.

Mayur's Verdict: This place is very popular with a lot of people who travel this highway including famous stars like Rajnikanth. If you like meat and if you like your food spicy, then stop here and enjoy a fiery, well-cooked meal.
Rating: Taste: 6, Ambience: 4, Service: 7, Value for Money: 6, Total: 23
Specialities: Ragi and mutton chops
Veg/Non-veg: Non-veg
Contact Details/Timings: One km short of Srirangapatnam on SH17. Jai Bhuvaneshwari Military Hotel, Baburaykoppal, SH17. Phone: 0-9740125168
Prices: Thali ₹ 45 (You do not get seconds of the meat)

Bengaluru

ALI BABA CAFÉ & RESTAURANT Situated on the first floor of a building on Bourdillon Road this restaurant is a pleasant surprise in every aspect. The interior with its dark wood furniture, brocade furnishings, ornate lamps, and ceilings painted to resemble sand dunes, Middle Eastern décor, and bric-a-brac, transports you to a place far far away.

The extensive menu makes very interesting reading thanks to exotic names like shish taouk, laun muriya maas, and zereshkh polo.

The alipeh, a wild mushroom curry, is redolent with spices and the little button mushrooms add a wonderful texture to the dish. The kadang fry (sweet potato slices coated with chilli paste and fried) and the mirza ghasemi (barbecued eggplant mashed and cooked with garlic and tomato) are both extremely flavourful and appetizing dishes.

Lovers of meat will be in ecstasy thanks to the wide range and preparations available, especially the shish bakhtiari (a combination of seasoned chicken and mutton pieces skewered and cooked over charcoal) and the shish taouk (chicken skewers). The mutton shaiya biryani, prepared with noodles instead of rice, has a unique texture, but do remember to ask for the traditional recipe, which uses sevai (vermicelli) for a more authentic, nutty flavour. Desserts on the menu are equally exotic and the shaufa pana pudding topped with dill leaf and cream is extremely tasty. Sip on the unique chilled tausha sherbet made from cucumber juice with little floating pieces of cucumber, or the Saudi champagne, which is a sweet, fizzy mixture of lemonade and apple juice.

SOMETHING ON THE SIDE Ali Baba serves a range of Bhatkali, Arabic, and Persian food and after you finish your meal do go up to the rooftop sheesha lounge to enjoy a fragrant smoke accompanied by kahwa (Arabian coffee) served with dates, Moroccan pot tea, or Irani chai.

> **Mayur's Verdict:** The variety of dishes available at Ali Baba is too vast to cover here and we highly recommend a visit there to discover the unique tastes for yourself.
> **Rating:** Taste: 9, Ambience: 9, Service: 9, Value for Money: 8, Total: 35
> **Certified:** Rocky and Mayur rating of excellence
> **Specialities:** Alipeh, Mirza ghasemi
> **Veg/Non-veg:** Non-veg
> **Contact Details/Timings:** Ali Baba, M.M. Road, Frazer Town. Phone: 0-9632126745.
> **Prices:** Chicken laun muriya maas ₹ 85, mutton shaiya biryani ₹ 125, sukka mass ₹ 135, shish khudar bbq (veg) ₹ 145, saudi champagne ₹ 65, lime mint cooler ₹ 30

THE EGG FACTORY   The owner Yogesh Mokashi started this venture thanks to his fascination with eggs, which he feels are the grey line between vegetarian and non-vegetarian food. The fascinating interiors are designed to make the restaurant look like a factory, complete with wrenches for door handles, music piped through siren tubes, and the furniture designed along clean, minimal, blocky lines.

The menu draws a lot of inspiration from international cuisine but with a great Indian twist. Huevos Rancheros, a TexMex dish consisting of stir-fried vegetables with a lot of seasoning and fried eggs on top are a spicy treat while the 'Chilli Eggs' taste like Chinese food. Egg Alfredo is a tasty penne pasta dish seasoned with cilantro, pesto, and with chunks of omelette added. Wash down your meal with one of many fresh fruit smoothies such as the Morning Burst, a tangy, filling combination of orange juice, banana pulp, and milk sweetened with honey.

SOMETHING ON THE SIDE   The menu is very funky, designed to look like a technical manual with the back page devoted to 'eggucation', containing interesting facts about eggs in English, Greek, and Chinese.

Mayur's Verdict: The Egg Factory lists seventy-five different egg preparations. Worth a try!
Rating: Taste: 8, Ambience: 9, Service: 9, Value for Money: 9, Total: 35
Certified: Rocky and Mayur rating of excellence
Specialities: Egg preparations
Veg/Non-veg: Veg/Non-veg
Contact Details/Timings: The Egg Factory, St Mark's Road, Bengaluru. Phone: 080-42110041.
Prices: Penne alfredo with cilantro pesto and eggs ₹ 110, huevos rancheros ₹ 90, egg chilli ₹ 50, ultimate veggies omelette ₹ 90

KOSHY'S   Koshy's is one of those places that truly represent the culture of the city. The restaurant has two separate rooms, an outside room for snacks, quick bites, and revolutionary intellectual conversations, and another inner air-conditioned room for more peaceful, relaxed, family dining.

What hits you as soon as you enter Koshy's is how busy the place always is. The menu is vast and has well over a hundred items which keep changing and yet somehow always taste just the same as you remember. Great pains are taken to get the food to you hot and it is a pleasant and relaxed dining experience. This is truly comfort food.

Koshy's claims to have over 850 items served every day from breakfast to lunch. The choice is staggering. We went with 'tender coconut soup', a delightful and delicate preparation, the famous roast mutton, the ever popular potato smileys, eastern chicken, Kerala pork, and the hot cross buns. They were all delicious. This is the place to get adventurous. Order anything that tickles your fancy and it will probably be good.

SOMETHING ON THE SIDE   The restaurant has been around for over sixty years and brothers Prem and Santosh Koshy are the third generation to run it. One of the reasons why it is so popular is that they stay connected to their clients on a very personal level. On Good Friday, for example, you can walk in and get hot cross buns, the foods of an old tradition. People make it a point to come here on this day and dig into these hot, tasty, and freshly baked treats. Koshy's is also environment friendly and has the only mahogany tree protected by a court order just outside.

Rocky's Verdict: A stalwart of Bengaluru, a must-visit for so many reasons.
Rating: Taste: 8, Ambience: 9, Service: 8, Value for Money: 7, Total: 32
Specialities: Hot cross buns and pork and meat dishes
Veg/Non-veg: Non-veg
Contact Details/Timings: Koshy's, St Marks Road, Bengaluru. Phone: 080-22213793
Prices: Pork ₹ 200, tandoori fish ₹ 220. Expect to pay about ₹ 350 a person while dining here.

MTR (MAVALLI TIFFIN ROOM)   This place is so popular that most days you will have to wait for anything between 10 to 40 minutes to get in. The wait though is worth it because seldom will you find the quality of MTR at these prices anywhere else.

The place is so popular that it has two waiting rooms and crowds of people standing by. The smell wafting out draws you in and gets you hungrier as you wait. Chances are you will meet Mr Janardhanam who is the mâitred' and a dynamic bundle of energy. He has been here for thirty-nine years and can teach the best a thing or two about customer service. The walls are lined with old black-and-white pictures but are themselves brightly coloured making for a cheery experience.

Customers are mostly regulars, some of whom have been coming here for the last fifty five years. There are family rooms, VIP rooms, and also common dining areas. Tables are well spaced and they do not rush you here. Your meal is sacrosanct and is meant to be enjoyed at leisure. Once you take a seat you will be served within minutes. We had a glorious breakfast here on a rainy morning and the dosa was delightful. Vadas are a speciality but are over by 9:30 am so be there early. The coffee is prepared in the traditional fashion and served hot.

The rava idli was good, as was the khara bhath. The turnover is tremendous and this place is a must-visit for its food and old-world charm.

SOMETHING ON THE SIDE   The preparation and serving of food in the entire state of Karnataka is viewed as a noble deed by most people involved in eating places. Great attention is paid to the cleanliness and food is served at the best possible prices. An increase, no matter how small, in prices, is usually an agonizing decision for most dhaba owners.

Rocky's Verdict: You will enjoy your meal here. Breakfast is highly recommended.
Rating: Taste: 8, Ambience: 8, Service: 8, Value for Money: 9, Total: 33
Specialities: Vadas, dosa, and coffee
Veg/Non-veg: Veg
Contact Details/Timings: For vadas you must be there before 9:30 am. Mavalli Tiffin Rooms, Lal Bagh Main Road, Bengaluru. Phone: 080-22220022/22235115
Prices: Dosa ₹ 30, rava idli ₹ 18, average cost per person ₹ 50

VIDYARTHI BHAVAN   This legendary eatery literally comes out smelling of roses thanks to its fragrant location behind a bright and colourful flower market. There are only eight items listed on the bilingual menu hanging on a wall (nine if you count the 'Hot Water Available') and these are available only in the morning. In the evening they make the choice even simpler by reducing the items available to two: dosas and vadas.

The heavenly masala dosa is a smaller, thicker, darker, and crisper cousin of the dosas you might be used to and each bite dipped in hot, tangy sambar is tasty. The fluffy idlis and the crisp, fresh, light vadas are served in a pool of sambar and are best eaten immediately while still hot. The puri sagu, a staple breakfast dish, is a delightful alternative to the idli–dosa option. Sweeten the deal at the end with the ghee-laden kesari bhath with the delicate flavour of kesar (saffron) or spice it up with a zesty khara bhath served with coconut chutney. Wash it all down with a steaming cup of aromatic filter coffee.

SOMETHING ON THE SIDE Take a little time out to chat with regulars at this iconic eatery and you will be sure to meet some very interesting characters. We did!

Mayur's Verdict: Vidyarthi Bhavan has a whole bunch of loyal diners some of whom have been eating there for over thirty years. Need we say more?
Rating: Taste: 9, Ambience: 9, Service: 10, Value for Money: 10, Total: 38
Certified: Rocky and Mayur rating of excellence
Specialities: Puri sagu and kesari bhath
Veg/Non-veg: Veg
Contact Details/Timings: Gandhi Bazaar Main Road, Gandhi Bazaar Road, Basavanagudi, Bengaluru, Karnataka. Phone: 080-26677588, Open weekdays: 6:30 am-11:30 am, 2 pm-8 pm.
Prices: Masala dosa ₹ 25, Puri sagu ₹ 18, idli ₹ 6, Kesari bhath ₹ 15, khara bhath ₹ 12

Coorg

COORG CUISINETTE Located on the first floor of a building in the centre of Madikeri this restaurant proudly announces that it serves traditional Kodava dishes. The inside is extremely clean with well-spaced glass-topped tables and comfortable chairs. The pandhi (pork) curry and the succulent pork chops dripping with fat are delicious. Both are made of extremely tender meat marinated in a special sauce called kachimpudi.

Vegetarians also have a range of options in the tender, tangy, and spicy baimbale (bamboo), kumm (mushroom) curry, and bale kamb (banana stem) curry. Curries are served with different forms of fragrant Sannakki rice ranging from akki otti (rice chapattis), nooputtu (noodle-like rice threads), and kadambuttu (rice balls) which are light and yet very filling. Chutneys and pickles made of pandi, baimbale, kumm, nellikai (gooseberries), and kaipuli (bitter oranges) make for interesting side dishes and add to the flavour of each bite.

SOMETHING ON THE SIDE   Kodavas are traditionally a martial race and their diet ensures they are well fuelled for the battle at all times.

Mayur's Verdict: If you are in Madikeri and not fortunate enough to eat at a Kodava home then your best bet is the Coorg Cuisinette for authentic, satisfying, and very reasonably priced traditional food. A must-visit destination for all food lovers.
Rating: Taste: 9, Ambience: 9, Service: 8, Value for Money: 9, Total: 35
Certified: Rocky and Mayur rating of excellence
Specialities: Pandhi curry, pork chops, and baimbale curry
Veg/Non-veg: Non-veg
Contact Details/Timings: Below the KSRTC Bus Stand. Phone: 08272-250097
Prices: Pandhi curry ₹ 50, pork chops ₹ 50, Pal puttu ₹ 20, Kadambuttu ₹ 15, akki otti ₹ 10

Gunnavante

HOTEL GURUKRIPA   Hotel Gurukripa is a local legend. Ask anyone for Bhattjee's place of the famous ghee dosa and they will guide you to a small one-room dosa eatery by the side of the road whose fame stretches at least a hundred kilometres in each direction. Be prepared for a basic establishment with simple fare—all you get with your ghee dosa is coconut chutney. Cooked over a wood fire on a basic metal plate, the first thing that hits you is the remarkable amount of ghee used to make these dosas. Thicker than most dosas, they are softened by the ghee and the aroma is delightful. Most are satiated with one dosa, maybe two. We ate seven each. We do not recommend this though, as these are some heavy dosas! Another option is the plain poha with yogurt and sugar.

SOMETHING ON THE SIDE The owner Manjunath Shankar Bhatt is a very religious man and is venerated by his customers. There are pictures of gods and gurus all over one wall, while another is adorned with images of bodybuilders and muscular men. Born of these two cults is the holy and powerful ghee dosa.

Rocky's Verdict: A hugely popular place. Don't even consider not stopping here!
Rating: Taste: 8, Ambience: 5, Service: 8, Value for Money: 9, Total: 30
Specialities: Ghee dosa
Veg/Non-veg: Veg
Contact Details/Timings: Hotel Gurukripa, Sea Face Road, Nani Daman, Gunnavante. Phone: 91-0-260-6452494, 91-0-922-7759265
Prices: Ghee dosa ₹ 8 per 2 pieces, dahi poha ₹ 8 per plate, idli sambhar ₹ 6 per 2 pieces

---

Karwar

SHWETHA LUNCH HOME The signboard of this famous lunch home proudly advertises 'Homely Food Served Here… Veg & Non Veg'. It is a basic eatery with a long room divided into a small cooking area and an eating area with rows of plastic tables and chairs. The customers are an eclectic mix and you could find yourself sharing a table and conversation with a shopkeeper, vegetable or fish seller, trader, or manual labourer.

The vegetarian and non-vegetarian thalis are very popular with the locals who flock here at mealtimes to tuck into them with great gusto. Everything is extremely fresh with the vegetables sourced at the local market round the corner and the seafood arriving fresh every day on fishing boats pulling into the harbour. The fish curry, daali toor, tomato subzi, cabbage, etc. are all very spicy and served with steaming hot white rice. The owner Mr Shyamsunder Basroor says that the family-run restaurant ensures the quality of its food by eating the same food that they serve their customers.

SOMETHING ON THE SIDE The payment desk at the entrance of the restaurant is modelled as a truck cabin—a little highway touch.

Mayur's Verdict: Definitely a great place to discover and enjoy the local Karwar experience. Try a little piece of fresh teppal, a spice that will leave a pleasant tingling sensation in your mouth.
Rating: Taste: 9, Ambience: 6, Service: 8, Value for Money: 10, Total: 33
Specialities: Fish curry, daali toor, and tomato subzi
Veg/Non-veg: Non-veg
Contact Details/Timings: Shwetha Lunch Home, Ananda Arcade, Green Street, Karwar. Phone: 0-9986675726
Prices: Veg thali ₹ 18, Chicken thali ₹ 25, solkadi free

Mangalore

HOTEL AYODHYA Mangalore, once a small laid-back town, is fast becoming a big city. Luckily for us all there is still Ayodhya. This place is unbelievably cheap and one of those places where you can still find authentic Mangalorean food and goodies. The mude is a prime example of the food offered here. It's like an idli but wrapped and steamed in a leaf which gives it a unique flavour. Other great specialities are pathrode, shemighe (idiappam), udi bhajji, soormali dosa, sanjeera roti, palak idli, and several others. This place changes its menu and serves seasonal preparations so the menu changes constantly. Be sure to top up your meals with some fresh seasonal and delicious juices. Remember, the most expensive item on this menu is only ₹ 12. Enjoy.

SOMETHING ON THE SIDE Mr Ramdass and his brothers are devoted to making those traditional and seasonal dishes that are no longer made in homes so you will often get to eat something quite unique here.

Rocky's Verdict: One of those places that must be visited when you come to Mangalore. Make the effort and enjoy the food.
Rating: Taste: 9, Ambience: 9, Service: 10, Value for Money: 10, Total: 38
Certified: Rocky and Mayur rating of excellence
Specialities: Mude, pathrode, shemighe, and sanjeera roti
Veg/Non-veg: Veg
Contact Details/Timings: Hotel Ayodhya, 13-12-1420, Kodialbail, Mangalore. Phone: 0824-2493681
Prices: Everything here is for ₹ 12 or under, believe it or not. Biscuit roti ₹ 5, mude ₹ 6, pathrode ₹ 4, soormali dosa ₹ 8, neeru dosa ₹ 8, sanjeera roti ₹ 6, pathrode ₹ 4

Mysore

BOMBAY TIFFANY Bombay Tiffany is a brightly lit, spotlessly clean sweet shop with lots of mirrors and glass-fronted shelves running along the length of the shop stacked with namkeens and packets of home-made chips. The display cases have neat rows and columns of a range of sweets such as many different burfis, laddus, jalebis, and other mouth-watering delicacies. There is a bright yellow menu up on the wall listing typical breakfast and snack food such as aloo-puri, papdi chaat, aloo and masala cutlets, samosas, dhoklas, kachoris, and dahi bhallas.

We suggest you get the delicious Mysore pak, a local sweet made of generous amounts of ghee, sugar, and besan. The golden yellow pak is stored and displayed in compressed bricks. It crumbles as you break it and literally melts in the mouth releasing a wonderful flavour reminding you of besan laddus and milk cake. It's not a cheap treat at ₹ 200 per kg but considering you can eat only 50 to 100 gm at a sitting and it is really delicious, it's money well spent.

SOMETHING ON THE SIDE Ever wondered about the coincidence that the main ingredient in Mysore pak is the similar sounding 'masoor' dal?

Mayur's Verdict: Another city with another great breakfast option to start your day with. You will emerge well fed and smiling wide enough to put every sweet tooth you have on show!
Rating: Taste: 8, Ambience: 8, Service: 8, Value for Money: 8, Total: 32
Specialities: Mysore pak
Veg/Non-veg: Veg
Contact Details/Timings: Bombay Tiffany, Sayyaji Rao Road, Mysore. Phone: 0-9845395054
Prices: Mysore pak ₹ 200 per kg, milk cake ₹ 180 per kg, Karachi halwa ₹ 240 per kg, chaat items ₹ 25–₹ 40

FOOD STREET This street lies just behind Marimalappa College in Mysore and is aptly named because every night the street is lined with mobile food stalls selling a range of food treats to happy visitors. Streetlights and small lanterns on the stalls provide a softly lit atmosphere while families, groups of students, and those returning from office feast on samosas, Chinese food, dosas, idlis, vadas, pulaos, kulfis, fresh sugarcane juice, and more.

Deep-fried gobhi manchurian served on pieces of old newspaper sprinkled with chilli powder redefines every meaning of hot. The vegetable pulao, also served on newspaper, is spiced with cardamom and cinnamon and is a gentler, healthier, and more filling option.

SOMETHING ON THE SIDE This place comes alive only in the evenings so have a light lunch.

> **Mayur's Verdict:** It's basically fast food but you do get a sense of adventure as you wander up and down the street discovering what the vendors have to offer. Feel free to get into conversation with people and try some of their recommendations. A nice place to eat a meal at and even better for a stroll with the family to nibble on kulfis.
> **Rating:** Taste: 6, Ambience: 8, Service: 7, Value for Money: 7, Total: 28
> **Specialities:** Gobhi manchurian and vegetable pulao
> **Veg/Non-veg:** Non-veg
> **Contact Details/Timings:** The street.
> **Prices:** ₹ 9–₹ 40 for most items off most carts

GAYATHRI TIFFIN ROOM Popularly called GTR, this place reminds you of a government school or railway station from the outside with its solid whitewashed construction and barred windows. The inside has sparkling clean, polished stone floors, counters, and tabletops and is humming with activity. There are signs posted on the walls with messages like 'No Smoking Please', 'No Table Service', and a stern 'Do not wash your hands in the plates'.

GTR is famous all over Mysore for its Mysore bonda, Mysore masala dosa, and kesari bhath. The restaurant has a horde of regular customers who swear by the food and have been eating here for over a decade.

The golden kesari bhath, cooked in pure ghee and served on a banana leaf set on a plate, makes for not just a delicious but a very colourful dish. The Mysore masala dosa has red chilli chutney smeared on the inside besides the potato and onion filling and butter. Try some delicious, hot south Indian filter coffee after your meal and make sure you slurp it from the bowl, desi style.

SOMETHING ON THE SIDE You will always find some fellow diner ready to take on a challenge to eat as many kesari bhaths as possible. See if you can eat eight in a row. Go on we dare you ☺

Mayur's Verdict: If you are in Mysore and want to get a taste of the local cuisine then the GTR is a must-visit.
Rating: Taste: 8, Ambience: 6, Service: 8, Value for Money: 9, Total: 31
Specialities: Kesari bhath, Mysore bonda, and Mysore masala dosa
Veg/Non-veg: Veg
Contact Details/Timings: As a tiffin room it opens only from 7:30 am to 11:30 am and 4 pm to 8 pm.
Gayathri Tiffin Rooms, Chamundipuram, Mysore.
Phone: 0821-2332170
Prices: Mysore masala dosa ₹ 12 and kesari bhath ₹ 7

Puttur

LINNET PRESIDENCY BAR AND RESTAURANT Inside the Linnet Presidency, the pride of place is given to a grand bar that serves customers drinks of all kinds. The section given over to the actual eatery is somewhat cramped, with most of the seating in small though private booths.

Non-vegetarian diners are handed a huge plate of steaming hot puffy rice, and they can choose from a number of meat and seafood curries. The kodiwassar (chicken curry) and the marwai (prawn) curry both taste the same since all you savour is the extremely spicy red curry and nothing of the meat. The plain rice with fish curry dish is quite popular with the regulars though it too is spicy in the extreme. The pepper fry chicken is a dry roasted chicken flavoured with fresh pepper and is the best available option if only because you can actually taste the meat. The vegetarian option available at this meat eater's paradise is a bland rice dosa with a stringy texture accompanied by boiled okra cooked with a minimum of spices.

SOMETHING ON THE SIDE The bar opens at 10 am and is busy from then on. If you like whisky for breakfast then this is a good bet.

Mayur's Verdict: Food is not the main concern here and is seen only as an excuse to get customers into the 'spirit' of things. Not an ideal destination for food lovers or families.
Rating: Taste: 5, Ambience: 5, Service: 5, Value for Money: 5, Total: 20
Specialities: Pepper fry chicken
Veg/Non-veg: Non-veg
Contact Details/Timings: Linnet Presidency Bar and Restaurant, Namana Tower, State Highway-88, Bypass Road, Puttur. Phone 08251-324502.
Prices: Pepper fry chicken, kodaiwassar, and marwai all ₹ 50 per portion and fish with rice ₹ 12 per portion, kori (chicken) masala ₹ 50, kori (chicken) pepper fry, ₹ 50, plain rice with fish curry, ₹ 12, dosa with veg chilli ₹ 10, thali, ₹ 20

Udupi

HOTEL ANUGRAHA   Hotel Anugraha is as good as it gets. Breakfasts here are the best. Dosas, idlis, vadas, and fresh juices are available, most for under ₹ 10. While you eat, the early morning smells of fresh jasmine and incense come wafting by. Add to this the peal of bells from hundreds of temples and the gentle pace of life surrounding you, and you're almost in heaven. Take your first bite and you realize that you are.

Political debate is welcome even at breakfast and most patrons will be happy to join your discussion.

SOMETHING ON THE SIDE   Udupi is famous throughout the world for having exported some of the finest chefs. There would hardly be a city or town in India without an Udupi hotel in it. Whole families of chefs train together and all members, be they male or female, become chefs. Most of them move away and start a little Udupi place of their own. Anywhere is a good place to eat in Udupi and we stumbled upon this little place by mere chance. Happily the food did not disappoint.

Rocky's Verdict: Just EAT!!!!
Rating: Taste: 9, Ambience: 9, Service: 10, Value for Money: 10, Total: 38
Certified: Rocky and Mayur rating of excellence
Specialities: Dosas, idlis, vadas, and fresh juices
Veg/Non-veg: Veg
Contact Details/Timings: Corporation Bank Road, Near Sree Krishna Temple, Hotel Anugraha, Udupi. Phone: 0-9900408066
Prices: Idli sambar ₹ 5 per plate, vada sambar ₹ 5 per plate, coffee ₹ 3.50 per cup

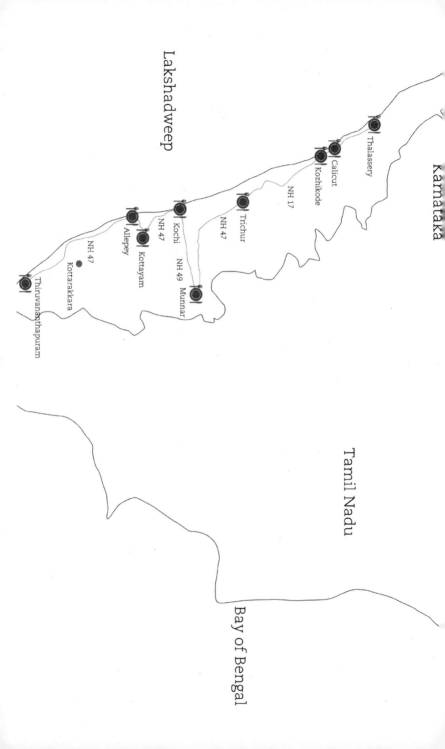

All Over Kerala

TODDY SHOPS Toddy is palm wine and is drawn and fermented every day. It is then served in large quantities to all comers, the locals in particular typically consuming two to three litres of toddy in one sitting. Toddy tastes like tart rice water and is usually served in little shacks, often accompanied by incredibly spicy snacks and food. These snacks and dishes truly represent the taste of Kerala. The matti, a small tasty fish either curried or deep fried with loads of chillies is a popular accompaniment.

SOMETHING ON THE SIDE   As a caution it is recommended that in case you do try the toddy, do so at a place registered by the government.

Rocky's Verdict: Toddy is a must-try, and a toddy-induced high is one of the gentlest and most pleasant highs any sort of alcohol can induce.
Rating: Taste: 5, Ambience: 9, Service: 9, Value for Money: 9, Total: 32
Specialities: Toddy with snack items like the matti
Veg/Non-veg: The snacks are non-vegetarian
Contact Details/Timings: All over Kerala.
Prices: ₹ 30 per bottle,. matti ₹ 20 per plate

Allepey

AMMU'S RESTAURANT   Lounging in your rented motorboat or traditional cane kettuvellam, cruising the lush, green, and peaceful backwaters that make Kerala a visitors' delight, can surprisingly work up quite an appetite. Hidden among the twists and turns of the palm-lined canals are little home restaurants catering to backwater tourists. In a little area called Kainakary one such restaurant is named Ammu's after the lady who owns it.

The single-page menu printed on both sides and wrapped in plastic, has a long list of meat and seafood items with a few vegetarian options thrown in. Meals or thalis cost ₹ 40 for the basic vegetarian option and you can order fish and other seafood as a side dish. Thalis are served on the ubiquitous banana leaves that make a bright backdrop for the colourful little heaps of different vegetables, pickles, and salads put on it. The freshly cooked ladyfinger, aviyal, thorran, beetroot khichdi, and rasam are served with large helpings of the slightly purplish, puffy grained Kerala rice and are quite filling. Every bite resonates with the underlying sweet flavour of the coconut used in most preparations.

The fried prawns and the karimeen are crisp, lightly spiced, and best enjoyed with rice (all to be eaten using your hands)! Seafood is priced by weight and size and can range from ₹ 150 upwards.

SOMETHING ON THE SIDE   The home-made toddy or fermented coconut palm wine offered is milky white, tart, and cool. It is made fresh every morning and evening and served in large plastic jugs. The fresher the toddy, the nicer it tastes and the milder it hits.

Mayur's Verdict: A cruise down the backwaters of Kerala is a must, and while you are doing this, a meal at one of these restaurants is highly recommended. Enjoy the feeling of home as the family cooks for you and little kids play by the water as the world goes by slowly in tune with the rhythm of lapping waves. Toddy shops will have mostly toddy and lots of drunken men so look out for one of the family-run places where food is the main course.
Rating: Taste: 8, Ambience: 10, Service: 8, Value for Money: 10, Total: 36
Certified: Rocky and Mayur rating of excellence
Specialities: Thali, fried prawns, and karimeen
Veg/Non-veg: Non-veg

> **Contact Details/Timings:** Ammu's Restaurant, Kainakary.
> Phone: 0-9847725838
> **Prices:** Seafood ₹ 150 per kg and upwards and thali ₹ 40

Calicut

ZAIN'S An elderly couple that wanted to share the taste of great home food with all their customers started this iconic eatery. Zain's is located in a quaint, old-style bungalow on a quiet road in Calicut but its reputation ensures it's well known by anyone who loves Moplah cuisine. Moplah cuisine, heavily influenced by its Arab roots, is famous for its non-vegetarian and seafood dishes. At Zain's the karimeen (fish) stew and mutton stew are exotic to taste, thanks to the gravy of chilli, coconut milk, and tamarind. Another unique dish is the roast chicken stuffed with spices and hard-boiled eggs, slow fried over a low flame to ensure the spices really soak into the meat. The vegetable stew with garden fresh vegetables simmered in a gravy of cashew nuts, poppy seeds, and home-made masalas is a must-try. All stews whether vegetarian or non-vegetarian can be enjoyed with rice flour breads called pathiris, which can be thin chapatti-like, thick or stuffed with keema or chicken and deep fried. If you love rice then there are a few different types of biryanis and pulaos on offer too.

The place has an amazing takeaway counter. There is a range of snacks like the fish fry masala and desserts like the elai adai (steamed rice pie with fresh coconut, and palm jaggery) available for selection from a glass-fronted cabinet in case you don't have time for a sit-down meal.

The mutta-mala, a traditional Moplah dessert consisting of long strands made from egg yolk cooked in syrup and fluffy, sweet, steamed egg whites, is a great ending to a great meal.

SOMETHING ON THE SIDE The owners are very interesting. The lady is immaculately dressed and adorned and runs the kitchen with military precision while the smiling gentleman who clearly adores his wife was a proud member of the Indian hockey team many a years ago.

Mayur's Verdict: The perfect example of a great result of love, passion, and personal attention blended into every recipe and dish that is served to customers. The food is delicious, the ambience relaxed and homely, and the prices reasonable.
Rating: Taste: 9, Ambience: 8, Service: 9, Value for Money: 9, Total: 35
Certified: Rocky and Mayur rating of excellence
Specialities: Fish stew, mutton stew, roast chicken stuffed with spices and eggs, and mutta-mala
Veg/Non-veg: Non-veg.
Contact Details: Mr Zainabi Noor 0-9847269041, 0495-2366311, 2761428
Prices: Roast chicken ₹ 160 per kg, fish and mutton stew ₹ 60 per portion, and vegetable stew ₹ 15 per portion

Kochi

FOUR FOODS Four Foods serves the traditional Naadan cuisine of Kerala. The place itself is rather modest looking and the thick coat of garish paint does little for its character. The location is great though, out facing a wide road and right next to a plush coffee shop called Coffee Beanz this place serves some really tasty dishes. We went with the kada (quail). Like with most of their meats, the kada is batter fried in hot oil.

SOMETHING ON THE SIDE The place is mainly for non-vegetarians and chilli gobhi and gobhi manchurian are the only vegetarian dishes on the menu.

Rocky's Verdict: The food is pretty good. Throw your diet plan out of the window as almost everything involves deep frying at some stage or the other.
Rating: Taste: 8, Ambience: 5, Service: 7, Value for Money: 9, Total: 29
Specialities: Kada
Veg/Non-veg: Non-veg (with a few vegetarian options)

Contact Details/Timings: Mr Girish 0484-2351026
Prices: Seafood ₹ 100 per portion, and other non-vegetarian
dishes ₹ 50. Average cost for one ₹ 200

SALT 'N' PEPPER RESTAURANT   The giant Chinese fishing
nets at Fort Kochi perform a more functional duty besides
providing a backdrop for picture-perfect sunset postcards.
Each night when the tide goes out, six or seven fishing nets are
manned by teams of up to six men who rhythmically lower
and raise them, and then transfer the catch into old buckets.
Flatfish, silver fish, exotic-looking fish with sharp spines, and
little crabs can all turn up in a catch.

You can go to any of the nets, examine the freshly caught fish,
and purchase as many as you want to be prepared and cooked
right away. You then take your fish to one of the shacks about
50 metres away from the nets. We suggest you head to Salt 'n'
Pepper. Hand them your purchase and sit outside at a table
under a beach umbrella sipping some fresh coconut water as
you wait for your fish to be prepared, cooked, and served. You
can choose the method of preparation for your fish and the
amount of chilli to be added. The deep-fried mackerel costing
₹ 150 per kg, is served with freshly sliced onions, tomatoes,
coriander, green chillies, and lime, and is a spicy, crisp delight
at every bite. Well worth the further ₹ 150 that Salt 'n' Pepper
charges to cook the fish.

SOMETHING ON THE SIDE   The nets were introduced in India
by Chinese traders from the court of Kublai Khan. Now they
provide these fishermen with their daily livelihood. Most of the
daytime fishing activity is for the sake of tourists, both Indian
and foreign, and the actual quantity caught is small.

Mayur's Verdict: Visit the Chinese fishing nets to get a sense
of history, and enjoy the view and a chat with the local
fishermen. You will really relish this meal as you sit by the
road and watch people strolling around at a gentle pace

---

along the tree-lined cobbled path. Be prepared to pay
separately for the fish and for the cooking.
Rating: Taste: 8, Ambience: 7, Service: 6, Value for Money: 8,
Total: 29
Specialities: Deep-fried mackerel
Veg/Non-veg: Non-veg
Contact Details/Timings: Salt 'n' Pepper Restaurant, Tower
Road, Fort Kochi.
Prices: Deep fried mackerel ₹ 300 per kg including cooking
charges

Kottayam

MANIPUZHA VYSALI FAMILY RESTAURANT Although the
restaurant serves Naadan, Chinese, and continental foods,
stick with the Naadan. You may be surprised to see turtles,
rabbits, and frogs on the menu in several places. Turtles and
frogs have now been banned and can no longer be served. A
few places continue to serve rabbits but these are farmed at
nearby locations and are always in short supply. We would
urge you not to indulge in exotic meats as this leads to the
exploitation of wildlife and there's plenty of choice available
even without them.

Start with the aviyal and dig into the beans and sambar
along with all the tasty chutneys and dals they offer. Eat
everything with a glass of 'moru' or buttermilk. Coconut
is a popular ingredient and finds its way into almost every
preparation. We highly recommend the crab Naadan style,
cooked with lots of onions with raw curry leaves sprinkled on
top. Also recommended are the konju (tiger prawns) cooked
with cashews. Rice is the staple and is ever present though you
could get a 'chapathi' as well. Try the naimeen molee (seer fish)
which is a local favourite. The restaurant is brightly lit, well
maintained and obviously popular with the locals.

SOMETHING ON THE SIDE The roads in Kerala are narrow and
very congested. Traffic still manages to flow smoothly as people
will almost always stick to the lanes. Be very careful near the

highways as people drive fast and do not expect careless people to wander on to the highways. While driving do remember to stick to your lanes, in fact do that anywhere in the country, why just Kerala.

Rocky's Verdict: Stop at this one and enjoy the meal, its very good and a fair representation of Naadan food.
Rating: Taste: 9, Ambience: 7, Service: 7, Value for Money: 8, Total: 31
Specialities: Naimeen molee
Veg/Non-veg: Non-veg
Contact Details/Timings: Manipuzha Vysali Family Resturant, M.C. Road, Kadimatha, Kottayam. Phone: 0481-2362486, 2360486.
Prices: Veg thali ₹ 40, crab ₹ 90, and konju ₹ 300

Kozhikode

CM HOTEL AND COOL BAR   Don't go to this bar expecting a drink, since Cool Bars only serve juices and soft drinks! The beef (buffalo meat) at the hotel is prepared by simply frying it with spices and lots of curry leaves. Almost everything we ate in this place was well fried: mattar masala, gobhi manchurian, prawns, and beef. Served up with the parota, the food was rather easy to eat though a bit heavy on the stomach later.

SOMETHING ON THE SIDE   In most places in Kerala you will get free 'kairangali', a mildly pink sort of hot water to drink with your food that has a few things in it to help aid digestion. It is quite pleasant to have with your meal and you can have as much of it as you like.

Rocky's Verdict: This is a mediocre place, feel free to move on without eating here, you wouldn't be missing anything.
Rating: Taste: 5, Ambience: 5, Service: 6, Value for Money: 4, Total: 20

Specialities: Beef
Veg/Non-veg: Non-veg
Contact Details/Timings: Mr Abdul Rehman 0496-2689824
Prices: Beef ₹ 20, prawns ₹ 100, and all vegetarian items below ₹ 20

Munnar

RAPSY RESTAURANT Here you get a touch of continental cuisine coexisting happily with authentic flavours from Kerala, a truly amazing range of food. Have fun when you get here, order like mad, and try out the variety. All of it is very good.

The main bazaar is a small cluster of tightly packed shops and narrow walkways dominated by the heavenly smell of incense and occasionally exotic spices. Most shops sell garments and household goods, and right in the heart of this little bazaar is Rapsy Restaurant. It has customers from over forty-three countries and has a sign outside that modestly claims that they were 'Amiably taken care (of)...Moreover astoundingly pleased...Their ecstasy is...Just with quality, not with looks'. Needless to say that the father and son duo that run this place are enterprising and very involved with their little restaurant. The menu is easy to understand, bright, and attractive. There are even little pictures of the way the dishes look when served.

SOMETHING ON THE SIDE Rapsy Restaurant has the good fortune of being located in one of the prettiest districts anywhere in this country. The old tea plantations of Munnar used to be owned and run by the British and this was their favoured retreat in the hot summer months. Most of the plantations are still functional and this place is truly a gem in God's own country.

Rocky's Verdict: A surprisingly good place. Nice home-cooked food at nominal prices.
Rating: Taste: 8, Ambience: 7, Service: 9, Value for Money: 9, Total: 33

Specialities: Shakshuka, Mexican salsa, and potato curry
Veg/Non-veg: Non-veg
Contact Details/Timings: Main Bazaar, Rapsy Restaurant,
Munnar. Phone: 04865-230456
Prices: Average cost per person Rs100, Shakshuka ₹ 30,
Mexican salsa ₹ 20, beef ₹ 25, and potato curry ₹ 7

Thalassery

NATIONAL HOTEL   One drawback of eating at the National
Hotel is the fact that it is situated so close to the highway that
clouds of smoke add a smoky flavour to your meal. On the
plus side, the inside of the hotel is spotless and even smells
of jasmine. Keralites pay attention to their food, and it shows
in the exceptional quality of food nearly all the restaurants
serve. The National Hotel is no exception to this. Like in most
other hotels in Kerala, you will be able to get crabs, prawns,
fish, vegetables, and dals. The local delicacy is the avoli fish
while the ayala fish is also tasty.

SOMETHING ON THE SIDE   Meals are served on banana leaves,
service is quick, and there are enough items for the vegetarians
prepared in the typical Kerala style. Food is served with hot rice
water which is supposed to clean your insides out!

Rocky's Verdict: Delicious and fresh, what could be better.
Rating: Taste: 9, Ambience: 6, Service: 8, Value for Money: 9,
Total: 32
Specialities: Vegetarian thali and avoli fish
Veg/Non-veg: Non-veg
Contact Details/Timings: National Hotel, Court Road, NH17,
Thalassery. Phone: 0490-2326035
Prices: Vegetarian thali ₹ 50, avoli fish and crab both for ₹ 30
per portion, and ayali fish ₹ 20

Thiruvananthapuram

INDIAN COFFEE HOUSE   Right next to the west entrance of the railway station, and by the bus stand, is a funky building that looks like a multi-tiered ship's funnel. Built in 1992, it houses the Thiruvananthapuram branch of the Indian Coffee House.

The Indian Coffee House is famous for its breakfast and you can choose from a truly extensive menu featuring fresh fruit juices, omelette, sandwiches, cutlets, chops, biryanis, pulaos, samosas, bondas, and four different types of filter coffee. Each item is cooked fresh and despite the rush there is no compromise on the quality of food served. With an average price of ₹ 10 to ₹ 15 per item, a filling breakfast here will not break the bank. Try the yummy toasted cheese and cucumber sandwiches dipped in sweet ketchup.

The inside has a corridor, which spirals upwards with stone table, and benches lining the wall and filled to capacity. Tables are numbered in ascending order and the last one, numbered thirty-two, is all the way up on the second floor.

SOMETHING ON THE SIDE   The Indian Coffee House is the precursor to the modern cafés. It has branches all over India that for decades have been the venues of intellectual conversations over a cup of java or chai.

Mayur's Verdict: A great way to start your day—with a full stomach and a smile. Get here early to avoid getting a place high up in the building as tables fill up fast and the only kitchen is on the ground floor. Chat with people around and see if long-time regulars will share some interesting anecdotes or historical facts related to the café.
Rating: Taste: 8, Ambience: 9, Service: 9, Value for Money: 9, Total: 35
Certified: Rocky and Mayur rating of excellence
Specialities: Toasted cheese and cucumber sandwiches and coffee

Veg/Non-veg: Non-veg
Contact Details/Timings: Indian Coffee House, Thampanoor,
Thiruvananthapuram. Phone: 0471-3214505
Prices: ₹ 10 to ₹ 15 per item

Trichur

HOTEL BHARATH   The delicious pure vegetarian fare at Hotel
Bharath is extremely popular with devotees going to church
on Sundays. It is a large, extremely clean place and really well
lit thanks to rows of large windows along the wall. The smell
of burning incense adds to the feeling of freshness as you dive
into a range of tasty and reasonably priced dishes. Seating is
communal and you can sit down to share any available table.

The idlis and vadas are cooked fresh and served with
coconut chutney and sambar as are the golden brown, piping
hot dosas. The traditional morning fare of puttu, made by
steaming moistened rice flour, and served with kadala curry
made from black chana, is a great way to start the day. Wash
your meal down with a glass of chilled badaam (almond) milk
or aromatic, freshly brewed filter coffee.

SOMETHING ON THE SIDE   If you are going on a Sunday, go early
and get there before the Sunday church service ends so you
can enjoy your meal at leisure.

Mayur's Verdict: A great destination any time of the day for
hot, fresh, and extremely affordable food.
Rating: Taste: 8, Ambience: 9, Service: 8, Value for Money: 10,
Total: 35
Certified: Rocky and Mayur rating of excellence
Specialities: Puttu with kadala curry
Veg/Non-veg: Veg
Contact Details/Timings: M. Sreekumar 0487-24217204
Prices: Idli ₹ 4 per piece, vada ₹ 7 per piece, puttu ₹ 2

MADHYA PRADESH

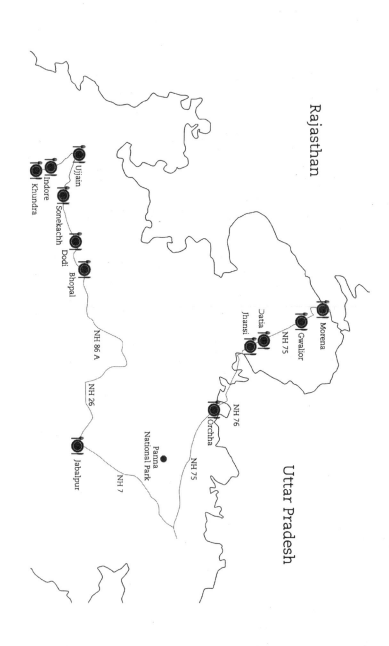

Bhopal

CHATORI GALI Chatori Gali is the place to go to if you like your meat. While seating is available in the form of shaky benches, we'd recommend that you stand outside the shop and watch the cooks prepare your meal.

The paaya is prepared by adding bone marrow and lots of cornflour to chunks of masala mixture. A generous helping of paaya slivers is added next, to prepare a tasty soup. The taste is more akin to thick Chinese soups for some reason!

The atmosphere seems alive; there is some kind of meat-related activity happening all around. Meat is cooking on a large-bicycle-tyre-sized tawa inside while seekhs are garnished with some coriander and served on a plate with buns and spicy chutney. A vertical grill across the road with rotating skewers with lots of masala smeared chickens ensures even grilling. Roasted chicken is cut into slices using a large pair of scissors, then sprinkled with a spicy masala and served with an unusual chutney of yogurt, salt, and red chillies.

SOMETHING ON THE SIDE The secret to the juicy taste is the fat mixed directly into the mixture before grilling, which helps the kebabs cook from the inside out too. The tender kebabs fall apart in your mouth sending off bursts of flavour.

Mayur's Verdict: Seekh kebabs, shammi kebabs, bade ke kebabs, meat biryani, paaya, roast chicken are all available and all delicious but vegetarians beware. The only thing you can eat here are the buns and they aren't even buttered! A must-visit though for lovers of meat.
Rating: Taste: 8, Ambience: 6, Service: 7, Value for Money: 8, Total: 29
Specialities: Meat preparations
Veg/Non-veg: Non-veg
Contact Details/Timings: A lane.
Prices: Average meal per person ₹ 75

JAMEEL HOTEL Down one of the lanes opposite Chatori Gali is Jameel Hotel started in 1947 and famed in this area for its mutton biryani and mutton stew. The biryani at Jameel is as close to perfection as it gets. The rice and meat are cooked separately with spices that subtly add to the taste without taking anything away from the succulent taste of the meat. The spices are freshly ground, the meat is fresh, and the rice cooked in dum style has a flavour all of its own. The mutton stew is very flavourful and the gravy is quite spicy and oily, adding to the taste.

Vegetarians can get a vegetable version of the biryani along with a spicy and tasty aloo subzi but the emphasis is definitely on the non-vegetarian menu. If you do have space left after your meal, you can feast on some sweet moong dal halwa dripping with ghee and sugar.

SOMETHING ON THE SIDE The hotel is on a lane full of little shops selling a variety of freshly baked breads, cookies, cream-filled and jam-filled bread rolls, and savoury, flaky salted breads for you to pick up and eat as you stroll around.

Mayur's Verdict: Rated by Rocky as the best biryani he has ever eaten.
Rating: Taste: 9, Ambience: 7, Service: 9, Value for Money: 9, Total: 34
Certified: Rocky and Mayur rating of excellence
Specialities: Mutton biryani and mutton stew
Veg/Non-veg: Primarily non-vegetarian but with some very tasty vegetarian options
Contact Details/Timings: Jameel Hotel, Ibrahimpura, Bhopal. Phone: 0-9229668827.
Prices: Mutton biryani ₹ 40, moong dal halwa ₹ 100 per kg

MANOHAR DAIRY AND RESTAURANT Manohar is brightly coloured, well lit, clean, marble floored, and famous for its chole bhature, Chinese bhel, puri bhaji halwa, and aloo tikkis. Each item is served in disposable Styrofoam dishes and is freshly prepared and served piping hot. The owner sits at the restaurant and his personal attention to everything is reflected in the quality of the ingredients and the attention to impeccable service. Manohar's also has several counters stacked with gajar halwa, gulab jamun, moong dal halwa, and other savouries catering to those that do not have time for a sit-down meal.

SOMETHING ON THE SIDE As you walk into this restaurant the first thing you see is a weighing machine right by a glass counter with trays of hot gajar halwa, moong dal halwa and gulab jamuns swimming in syrup. So go on check your weight as you wait ☺

Mayur's Verdict: This is an excellent place to eat a meal with family or friends thanks to its neat and clean surroundings, comfortable seating, great attention to service and quality. The tastes are not spectacular but everything is well cooked.
Rating: Taste: 7, Ambience: 7, Service: 8, Value for Money: 8, Total: 30
Specialities: Chole bhature, Chinese bhel, puri bhaji halwa, and aloo tikki
Veg/Non-veg: Veg
Contact Details/Timings: Manohar Dairy and Resturant, Bus Stand, Bhopal. Phone: Murali, 0-9826053245.
Prices: Chole bhature ₹ 35, Chinese bhel ₹ 36, and puri bhaji halwa ₹ 44

Datia

MP TOURISM TOURIST MOTEL In typical government fashion, there was no one present at this establishment when we reached. We found the chef first, snoozing behind the kitchen. When asked to cook us a meal he told us to find the waiter to take the order, as it wasn't the chef's job to do that! It took us about fifteen minutes to find the waiter, give our order, and hey presto!...within an hour our food was ready. Our second order of rotis took another ten minutes to come.

The food was tasty enough consisting of standard roti, subzi, and dal. It just took too long to arrive.

SOMETHING ON THE SIDE   The first thing to do in this sleepy (almost dead) little restaurant is to wake the staff from their deep slumber. After that you can enjoy the stunning views from the back garden which overlooks four palaces and two lakes. The most dominant one is Raja Bir Singh's palace, an imposing structure. With a good camera this should be a perfect place as you can take as many pictures as you want while you wait endlessly for your food.

> **Rocky's Verdict:** Eat at your own risk. Be ready to wait for a long time.
> **Rating:** Taste: 6, Ambience: 9, Service: 1, Value for Money: 5, Total: 31
> **Specialities:** The view.
> **Veg/Non-veg:** Veg
> **Contact Details/Timings:** Between Gwalior and Jhansi.
> **Prices:** Cost per person ₹ 150

Dodi

HIGHWAY TREAT   Highway Treat is a self-service joint. Buy your coupons from the counter, go across to a row of very busy and grumpy men behind a glass and metal counter, and trade in your coupon for food. The menu is very extensive with more than forty items on offer representing cuisine from all parts of India, although the dishes all taste alike.

SOMETHING ON THE SIDE   Vending machines are present should you wish to drink a bottle of cold water or soft drinks.

> **Mayur's Verdict:** It's clean, spacious, and has clean bathrooms and a little play area with swings for the kids.

By all means stop here for a little rest and sip some tea or coffee. Eat, but don't expect anything great.
Rating: Taste: 5, Ambience: 7, Service: 4, Value for Money: 5, Total: 21
Specialities: Rajma chawal is decent.
Veg/Non-veg: Veg
Contact Details/Timings: Highway Treat, Dodi, NH 86.
Prices: Rajma chawal ₹ 40, kadi chawal ₹ 40

Gwalior

BHOJ Bhoj or Food Dhaba has just one item on their menu, the thali. But it is a good one indeed and well worth the trip. You start with four kinds of roti—potato and mattar roti, methi or palak roti, plain roti with ghee, and a missi roti. The thali changes every day but the regular features are the sour kadhi, peas and potatoes, seasonal vegetable, potato gravy, dal, yogurt, raita, pickle, onion and tomato salad, and buttermilk. It's 'All You Can Eat' though the sweets are limited. This is a no-frills place so just walk in, grab a seat, and attack your thali.

The place is well lit and has basic tables and chairs packed in tight. The staff is smartly dressed and you can expect them to serve you delicious, hot, local food.

SOMETHING ON THE SIDE Bhoj is in the process of modernization. Located above 'Cooks Fast Food' which has a bright neon pink signboard is the more modest Bhoj.

Another famous Gwalior landmark eatery is the Bahadura ke Laddu in Naya Bazaar at Lashkar, where the popular breakfast is laddu and jalebis. India's mightiest hockey legends Dhyan Chand and Roop Singh used to eat their breakfast here. Even today you will find Roop Singh's son, also an ex-India hockey player, coming here for this breakfast.

Rocky's Verdict: A delicious thali prepared by local chefs. Pop into Cooks below for some ice cream after your meal.

Rating: Taste: 8, Ambience: 6, Service: 9, Value for Money: 8,
Total: 31
Specialities: Thali
Veg/Non-veg: Veg
Contact Details/Timings: Bhoj, Patankar Bazaar, Gwalior.
Phone: 0751-2325577
Prices: 'All You Can Eat' thali for ₹ 60

Indore

DILBAHAR GHAMANDI LASSI   Sunil, the owner of Ghamandi,
is so proud of his lassi that he calls it ghamandi (arrogant).
The ghamandi lassi is made with yogurt, rabri, sugar, ice, and a
touch of saffron. It is eminently drinkable.

SOMETHING ON THE SIDE   Right next to Ghamandi Lassi is Apna
Sweets; a place famous for its sabudana (pearl sago) khichdi.
This is puffed pearl sago prepared like a bhelpuri or a chaat.
It has puffed pearl sago, peanuts, chillies, coriander, and lots
of lime. It is an eminently edible little snack. In addition to
the khichdi you will also get lots of traditional sweets and
plenty of savouries here. The place is neat and clean and air
conditioned.

Rocky's Verdict: A mighty lassi indeed. Well worth the
trip. Tasty food and lively people make for a great dining
experience.
Rating: Taste: 8, Ambience: 8, Service: 7, Value for Money: 9,
Total: 32
Specialities: Ghamandi Lassi
Veg/Non-veg: Veg
Contact Details/Timings: Dilbahar Ghamandi Lassi, Sapna
Sangeeta Road, Indore. Phone: Sunil, 0-9926811791.
Prices: ₹ 25 per glass

SARAFA BAZAAR This is a bustling, lively and charged little market with everyone making their way to their favourite food stalls for a snack or two. The Joshi Bada House should be your first stop. You will be greeted by Mr Joshi whose continuous banter distracts you as he magically produces one spice after another from his empty hand to put into your dahi bhalla. The next stop should be the giant jalebi maker near the mandir. Mr Gupta makes a 'family' jalebi called kesaria jalebi that he claims cannot be finished by a family of four. A thick, fat, and sweet jalebi, it is very edible as the syrup cannot find its way into the jalebi and so it's not cloyingly sweet. It is still crunchy on the outside and soft and gooey on the inside. You can also get the very popular fried garadu (tapioca or yam) chunks with a variety of spices and chutneys. This is a surprisingly light and delicious snack.

SOMETHING ON THE SIDE No need to step back as Mr Joshi tosses and twirls the dahi bhallas in the air. His well-practised moves show how expert he is at the manoeuvre.

Rocky's Verdict: You have to visit this market for a true-blue Indian street food experience complete with the smells, the colours, and the people.
Rating: Taste: 7, Ambience: 7, Service: 7, Value for Money: 9, Total: 32
Specialities: Street food of all kinds, dahi bhallas and jalebis
Veg/Non-veg: Veg
Contact Details/Timings: Near Indore Bus Stand
Prices: ₹ 40 per head.

Jabalpur

CHAUPATI The Civic Centre area of the busy city of Jabalpur really comes alive at night with a square filled with brightly lit shacks offering a wide range of street food and snacks to its many visitors. The food on offer ranges from soups to pav bhaji, dosas, besan chillas, bhelpuri, ice cream, and even stir-fried chowmein and veg fried rice all prepared right in front of you and served piping hot. All these and more at prices that range from ₹ 10 to ₹ 30. Try the giant dosas, the besan chillas, and the hot almond milk which are all available within ten steps of each other.

SOMETHING ON THE SIDE It is a fun place with the delicious sights, sounds, and smells of snacks being fried, mixed, and served. A lot of families and couples come to eat here and you also have the occasional well-oiled drunk enjoying the deep-fried offerings.

Mayur's Verdict: A must-visit, as much for its carnival atmosphere as for the food factor. Enjoy a nice evening out satiating your taste buds and filling your belly.
Rating: Taste: 7, Ambience: 7, Service: 8, Value for Money: 10, Total: 32
Specialities: Giant dosas, besan chillas, and hot almond milk
Veg/Non-veg: Veg
Contact Details/Timings: Civic Centre Area
Prices: Kesar garam milk ₹ 10, aloo basket chaat ₹ 15, pav bhaji ₹ 20

DEVA MANGORI WALA In the neighbourhood of Fountain, sits an impressive elderly man in a single-room shop. Deva Bhai, with his long, curling moustache, cooks and serves hot, deep-fried snacks to a fast moving clientele. Deva will usually serve samosas, bondas, and mangoras or moong dal pakoras in leaf pattals along with onions and green chillies. As the day draws to a close and some of his long-time regulars drop in, he will use the remaining ingredients to fry some aloo pakoras as a treat. At ₹ 5 per plate for anything, this is great value for money too.

SOMETHING ON THE SIDE While most get their snacks and go, some stay on to watch Deva perform an amazing act. With a small prayer to his guru, Deva immerses his hand into the boiling oil and picks up the fried pakoras with no sign of discomfort. On

examination, his hand feels cool and shows no sign of burns.
You figure it out...

Mayur's Verdict: A must-visit in Jabalpur for the delicious
snacks that drop down to the belly, or for the jaw-dropping
sight of Deva Bhai dipping into the frying pan with
indifference.
Rating: Taste: 8, Ambience: 6, Service: 10, Value for
Money: 10, Total: 34
Certified: Rocky and Mayur rating of excellence
Specialities: Moong dal pakoras
Veg/Non-veg: Veg
Contact Details/Timings: Deva Mangori Wala, Bada Fuhara,
Jabalpur. Phone: 0-9827209794
Prices: Everything for ₹ 5 per plate

HIRA SWEETS   Here you can find Jabalpur's favourite sweet,
the gajak. Made from cane sugar or jaggery, these sweet, flaky
rectangles are great to keep you warm in the winter. The shop
also sells other traditional sweets like chikki but the highlight
is the different types of gajak.

Mayur's Verdict: A great stop to pick up some sweet
memories of your time in Jabalpur.
Rating: Taste: 8, Ambience: 6, Service: 8, Value for Money: 8,
Total: 30
Specialities: Gajak
Veg/Non-veg: Veg
Contact Details/Timings: Hira Sweets, Russell Chowk,
Jabalpur. Phone: 0-9893272444
Prices: ₹ 110 per kg upwards, dry fruit chikki ₹ 40

Jhansi

NARAYAN CHAAT BHANDAR This place has the reputation for being one of the best chaat joints in Jhansi. On a quiet street with a lot of parking space lies this little place. As you enter you are greeted with the smell of incense and the many pictures of gods hung on the walls.

I enjoyed the karela which is a bitter-gourd-shaped paapdi crushed and served with saunth (sweet chutney), hari chutney, and yogurt along with a dash of spices to suit your palate. The delicious golgappas come with two options of water, both of which are good. Jhansi still has small town prices and the karela is for ₹ 7 and the aloo tikki is ₹ 12.

Narayan Chaat Bhandar has two outlets on the same street. The place is very popular and starts filling up as night falls. The people of Jhansi will vouch for this one.

SOMETHING ON THE SIDE Rani Laxmibai of Jhansi is famed throughout India for the valour she displayed fighting British rule. The people of Jhansi venerate their queen to this day and you can hear the famous poem on her life from most people on the street. Even the kids will sing it for you.

Rocky's Verdict: A pleasant outing and nice chaat.
Rating: Taste: 7, Ambience: 6, Service: 8, Value for Money: 8, Total: 29
Specialities: Karela
Veg/Non-veg: Veg
Contact Details/Timings: Narayan Chaat Bhandar, Sadar Bazaar, Jhansi. Phone: 0-9415179686
Prices: Karela ₹ 7, and aloo tikki ₹ 12, cost per person ₹ 25

Khundra

CHAURASIYA DHABA   This dhaba is a visual treat with bright blue walls featuring multi-coloured advertisements and signs. It caters mostly to the truck drivers that move along this long highway. The palak paneer, dal, aloo jeera, and hot tandoori rotis on offer ranged from ₹ 15 to ₹ 30 and were satisfying. The speciality of the place is a pickle made from kadam, a golf-ball-sized fruit covered with soft spikes. It is a fibrous fruit with a tart taste and a bite to it.

It is an open dhaba with the cooking area cordoned off by a low wall on which numerous containers of food rest. The sky blue tables are long, wide, and low with the customary plastic chairs to rest your weary selves on.

SOMETHING ON THE SIDE   Besides eating, the drivers also use this dhaba to bathe, wash their clothes, and clean their trucks.

Mayur's Verdict: The food is fresh, hot, and satisfying and it's great to just watch the goings-on as you eat. It's quite noisy as it sits right on the highway and there were no travelling families or couples eating here.
Rating: Taste: 6, Ambience: 6, Service: 6, Value for Money: 8, Total: 26
Specialities: Kadam pickle
Veg/Non-veg: Veg
Contact Details/Timings: 162 km short of Jabalpur. Chaurasiya Dhaba, Khundra, NH7. Phone: 0-9893346641
Prices: ₹ 70 to ₹ 80 per head

Morena

ASLI KAMAL GAJAK BHANDAR   This is one of the most famous gajak shops in a city famous across the world for its gajak. The Morena gajak is a crunchy sweet made with jaggery, sugar, dry fruit, and other delicious ingredients. Sheets of jaggery are heated with sesame and dry fruits. They are then stretched and pulled repeatedly till they are just the right texture, after which they are beaten with giant hammers and cut or rolled into the desired shape. They say that the air and water of Morena is more suited to gajak than anywhere else in the world.

You may have had gajak before but it is unlikely that you have sampled the over forty varieties available in this little shop including til (sesame), kaju (cashew), dry fruit roll, pista, and even chocolate and strawberry.

SOMETHING ON THE SWEET: The Diwali season brings with it the gajak season, a favourite throughout the year but most preferred during the winter months, Morena's gajak is exported throughout the world and you would be lucky to get your hands on some in your city. Exceptional stuff.

Rocky's Verdict: If in Morena, lay your hands on as much gajak as you can carry. Taste all the flavours and take home the ones you like.
Rating: Taste: 9, Ambience: 2, Service: 9, Value for Money: 9, Total: 29
Certified: Rocky and Mayur rating of excellence
Specialities: Gajak of all flavours
Veg/Non-veg: Veg
Contact Details/Timings: Asli Kamal Gajak Bhandar, Opposite Collectorate, Morena. Phone: 0-9301689879
Prices: Prices range from the plain gajak at ₹ 80 per kg up to ₹ 140 per kg for the cashew gajak

---

Orchha

BHOLA CAFÉ On Sheesh Mahal Road lies a row of shops and restaurants catering to the numerous tourists both Indian and foreign who visit the temples and tombs of Orchha. Of these eateries Bhola Café, run by a young man named Birju, is very popular. You eat at plastic tables set out on the sidewalk, ordering from an extensive menu, featuring Korean, Dutch, and Israeli food in distinct sections besides the usual pancakes, parathas, and of course, chopsuey and noodles.

The breakfast menu has over forty items on offer and includes a variety of freshly squeezed juices and milkshakes. The butter honey pancake and the 'Dutch pannekoek met honing' differ only in that the latter is thicker and more filling. Both are priced the same at ₹ 40 but the butter honey pancake is recommended for its lighter texture. The pannekoek with kaas was fun to eat with the melted cheese dripping out of it, while the honey paratha is fried and dripping with honey and at ₹ 15, a real bargain. The mixed juice is refreshing and surprisingly filling and you can also get the fruits chopped and served on a plate or on your pancake. Most items on this menu range from ₹ 15 to ₹ 40 and each is best enjoyed with a glass of fresh juice as you sit and watch the hustle and bustle on the street.

SOMETHING ON THE SIDE If you are fortunate you might have your meal accompanied by the melodious sounds of some wandering holy man strumming on an ektara while singing a religious hymn.

Mayur's Verdict: Have fun rolling your tongue around not just the delicious food but the exotic names like ramyun, malawach, pannekoek, and fatut as you enjoy the crisp morning sun while sipping on some fresh fruit juice. Highly recommended!
Rating: Taste: 9, Ambience: 9, Service: 8, Value for Money: 9, Total: 35
Certified: Rocky and Mayur rating of excellence
Specialities: Butter honey pancake, dutch pannekoek, and fresh juices
Veg/Non-veg: Veg

Contact Details/Timings: Bhola Restaurant, Sheesh Mahal
Road, Orchha. Phone: 0-9424344378
Prices: Butter honey pancake ₹ 40, pannekoek met honing ₹
40, honey paratha 15

RAMRAJA RESTAURANT   This restaurant proudly displays a
sign advertising its temple view, its mention in the *Lonely Planet*
guide for travellers and the fact that it serves Italian, Korean,
and continental food along with fresh juice for breakfast,
lunch, and dinner.

Ramraja is famous for its Indian thalis with rotis, rice, dal,
mattar-gobhi, paneer, chana, and dahi. The vegetables can
change from day to day but everything is as delicious as home-
cooked food. If you are really lucky you can try a vegetable dish
made from jasmine flowers that the old grandmother of the
house sits and cleans.

The kimchi, a Korean dish of pickled vegetables with
seasoning, is made of radishes here and is strong and pungent
while the shakshuka, a dish consisting of poached or fried eggs
cooked in a sauce of tomatoes, peppers, onions, and spices
(often including cumin, turmeric, and chillies), and usually
served with white bread, is like eating a combined breakfast
and lunch. The pizza verdure is full of vegetables and cheese
with a really nice smoky taste thanks to the wood-fired home
made oven the family uses.

There is an outside section with walls that display numerous
religious posters and tabletops covered with quaint red-and-
white checked tablecloths. Go inside, through the family's
living space, and then a large poorly lit kitchen and storage
area, to get to the open backyard. Here there is seating for
about twenty people and a magnificent view.

SOMETHING ON THE SIDE   Look out for the owner's friend who
will be happy to sit at your table and regale you with songs and
poetry from the good old days.

Mayur's Verdict: A great variety of clean, tasty, freshly cooked food, the feel of home thanks to the family that runs the place, a great view of the palace all lit up at night, and the chance to converse with people from different countries and learn about their food. Enjoy a nice, relaxed evening here.
Rating: Taste: 7, Ambience: 8, Service: 9, Value for Money: 9, Total: 33
Specialities: Indian thalis, kimchi, shakshuka, and pizza verdure
Veg/Non-veg: Veg
Contact Details/Timings: Ramraja Restaurant, Sheesh Mahal Road, Orchha. Phone: 0-9425881378
Prices: Shakshuka ₹ 40, lamiya ₹ 30, pizza al verdure ₹ 100

Sonekachh

PAPPU KA DHABA The food here is indifferent and unappealing with standard dishes such as paneer bhurji and dal being barely edible, and rotis being just passable. The place has really nothing to offer barring some ice cream. It's also only vegetarian.

SOMETHING ON THE SIDE Run by the very large and politically active Pappu Chauhan, this place boasts great security for families and is a great place to get on a political chat with the owner or one of his brothers.

Rocky's Verdict: Stop here only if you must.
Rating: Taste: 3, Ambience: 2, Service: 5, Value for Money: 1, Total: 11
Specialities: None
Veg/Non-veg: Veg
Contact Details/Timings: Pappu ka Dhaba, Sonekachh, NH 86.
Prices: Paneer bhurji ₹ 50 and dal ₹ 20

Ujjain

BANKS OF THE KSHIPRA RIVER Early morning by the banks of the holy Kshipra, hymns can be heard as incense fills the air and people take purification dips in the holy river. Along the banks are a few small shacks offering devotees hot and fresh breakfast.

Pre-boiled poha (flattened rice flakes) with liberal amounts of sugar added is kept ready and the tadka of green and red chillies, salt, pepper, onions, curry leaves, and tejpan is fried together with the poha in giant kadahis to make a wholesome breakfast. Sev is added to make the mixture crisp and the delectable poha is served hot along with extremely sweet, milky tea to wash it down. If the sugar in the poha and the tea is not enough you can always please your sweet tooth with hot, sweet, and crunchy jalebis fried on order and served on pieces of old newspaper.

SOMETHING ON THE SIDE The evening aarti is a beautiful sight with ringing bells accompanying the pujari as they move burning flames in circular motions at the riverbank accompanied by the chanting of hymns.

Mayur's Verdict: A perfect way to start the day. Enjoy a hot, sweet snack as you breathe in the incense and enjoy the sights and sounds of people offering devotions at the riverside.
Rating: Taste: 8, Ambience: 9, Service: 8, Value for Money: 10, Total: 35
Certified: Rocky and Mayur rating of excellence
Specialities: Poha and jalebi
Veg/Non-veg: Veg
Contact Details/Timings: By the Kshipra
Prices: Poha ₹ 8, tea ₹ 2, jalebi ₹ 10 for a double handful

SRI MAHAKALESHWAR BHANG GHOTA   Ujjain is a temple city and the devotees of Shiva take daily doses of bhang as part of their rituals. The ever-smiling Vyasji sells bhang just outside the Mahakaleshwar temple. Bhang leaves are pounded to a powder, which is then mixed with water to make a green paste. Beside Vyasji are a number of thalis stacked with little balls rolled from the bhang paste. These bhang balls are blended with milk, thandai (milk-based blend of dry fruits, nuts, seeds, and spices), lime water, or jaljeera (cumin, mint, and rock salt drink) and served to customers.

SOMETHING ON THE SIDE   As you drink the bhang, encourage the ever-present jovial crowd around you to join in as you call out a salutation praising Shiva, and then, glug down your chilled glass of bhang thandai. Do it real quick and let some of it escape the glass to run down your chin.

Mayur's Verdict: For the daring, we would recommend the thandai. We warn, however, that bhang can induce a high, if too much is taken.
Rating: Taste: 10, Ambience: 10, Service: 10, Value for Money: 10, Total: 40
Certified: Rocky and Mayur rating of excellence
Specialities: Bhang
Veg/Non-Veg: Veg
Contact Details/Timings: Outside the Mahakaleshwar temple.
Prices: Bhang makes you forget ☺

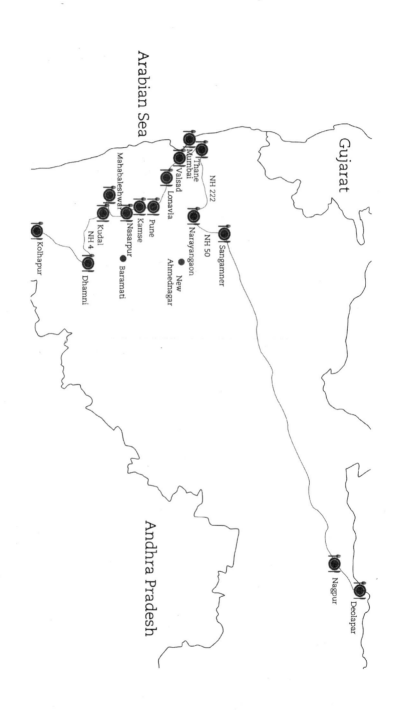

Deolapar

SARDAR DHABA   On this long, continuous stretch of NH7, this quaint little dhaba is a welcome stop. Sardar Dhaba is run by Avtar Singh and his aged father. Simple, honest, and straightforward, they can best be described as the 'salt of the earth' kind of people.

Dhabas in this area are less about choices and more about pure sustenance so most people will simply order 'khana' (food) as opposed to choosing items from a menu. When we ate here on a cold winter night the choices were dal and ande ki bhujiya (scrambled eggs with onions, tomatoes, green chillies, and some salt and chilli powder) and they tasted as good as any gourmet meal. The tandoor radiates plenty of heat and is the most popular place in the house to sit around on a cold evening. With the dal costing ₹ 15 and the bhujiya ₹ 20, value for money takes on a whole different meaning here. There is even a tap to bathe under after you have spent a night sleeping on the manjis (beds), and all this comes at the price of a meal!

SOMETHING ON THE SIDE   This highway has very little in terms of eating places and even less in terms of villages and civilization. The forest air is clean enough to drink and the verdant foliage makes this a great drive. There are some problems with 'bhai log' or the new avatars of dacoits, who have been known to stop vehicles and demand money. It is a stretch, better negotiated during the day.

Rocky's Verdict: A great place to stretch your legs and have a hot bite. Very simple and basic.
Rating: Taste: 7, Ambience: 9, Service: 9, Value for Money: 7, Total: 32
Specialities: Dal and hot tandoori rotis.
Veg/Non-veg: Non-Veg
Contact Details/Timings: Sardar Dhaba, Deolapar, NH7. Phone: 0-9422821233
Prices: ₹ 100 per head

Dhamni

HOTEL SHRADHHA LODGE   This dhaba calls itself a 'hotel' like most others in the area, and claims to specialize in Konkani food. The staple gravy for both vegetarian and non-vegetarian dishes is the usal, a kind of sambar containing coconut. The vegetarian food is very nice but the highlight here is the meat.

The Bangda fish in particular is popular in these parts and is a pungent though tasty fish. The 'solkadi' offered is watery coconut milk coloured pink by the use of kokam. Mildly spiced and soothing, it is drunk before a meal and is refreshing, light, and a great appetizer. We recommend that after your meal you try the strong filter coffee.

For those who want less adventurous food, they offer chana masala and dum aloo Kashmiri. This being the land of vada pav and tea, the two taste great wherever you order them. Most of these places are neat and clean, and maintain pretty gardens on the premises.

SOMETHING ON THE SIDE   Most dhabas here compete to see who has the best-maintained and most beautiful place. This accounts for some wonderful gardens, flowers, and brightly lit and coloured places. Owners are justifiably proud and can be seen showing regulars the latest improvements that have been made. Also, a lovely area to drive through in the monsoons.

Rocky's Verdict: The hotels are great to stop at for a good wholesome meal.
Rating: Taste: 7, Ambience: 8, Service: 6, Value for Money: 7, Total: 28
Specialities: Bangda fish, solkadi, and vada pav
Veg/Non-veg: Non-veg
Contact Details/Timings: 265 kms short of Panaji on NH17. Shradhha Lodge, Dhamni.
Prices: Cost per person ₹ 100

Kamse

TONY DA DHABA   The food is very typical of a Punjabi dhaba with a huge range of food both vegetarian and non-vegetarian. The highlight of the place is the variety of birds on the menu, either roasted in a tandoor or cooked with a variety of gravies. Equally interesting for vegetarians is the range of breads made of different grains including wholewheat, maize, barley, jowar (sorghum), bajra (millet), and chana (chickpea), and in different styles such as tandoori, parathas, rotis, etc.

This legendary dhaba is famous not just for its food but for its eccentric and colourful owner Tony Paaji, as he likes to be called. There are large signs advertising the place on the highway and when you arrive you are greeted by a sign promising fresh fish, a kebab corner, and 'Arebian (sic) Nights with Hookas'. Unusually for a 'dhaba', this one also has a sign informing you that they accept MasterCard and Visa.

The dhaba is an open space with a metal-framed covered roof and you sit down to eat at Formica tables and a choice of plastic chairs or manjis. It is a large space and can seat over a 150 patrons many of whom come down from Mumbai or Pune just to enjoy a hearty meal and maybe a hookah.

SOMETHING ON THE SIDE   The dhaba is spread over a large open area including a grassy lawn with a children's playground complete with swings, slides, and see-saws. Bordering the lawns are a series of hutches and coops housing varied species of birds many of which are running around on the lawn. These include ducks, geese, guinea fowl, junglefowl, quails, and chickens. Off to the side there is a large wire enclosure with turkeys and five and a half feet high emus!

Mayur's Verdict: Stop at Tony da Dhaba for decent food and for the whole experience which will only be complete if you are fortunate enough to meet Tony Paaji. This is a man whose character and language are as colourful as the plumage of the birds that you can sample at his dhaba. The popularity of the dhaba has led to a steep increase in prices and it's no longer a cheap option. The open kitchen is well worth a look.

Rating: Taste: 7, Ambience: 8, Service: 8, Value for Money: 7, Total: 30

Specialities: A variety of birds and rotis

Veg/Non-veg: Non-veg

Contact Details/Timings: On NH 4 about 50 km from Pune. Tony da Dhaba, Kamse, NH 4. Phone: 0-9890695937

Prices: Cost per person ₹ 300

Kudal

HOTEL KONKAN DHABA   When here, we recommend you try the vada sagoto—chicken cooked in rich gravy with the Konkani touch—or the variety of fish offered. The spices of Konkani food are hot and exciting, and appeal to most Indian palates. The coconut is ever present but is not an obtrusive taste. The bhindi found in this area is of a different variety, and also cooked with coconut. We suggest you try this dish.

There is no dearth of variety here, and the well-illustrated menu will help you choose your meal. This town will give you a good bang for your food buck.

SOMETHING ON THE SIDE   Goan spices are so popular that they are now sold throughout the region in neatly packed polybags or plastic bottles. There are umpteen companies employed in this business. Sadly, the mixes are usually far inferior to freshly ground traditional masalas and are used by most little eating places to prepare overspiced food with lots of food colouring.

Rocky's Verdict: Goa is only an hour and a half away. Stop here if you're very hungry but the food is average.

Rating: Taste: 6, Ambience: 6, Service: 6, Value for Money: 6, Total: 24

Specialities: Vada sagoto and bhindi
Veg/Non-veg: Non-veg
Contact Details/Timings: About 80 km short of
Panjim on NH 17. Hotel Konkan Dhaba, Kudal, NH 17.
Phone: 0-9960930650
Prices: Cost for one person ₹ 100. For seafood it can go up
dramatically depending on the size of the fish/shellfish you
order. Check in advance to avoid any unpleasant surprises.

Kolhapur

ALL INDIA SPECIAL BHEL Ask for Raja Bhau pretty much
anywhere in Kolhapur and the directions will lead you to
the Khasbaug area. There in a side street you will find a little
booth-like shop surrounded by crowds of people. Welcome
to the All India Special Bhel, which in its own words (painted
on the front in Marathi) has no other branches. The stand is
now run by Babu, the son of Raja Bhau, and he continues the
tradition by having his son and nephew work for him though
only in a helping role. This man single-handedly takes orders,
prepares the bhelpuri complete with special requests, hands it
over, accepts the money, and starts the cycle all over again. He
does this every day from 4 pm until 2 am and we clocked him
making one helping of bhel every ten seconds.

The scrumptious bhelpuri is to die for with an excellent
balance in all things be it sweet-spicy or crisp-chewy. The
ingredients are fresh and you can eat there or take away a
family pack with all the ingredients packed separately and
ready to be mixed at your convenience.

SOMETHING ON THE SIDE The action is non-stop as Babu moves,
bobs, and dips at great speed doling out ingredients into different
pateelas, mixing it all up before ladling out precise portions
into disposable paper bowls or pre-cut paper rectangles,
which he twists into cones. His alert helpers are responsible
for refilling any of the boxes in which the ingredients run out
and the crowd never seems to thin. The most amazing thing
though is that he does it all with a happy smile on his face

and a very pleasant manner in dealing with his customers and his staff.

> **Mayur's Verdict:** One bite of the bhel will explain the constant crowd at this booth and the fact that the popularity of this place has led to a thriving street food market being set up along the whole lane.
> **Rating:** Taste: 9, Ambience: 7, Service: 10, Value for Money: 10, Total: 36
> **Certified:** Rocky and Mayur rating of excellence
> **Specialities:** Bhelpuri
> **Veg/Non-veg:** Veg
> **Contact Details/Timings:** All India Special Bhel, Khasbaug, Kolhapur.
> **Prices:** Bhelpuri ₹ 8

FADTARE MISAL PAO The misal served at this shop is a light and very spicy soup which is poured into a small bowl containing sev, poha, peas, sprouts, and other crunchy ingredients. It is then topped with onions, a lemon is squeezed on top and finally the 'kut' is added. This is a sharp, spicy, and chilli oil that adds a tangy flavour to the misal. Top it off with tea which is only available outside the little shack.

SOMETHING ON THE SIDE Be prepared to wait in line as this seems to be Kolhapur's favourite breakfast. Grab a cup of tea from the chaiwallah as you wait.

> **Rocky's Verdict:** An awesome breakfast and a delightful snack. It is eminently edible.
> **Certified:** Rocky and Mayur rating of excellence
> **Rating:** Taste: 9, Ambience: 10, Service: 10, Value for Money: 10, Total: 39
> **Specialities:** Misal
> **Veg/Non-veg:** Veg

> **Contact Details/Timings:** Fadtare Misal Pao, 1243/1, Shivaji Udyamnagar, Kolhapur.
> **Prices:** ₹ 20 per plate of misal

HOTEL PARAKH Hotel Parakh serves authentic Kolhapuri cuisine. The vegetarian thali consists of usal, bhaji, amti, yogurt, papads, and onions. The singdana chutney is served with it which is crushed peanuts in red chilli. The preferred food of choice with Kolhapuris though is mutton. The non-vegetarian thali consists of meat cooked in an onion base. The taste of the meat itself is complemented by the awesome spices. Two bowls of curry are served separately. The tambda rasa (spicy red curry) and pandra rasa (coconut-based spicy curry, white or greenish in colour) are the gravies that the meat is dipped into before being eaten. The staple is a bhakri and this is liberally dipped into the curries and eaten with the spicy singdana and onions. To wind up your meal dig into some delicious shrikhand.

SOMETHING ON THE SIDE This is possibly one of the best-known places for Kolhapuri cuisine. Most people anywhere in the city will be able to point you in the right direction when you ask for 'Parakh'. Surprisingly well known for such a humble place.

> **Rocky's Verdict:** The people of Kolhapur are like their food, spicy and lively. Stop in Parakh for a delicious bite and authentic Kolhapuri cuisine.
> **Tip:** Spice it up, Kolhapuris love spicy food.
> **Rating:** Taste: 8, Ambience: 7, Service: 9, Value for Money: 10, Total: 34
> **Specialities:** Veg and non-veg thali
> **Veg/Non-veg:** Non-veg
> **Contact Details/Timings:** Hotel Parakh, Patolewadi, Kolhapur. Phone: 0-9423281343.
> **Prices:** Veg thali ₹ 60 and non-veg thali ₹ 100

MORNING JUICE For those that believe in the old adage 'health is wealth', the vendor of fresh juices made of neem, karela (bitter gourd), and amla (Indian gooseberry) at Tara Bai Park comes as an added boon during the morning jog.

SOMETHING ON THE SIDE If it's vegetable or fruit and it tastes terrible you will be able to buy a glass of its juice here. The variety is surprising. Mixing and matching seems to be the mantra here.

Rocky's Verdict: Drink it only if you're a health freak.
Rating: Taste: 0, Ambience: 1, Service: 9, Value for Money: 9, Total: 19
Specialities: Fresh vegetable juices
Veg/Non-veg: Veg
Contact Details/Timings: Tara Bai Park
Prices: ₹ 30 per person

SHYAM VADA PAV If you cook it well they will come and if you cook it well and set up shop at the right place they will bring all their friends. Shyam has worked that out really well and for the past twenty-five years he has set up his makeshift food stall every day in a little open area on the old Pune–Bengaluru road within shouting distance of three colleges. The reason for his popularity is his quality which has remained the same for over two decades. His offering is the same: giant vadas, deep fried as you watch, are served with thick slices of fresh pav, and piping hot cups of chai. The giant potato vadas are hot, fresh, tasty, spicy, and filling to the extreme and best enjoyed squashed between two pieces of the fresh bread.

Pretty much every student, every teacher, and every professor in the area has eaten here at some stage and many eat here every day.

SOMETHING ON THE SIDE Shyam refuses to move to a larger, better location because he wants to be there for customers and friends who return here, some after a decade. Food and love make a great combination.

> **Mayur's Verdict:** Indian street food at its best not just for the taste but also for the humility and love shown by Shyam Kaka who refuses to leave this spot since it is the place where his old customers can come find him. A must-visit if you are in Kolhapur.
> **Rating:** Taste: 9, Ambience: 7, Service: 9, Value for Money: 7, Total: 32
> **Specialities:** Vada pav
> **Veg/Non-veg:** Veg
> **Contact Details/Timings:** Near Rajaram College, Kolhapur. Phone: 9730401366.
> **Prices:** Vada pav ₹ 9 and chai ₹ 3

VAAMAN GUEST HOUSE Vaaman specializes in Malwani food, which is not too spicy unlike Kolhapuri food. It has a subtler taste and at Vaaman they specialize in seafood. The mandheli fish is a local favourite and is deep fried with minimal batter. The clam curry is big on flavour and of course the fried prawns are a must-have. The crab curry is a great mix of spicy gravy and sweet crab meat. The delicious solkadi, usal or peas in gravy, bhaji (cauliflower in mustard), amti (lentil), and onions make up the vegetarian thali. The non-vegetarian thali has the tambda rasa (red spicy curry made with mutton stock), solkadi, and spicy mutton served with rotis. Roti is the staple here and onions are an important accompaniment with your food.

SOMETHING ON THE SIDE This place serves what is best described as Kolhapuri fast food. You will get served within five minutes flat of ordering by the enterprising staff. This is a cuisine under constant evolution.

Rocky's Verdict: Decent food. Come here only for the
seafood.
Rating: Taste: 7, Ambience: 6, Service: 8, Value for Money: 9,
Total: 30
Specialities: Seafood
Veg/Non-veg: Veg and non-veg are served but it is known for
its seafood.
Contact Details/Timings: Vaaman Guest House, Ist lane,
Shahupuri, Kolhapur. Phone: 9890098805, 0231-2652224.
Prices: Veg thali ₹ 30 and non-veg thali ₹ 60

Lonavla

CHIKKI HEAVEN   On either side of the railway station are
roads where EVERY shop is a chikki shop selling dozens of
varieties of this sugary nut-laden sweet. Originally made using
jaggery, liquid glucose, sugar, and roasted groundnut, the chikki
is now available in so many variations and flavours, it bewilders
the mind. Pineapple, fig, cashew, chocolate, butter crush, and
mint crush are just some examples of the many flavours that
feature on this endless list that grows longer each year as the
vendors try to keep customers interested.

SOMETHING ON THE SIDE   Lonavla was so named because of the
word 'lenya' which means caves in Marathi. There are many
rock-cut caves which surround Lonavla. It is claimed that
chikki first came to Lonavla more than 125 years ago when Shri
Maganlal Agarwal began selling 'gurdana', a mixture of jaggery
and groundnuts in a huge sack to the labourers who were
laying tracks on the Khandala–Pune railway line. 'Gurdana' is
rich in protein and iron and the labourers used to consume
it for instant energy. Later, the simple 'gurdana' graduated to
groundnut chikki and over the years other chikki varieties were
introduced.

Mayur's Verdict: The chikki vendors of Lonavla have lost a lot of business thanks to the new expressway, which bypasses the town. However, you can still exit off the expressway and take a small detour to go stock up on some fresh and tasty chikki in whatever form or flavour that takes your fancy. This is a great reason to get off the beaten track, so pack some and take it home to enjoy with friends and family.
Rating: Taste: 10, Ambience: 6, Service: 6, Value for Money: 8, Total: 30
Specialities: Chikki in all its flavours
Veg/Non-veg: Veg
Contact Details/Timings: Maganlal Chikki, Lonavla. Phone: 02114-272816
Prices: The price per kilo starts at ₹ 80 for groundnut and chana chikki to ₹ 520 for kesar pista

Mahabaleshwar

DADA CHANAWALA The famous Mahabaleshwar chana, believe it or not, comes from Uttar Pradesh! The reason it tastes so good here is because the 'air' of Mahabaleshwar helps it bloat nicely when roasted. Roasted and salted, this chana is a great snack. There's also nothing better than the 'Maharashtra mewa', which is what they call their bhutta (whole corn) roasted on a fire. The corn is plump, full, soft, and sweet. You must look out for the mewa when in this region. In season it's sold on every street corner and is hard to miss.

Mama Chanawala, next door to Dada, is also famous for his natural strawberry, mulberry, and raspberry jams along with other natural produce. Made with whole fruits, the jams have solid berry chunks in them. Make sure you grab a bottle.

SOMETHING ON THE SIDE Mahabaleshwar offers cool climes not too far from Mumbai and is a popular getaway for those stifled by Mumbai's packed streets. There are plenty of good walks and fresh air for those willing to take them.

> **Rocky's Verdict:** Light snacks and fun jams. You must try
> them.
> **Rating:** Taste: 7, Ambience: 9, Service: 7, Value for Money: 8,
> Total: 31
> **Specialities:** Mahabaleshwar chana, the Maharashtra mewa,
> and fruit jams
> **Veg/Non-veg:** Veg
> **Contact Details/Timings:** Dada Chanawala, Shivaji Chowk,
> Mahabaleshwar, Mama Chanawala, Shivaji Chowk,
> Mahabaleshwar. Phone: 0-9422404057
> **Prices:** Snack at ₹ 20 per head

Mumbai

BADE MIYAN   Md Yasin, father of the present owner Md Ismail
Sheikh, started the place and was affectionately referred to as
'Bade Miyan'. It was started in the 1960s by Bade Miyan with
the recipes he has passed on to his children who now run the
place. It has a reputation for serving authentic tikkas, kebabs,
and stuffed rolls. Frequented by the who's who of Bollywood
this place comes alive as the sun sets and you can smell the fat
in the fire from a few hundred metres away. There's something
here for the veggies and non-veggies—in fact there's a lot.

Place your order with one of the many super efficient
waiters who buzz around like bees. Make sure you have a car
to eat in or at least a taxi bonnet to put your food on. The rolls
are spectacular and are recommended (go with chicken bhuna
roll and the paneer roll). The kebabs are fairly good and the
chicken tangri is up there with any tangri anywhere else. The
paneer tikkas are pretty good too and the mutton seekhs are
pleasant but must be had hot or they are just average.

SOMETHING ON THE SIDE   This is one place that highlights the
character of Mumbai and rickshaw pullers can be see dining
with BMW owners side by side. We love that. Hang around long
enough or late enough into the night and you may be rewarded
by and actor or two showing up to nibble on the goodies.
Closing time varies depending on who you ask. Around 2 am

is a safe bet but it has been known to carry on even later into the night.

Rocky's Verdict: These may be the best kebabs and tikkas in Mumbai—we did not find any better. The place has lots of energy and is efficient. You will just have to bear the heat though.
Rating: Taste: 7, Ambience: 8, Service: 9, Value for Money: 6, Total: 30
Specialities: Chicken bhuna roll
Veg/Non-veg: Non-veg
Contact Details/Timings: Bade Miyan, Colaba, Mumbai.
Prices: Paneer roll ₹ 90, chicken tangri ₹ 150 for four pieces, paneer tikka, ₹ 80, and mutton seekh ₹ 80

BRITANNIA AND COMPANY   The story behind the name of this old-fashioned eating joint is very amusing. In 1923 when it started, it was a lot easier to get a licence from the British government if you had a British sounding name. Thankfully the licence was gotten and the place is still going strong. Antiquity and age hit you as soon as you walk in, the furniture itself is pre-World War II and the owner and overall in charge Mr Boman Kohinoor will be happy to tell you old stories.

The Iranian chicken berry pulao and the vegetable pulao are the favourites at this place and use Iranian barberries to flavour their pulao. The sali boti (mutton with potato strips) and dhansak (Parsi-style meat cooked with many lentils and sometimes even vegetables) are popular as well. There are funky and bright coloured drinks like Rosy Raspberry and a choice of others. There is a strict queue outside and the place is always full. There is plenty for vegetarians as well. Try the old-style caramel custard for dessert.

SOMETHING ON THE SIDE   Boman Kohinoor's job is to walk about and take personal care of his customers. He will be delighted to show you one of his many glowing reviews in journals and magazines which he carries with himself. He has the original pages cut out and laminated and he is justly proud of them. The man's an institution.

Rocky's Verdict: A little piece of unchanged Bombay (Mumbai). The place is ageless and a must-visit if only to chat with Boman.
Certified: Rocky and Mayur rating of excellence
Rating: Taste: 9, Ambience: 10, Service: 10, Value for Money: 7, Total: 36
Specialities: Iranian chicken berry pulao, veg pulao, sali boti, and dhansak
Veg/Non-veg: Non-veg
Contact Details/Timings: Britannia and Company, Ballard Estate, near RBI, Mumbai.
Prices: Iranian chicken berry pulao, ₹ 250, vegetable pulao ₹ 150, and sali boti ₹ 230

GAJALEE This legendary place whose name means 'casual chitchat' serves up some of the best seafood in town. The interior is air conditioned, luxurious with lots of wood and marble, and has a well-stocked bar and extensive wine list.

Gajalee specializes in Malwani food, coastal cooking that features hot coconut-based sweet and sour curries with fish and seafood. The pomfret butter pepper dish with pomfret chunks coated in a cream and pepper base and roasted in a tandoor is served on a bed of salad and is rich, creamy and yet has an extremely delicate taste. The chef's speciality, the bombil fry has delicate fillets of fish coated with rice powder and deep fried to a golden brown colour. The flavour of the fish permeates every mouthful and it is easy to see why it is such a prized delicacy. The crab is cooked in a delicious tandoori batter that adds flavour to the intrinsically sweet meat, which in turn provides an interesting counterpoint to the super spicy seasoning.

Vegetarians do not despair as you can get a vegetarian thali also cooked in the Malwani style. The beautifully presented thali comes with bowls of amti (sweet-sour dal), usal (marinated green peas), suran (spicy yam), and pink, creamy solkadi along with rice and rotis. It is a tribute to the chef that each dish has a unique taste but sadly you get only one helping of everything. You can choose to order these dishes a la carte too and add items such as vegetable kolhapuri, vegetable kadahi, and vegetable makhanwala besides a range of paneer dishes.

SOMETHING ON THE SIDE   This is one of the four Gajalee branches and at the entrance you are greeted by a huge billboard depicting a cartoon scene of a fish marketplace featuring several well known Bollywood stars. The bank has a relaxing view of a little lake while the front looks down on a busy main street.

Mayur's Verdict: Visit Gajalee for an eating experience that combines conventional recipes with improvised cooking to please your palate. It is expensive dining but well worth the price.
Rating: Taste: 8, Ambience: 10, Service: 10, Value for Money: 8, Total: 36
Certified: Rocky and Mayur rating of excellence
Specialities: Malwani food
Veg/Non-veg: Non-veg
Contact Details/Timings: Gajalee, Vile Parle, Mumbai.
Prices: Vegetarian thali ₹ 100, pomphret butter pepper ₹ 3200, pomphret kapri ₹ 3200, crab tandoori ₹ 2000

HAJI ALI JUICE CENTRE   There is a wide array of juices and they are all freshly squeezed. You can mix and match as you like. We went with pomegranate, guava, strawberry, and kiwi, which frankly was disastrous but it sounded really good. They now also sell the usual variety of chocolates and candies that are becoming extremely popular with young people. They also have an assortment of 'natural' ice creams like kiwi and sitaphal (sharifa or custard apple). These are well made and hit the spot. It is a good place to start and the unique and beautiful shrine of Haji Ali is right next so you can walk to this holy place to pay your respects at the tomb of Sayed Peer Haji Ali Shah Bukhari.

Rocky's Verdict: No visit to Mumbai would be complete without going to this shrine. On a hot day you will appreciate the perfect location of the Juice Centre.
Rating: Taste: 8, Ambience: 9, Service: 5, Value for Money: 6, Total: 28
Specialities: Natural ice creams
Veg/Non-veg: Veg
Contact Details/Timings: Open from 5 am to 1 am. Haji Ali Juice Centre, Haji Ali, Mumbai.
Prices: Vary according to order

KAILASH PARBAT VEGETARIAN RESTAURANT Take your pick from the dozens of items on display in the glass fronted display and eat sitting indoors or outside on the pavement. The famous ragda patties dish is delicious with golden brown potato patties competing for taste with the ragda in which the gram flour adds a nice thick gravy-like consistency. The dal-pakwaan is a filling snack with the deep-fried crisp pakwaan serving as a tasty spoon to scoop the dal with. The fact that these are so rich in taste without the use of any onion or garlic in the cooking is quite remarkable.

There is a range of sweets including the mohan thal, til laddu, tosha, murmura mithai, and ghevar which are all truly delightful and sweet as sin. The til laddu made entirely of til held together by honey and covered with raisins is a true winner.

SOMETHING ON THE SIDE This eatery has two outlets across the road from each other and though they serve a range of dishes, they are best known for their Sindhi food. One outlet does full meals while the other specializes in sweets and breakfast snacks, which you can eat sitting indoors or outside on the pavement.

> **Mayur's Verdict:** Fresh food of excellent quality served in
> extremely clean surroundings ensures that Kailash Parbat
> is a great place to start your day with. Sit outside and enjoy
> a meal as you watch the world go busily by or order your
> sweets and savouries to take away.
> **Rating:** Taste: 9, Ambience: 7, Service: 9, Value for Money: 7,
> Total: 32
> **Specialities:** Til laddu
> **Veg/Non-veg:** Veg
> **Contact Details/Timings:** Kailash Parbat, Colaba, Mumbai.
> Phone: 022-22812112.
> **Prices:** Ragda patties ₹ 35, dal-pakwaan ₹ 25, til laddu ₹ 300
> per kg, tosha ₹ 200 per kg, and ghevar ₹ 220 per kg

Narayangaon

WINE TASTING CENTRES AND SHOPS When we first
entered this place, we were greeted with quite an amusing
sight—three local Maharashtrian villagers, with their Gandhi
topis in place, were sipping on Chardonnay. The area is well
known for some of the finest grape production in India and
produces the Chardonnay, Merlot, and Cabernet Sauvignon
varieties amongst others. The vineyards are along the highway
(NH50) and have café-style wine tasting centres serving wines
and, believe it or not, delicious Italian food to all comers. At
₹ 150 for six glasses of three red and three white wines the
prices cannot be beaten.

At one time Indian wines were considered to be substandard
but have now come a long way and some very acceptable
wines are now available. The wine tasting centres provide the
six wines with some rudimentary tips on how wine should be
drunk and enjoyed. It must be added here that much attention
is given to adhering to the wine tasting ritual, making this an
educative and enjoyable experience.

SOMETHING ON THE SIDE Indian wine has come into its own in
the last few years. We are still a young wine producing nation
but the variety that is available within Indian wines itself will

surprise you. At any of these little places you can expect to find at least fifteen varieties of wines at any given time.

Rocky's Verdict: A truly unique experience to be got on the Indian highway. You must check it out.
Rating: Taste: 7, Ambience: 9, Service: 9, Value for Money: 9, Total: 34
Specialities: Red and white wines, Italian food
Veg/Non-veg: Non-veg
Contact Details/Timings: Chateau Indage, Narayangaon.
Prices: ₹ 150 for six glasses of red and white wines (three of each), ₹ 150 + for most dishes

---

Nagpur

HALDIRAM'S All the usual Haldiram's snacks and mithais are available here but what we found especially good were the orange burfi and orange sohan papdi. The soft sohan papdi lacks the cardamom and usual spices but has an orange flavour that literally bursts in your mouth with every bite, before melting away. The orange burfi is different from most things you would have had and makes for a great sweet. More orangey than the sohan papdi, it is a bit strange to eat at first but as you keep going you will find it is tough to put down

SOMETHING ON THE SIDE Our tip is to pack plenty of it because I can assure you once you leave Nagpur you will want more.

Rocky/Mayur's Verdict: Nagpur is famous throughout India for the finest oranges. During the orange season you can see them everywhere in the city. There are more foods and drinks done with oranges in Nagpur than possibly anywhere else in the world.
Ratings: Taste: 8, Ambience: 6, Service: 7, Value for Money: 7, Total: 28

Specialities: Orange sohan papdi, orange burfi
Veg/Non-veg: Veg
Contact Details/Timings: Haldiram's Hot Spot, Nagpur.
Phone: 0-9373107405
Prices: Unknown

RUPAM POHA WALA This is one of those places that have made a great name for themselves by putting out consistently delicious fare for years. Mr Rupam serves his poha with chana (chickpeas) and chutneys. Freshly chopped onions and coriander on top make this treat colourful and tasty. This is a substantial snack and served hot to customers waiting in line and at ₹ 7 a plate, makes for brilliant street food.

SOMETHING ON THE SIDE Make sure you get here early as the food always runs out fast.

Rocky's Verdict: Grab some poha for a great Nagpur taste.
Rating: Taste: 8, Ambience: 6, Service: 4, Value for Money: 7,
Total: 25
Specialities: Poha
Veg/Non-veg: Veg
Contact Details/Timings: It is usually open till 6 pm but runs out by noon on Sundays. Rupam Poha Wala, Kasturjung Park, Nagpur. Phone: 0-9822563350
Prices: ₹ 7 a plate

SAOJI JAGDISH BHOJNALAYA In this place one can sample the unique Saoji cuisine. It claims to be the 'hottest' cuisine in the world and we have not found anything else that outdoes it in terms of sheer spice. It has to be tasted to be believed. Predominantly non-vegetarian, the cuisine includes hot, rich gravies, darkened by chilli powder that make your mouth water. Seconds later your mouth is on fire but you will find you just cannot stop eating. Apart from tons of chilli, this cooking uses plenty of oil and so is not something we recommend for the faint hearted!

SOMETHING ON THE SIDE   This Maharashtrian community from the Vidarbha region runs plenty of restaurants and most of them are family owned and operated. You will find the men taking care of the customers' orders and at the counter, whereas the women are busy cooking and telling the men what to do. The matriarch lords over the kitchen while her daughters-in-law cheerfully prepare food for the customers. We believe that the attention the women pay to the food makes it that much more special.

Rocky's Verdict: A must for suicidal chilli maniacs. A formidable cuisine indeed. You haven't lived till you've eaten this.
Rating: Taste: 8, Ambience: 8, Service: 9, Value for Money: 9, Total: 34
Certified: Rocky and Mayur rating of excellence
Specialities: All non-vegetarian items. Keema (mutton mince) curry and local seasonal fish are a must have.
Veg/Non-veg: Non-veg
Contact Details/Timings: Saoji Jagdish Bhojnalaya, Subhash Road, Nagpur. Phone: 0-9422822465
Prices: About ₹ 60 a plate for the meat items and ₹ 55 for a generous vegetarian thali

---

Nasarpur

HOTEL JAI BHAVANI GARDEN   This eatery on NH4 en route to Kolhapur is one of three adjacent hotels offering pretty similar fare. The hotel has indoor seating under a tin roof or you can sit outdoors and watch traffic whizzing by as the food whizzes down your gullet.

The chicken malwani is a flavourful combination of fried masala chicken and spicy gravy made from the chicken stock served separately and mixed just before eating. The vegetable kolhapuri is a mishmash of available vegetables flash fried with heaps of spices, especially chillies and if you do not have a taste for chillies, this dish is hard to eat. The baingan bharta made by roasting brinjals in the tandoor before mashing and frying them with spices, is a delightful taste with a unique charred, smoky flavour. In case you find that the huge amount of chillies put in the food are not enough try the thecha. This side dish is made by frying a mashed heap of green chillies, garlic, and unripe peanuts and is an eye-watering yet amazingly piquant taste. All these dishes are best enjoyed with bhakris as they are called here. Besides wheat you can also get piping hot, large, tandoor-charred bhakris made of bajra (millet) or jowar (sorghum).

SOMETHING ON THE SIDE   Look out for the giant multicoloured billboard listing the specials on the menu along with images of a thali, a rooster, and a chef in uniform.

Mayur's Verdict: The range and quality of dishes that come out of dark, smoky kitchens never fail to amaze and Jai Bhavani is no exception. Stop here for a hot, fresh, and extremely tasty meal.
Rating: Taste: 7, Ambience: 6, Service: 8, Value for Money: 7, Total: 28
Specialities: Baingan bharta and thecha
Veg/Non-veg: Non-veg
Contact Details/Timings: Hotel Jai Bhavani, NH 4, Nasarpur, Kolhapur. Phone: 0-9271806944.
Prices: Chicken malwani ₹ 250, vegetable kolhapuri ₹ 50, baingan bharta ₹ 45, and thecha ₹ 15

Pune

KAYANI BAKERY   This is the mother of all Indian bakeries. Most famous for its delicious Shrewsbury biscuits, this place churns out mawa cakes, breads, cheese papdi, patasas, and many other baked items. At the counter you will find either Pervez or Rustam. Started by Pervez's father and Rustom's grandfather in 1955 the place still retains the old décor and an air of timelessness. As you walk in you are greeted by the heavenly smell of freshly baked foods.

At Kayani, the ingredients used are of top quality, the strictest standards of hygiene are maintained and the recipes... well, they are top secret. The taste of the food comes from the large firewood ovens in which it is prepared, says Rustam, while Pervez attributes it to 'lots and lots of maska (butter)'.

They recently had to install two more ovens to increase their capacity, as they were selling out by lunch and had to turn away many disappointed customers empty handed. There's plenty and more to go around now, so visit Kayani Bakery when in Pune and enjoy the delights.

SOMETHING ON THE SIDE   No one goes to Pune and comes back without the famous Shrewsbury biscuits. Many an old 'Sahib' will still only have these famous biscuits with the 'Cup o Cha' to this day.

Rocky's Verdict: The Shrewsbury lives up to its reputation. The rest is just pure bonus. Must-have!!
Rating: Taste: 8, Ambience: 9, Service: 9, Value for Money: 9, Total: 35
Specialities: Shrewsbury biscuits
Veg/Non-veg: Veg
Contact Details/Timings: Kayani Bakery, East Street, (opposite Victory theatre), Pune. Phone: 020-26360517
Prices: Shrewsberry ₹ 160 per kg, mawa cake ₹ 40 per pound, cheese papdi ₹ 120 per kg

---

VADE WALE JOSHI   The speciality of the house is vada pav—spicy potato patties deep fried in gram flour batter, and served with bread or buns and chilli chutney. A fair description of its effect would be 'Heaven on the tongue and hell on the arteries'. Interestingly, on the days that people are fasting for religious reasons, Joshi makes a sabudana (pearl sago) vada, a chewier and slightly sweeter variation. You can also enjoy some other 'light' snacks such as samosas, patties, vegetable pulao, and different types of 'bhaji', all served with pav.

You can order a snack and eat it at the counter or at the 'standing room only' tables on the pavement outside as you watch and hear the streams of traffic go by.

SOMETHING ON THE SIDE This is one of the last places standing on this stretch of the highway, most people preferring to zip by at such a speed they can't smell the roses, let alone the vadas.

Mayur's Verdict: Slow down, and take a little time to try the delicious fresh, hot, and spicy snacks at Vade Wale Joshi. Savour each bite while watching the world speed by on the expressway.
Rating: Taste: 8, Ambience: 5, Service: 6, Value for Money: 8, Total: 27
Specialities: Vada pav
Veg/Non-veg: Veg
Contact Details/Timings: Outskirts of Pune, on NH 4. Vade Wale Joshi, Pune.
Prices: Vada paav ₹ 12 per plate

Sangamner

JAMMU PUNJAB CHAUDHARY DHABA The owner of this dhaba, Dinesh Sharma, is from Jammu and prides himself on his kaju curry made with almonds and yogurt. This dish is a favourite at the shrine of Vaishno Devi in Jammu. In addition to the kaju curry there is also Gujarati, Rajasthani, Punjabi, and of course, Maharashtrian food available here. Unfortunately it all tastes about the same and is not very good.

There are several dhabas in Sangamner but their food is rather ordinary and can be easily avoided. We would have talked about the kaju curry but it is seldom available as it is expensive. The best part about this eatery is the signage which is bright, colourful, and attractive. Don't be lulled by the boards though, give this one a miss!!

SOMETHING ON THE SIDE   Started in 2005, this dhaba was a gift to Dinesh from his previous boss. Dinesh worked hard for his boss for fifteen years after which his boss set up this dhaba for him. Such stories of largesse abound on the highways of our country.

Rocky's Verdict: Highly avoidable and dull food.
Rating: Taste: 3, Ambience: 5, Service: 7, Value for Money: 4, Total: 19
Specialities: Kaju curry
Veg/Non-veg: Veg
Contact Details/Timings: Lies just 60 km out of Nashik en route to Pune. Jammu Punjab Chaudhary Dhaba, Ahmednagar, Sangamner.
Prices: Cost per person: Dal fry ₹ 20, paneer butter masala ₹ 50, kaju curry ₹ 40

ATHWAN POHA CENTRE   A small place that has truly captured the taste buds of the local populace by serving delicious poha. Poha is made by soaking dried rice flakes in water for fifteen minutes and then cooking it along with onions, green chillies, coriander, salt, and turmeric. Using these standard ingredients, Athwan Poha has mastered the making of this dish, ensuring that the place is always packed. Made fresh in a huge kadahi, you will have to wait for about five to ten minutes to get your share.

Kailashji, the owner, is a bit of a character and shuts at 7 pm so that he can have a few drinks before dinner. We pulled him out between drinking sessions and though he swayed through the whole shoot, his poha was still brilliant. 'The magic for making good poha lies in the hand,' says Kailashji, and as if to prove it he frequently puts his hand into the hot poha to give the ingredients a bit of a stir. He was charitable enough to mention though that the only poha that tastes better than his is made by his mother!

If you pass this way and the time is right, you have to stop and grab a plate.

SOMETHING ON THE SIDE The same recipe is used across the state to prepare this popular snack yet this one is strangely better than most. Locals will grab a pack or two while heading home as a part of their routine. This place exemplifies how street food is so important for most Indians.

Rocky's Verdict: If you are a fan of the snack, you must stop here as it is unlikely you can find such good poha anywhere else.
Rating: Taste: 8, Ambience: 5, Service: 5, Value for Money: 9, Total: 27
Specialities: Poha
Veg/Non-veg: Veg
Contact Details/Timings: Open from 3 to 7 pm every day. Athwan Poha Centre, Sangamner. Phone: 0-9960280495
Prices: ₹ 8 per plate

Thane

ANKUR LAKE VIEW DHABA Away from the main highway and just off SH37 sits this little gem of a place. The food is basic, consisting of dal, rice, tawa rotis, and vegetables cooked 'home style'. Set amidst rolling green hills with a beautiful lake at its doorstep, there is an indoor seating area but the outdoor open-air thatch roof areas are where the best tables are to be had.

SOMETHING ON THE SIDE The owner came to this area as a visitor, went back home, saved enough money, and returned here to buy land and set up this dhaba. When you visit here you will see why following your passion is a great thing.

Mayur's Verdict: The place is quite off the beaten track but if you do find yourself taking this scenic route to Nashik, be sure to stop at this dhaba to enjoy a cup of hot, sweet, milky tea and piping hot vegetable and paneer pakoras.
Rating: Taste: 7, Ambience: 10, Service: 7, Value for Money: 7, Total: 31
Specialities: The pakodas
Veg/Non-veg: Veg
Contact Details/Timings: About 80 km short of Nashik. Ankur Lake View Restaurant, Jawhar, Thane. Phone: 0-9223360056
Prices: Cost per person ₹ 75–₹ 100

Valsad

DESI DHABA   Staying true to its name, this dhaba is a modern-day recreation of a village scene. Brightly coloured charpais and mudaas around tables spread all over a pristine garden with props such as cart wheels and even a bullock cart (sans the bullocks of course). There is a clean, well-constructed indoor dining area with open sides and a view of the lawn too.

The menu aspires to look like a true Punjabi dhaba and then things go rapidly downhill. The kitchen though large is none too hygienic and the food they churn out would be average if they tried really hard. The bhindi jaipuri masala, the desi dal fry, paneer methi are all drowned in so much oil, garam masala, and chillies that you half expect to see the cook come running out and start throwing about large ladles of these everywhere. The only saving grace is the dry bhindi masala that is crisp (well for a while) and makes up for the tandoori rotis which are not!

SOMETHING ON THE SIDE   Traffic from here on into Mumbai can get really crazy so do try and stop somewhere to eat and freshen up because who knows when the chance will come next.

Mayur's Verdict: The location and setting of the dhaba is great as is the service. Now only if they get their act together and get a new cook then this will be an excellent stop. For now though just drive on and find somewhere else to stop and munch.

Rating: Taste: 3, Ambience: 8, Service: 8, Value for Money: 3, Total: 22

Specialities: Dry bhindi masala

Veg/Non-veg: Non-veg

Contact Details/Timings: Just off the highway near the town of Atul.

Prices: Bhindi jaipuri masala ₹ 89, desi dal fry ₹ 49, paneer methi ₹ 89, and masala papad ₹ 19

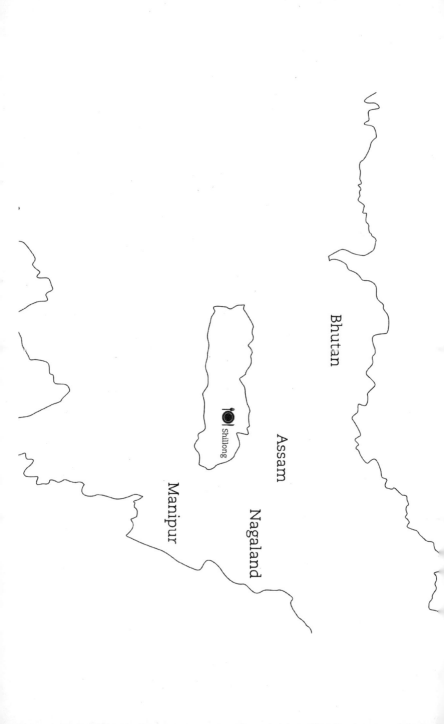

Shillong

JADOH STALL   The food of choice is pork in many different forms and rice. The dokhlieh is a meat salad with filleted beef or more commonly boiled pork pieces, mixed with onion, ginger, and chillies. It tastes like a salad though one with a strong flavour to it. The dohneiiong, another pork dish served hot in a gravy of chillies and black sesame seeds, is a dark dish with an interesting nutty flavour to the pork. The dohjem made from pork liver, intestines, and heart has a strong flavour, which is definitely not for those who prefer subtle tastes. The dohshe, fried spiced meat patties, are highly recommended for their taste and texture.

The vegetarian dishes on offer are fried potato patties and mixed fried vegetables called jhurkleh, which have a strong yet pleasant flavour of ginger and garlic. The meat or vegetable dishes can be eaten with the jadoh (red hill rice cooked with pork pieces) or jastem (rice cooked with pork gravy, onions and ginger and sometimes pig's blood) both of which have lots of turmeric giving them the characteristic yellow colour. The rice itself is very flavourful and can be eaten as a stand-alone dish accompanied by turumbai, a pungent paste of garlic, and fermented soya beans, or with tungtap, a paste of dried fermented fish, garlic, and a lot of red chillies.

All dishes are priced per 'spoon' though it is a large ladle that is used to measure, and at an average price of ₹ 5 per spoon it is definitely a great value meal.

SOMETHING ON THE SIDE   Named after jadoh the traditional Khasi version of biryani made with red hill rice cooked with pork, Jadoh Stall is a small one-room eatery run by a smiling mother–daughter team. A small wood and glass case has shelves heaped with the dishes cooked for the day and you eat sitting on benches lining the periphery of the room.

Mayur's Verdict: Visit here to get a taste of authentic and delectable Khasi food and wrap up your meal with some khoi, betel nut wrapped in a paan leaf, which almost everyone in Meghalaya can be seen chewing.
Rating: Taste: 8, Ambience: 6, Service: 10, Value for Money: 10, Total: 34
Certified: Rocky and Mayur rating of excellence
Specialities: Khasi cuisine
Veg/Non-veg: Non-veg
Contact Details/Timings: Jadoh Stall, Polo, Shillong.
Prices: ₹ 5 per spoon for all dishes

MATTER OF TASTE 'Where coffee meets art' is the pitch MOT makes to people passing by and it takes pride in promoting local arts and music. Situated in an office complex building on a busy road, the café is clean, brightly lit with one corner set aside as a stage for musicians and poets that perform here Sunday evenings. Seating is modern steel and leather with comfortable sofas in case you want to lounge as you listen to some brave soul strumming a guitar and singing to an attentive audience.

Steel and glass counters showcase a salad bar that offers fresh, colourful vegetables, and fruits. If you want to eat 'healthier' then there are counters with chocolates, cakes, muffins, burgers, and sandwiches. If that is still not enough then grab a menu that offers interesting titbits of information such as the origin of the coffee or sandwiches along with an extensive list of coffee, shakes, pizzas, and pastas. The triple-decker Khasi sandwich, the triple-decker vegetable sandwich, and vegetable burger are nothing special in taste but the ingredients are fresh and the dishes well presented on a bed of healthy salad. The chocolate éclair and the tiramisu are a sweet accompaniment to the freshly brewed coffee be it a cappuccino or a frappe. The winner is the succulent and scrumptious pork available as deep-fried sausages or hot dogs.

SOMETHING ON THE SIDE Sketches, paintings and sculptures from local artists adorn the walls of the café and are on sale if you find something you like. They also have 'open mike' evenings where anyone can come up and entertain the guests (and themselves).

Mayur's Verdict: A relaxed atmosphere, clean surroundings, well-lit area, friendly and fairly efficient staff makes MOT a great place to visit for a light snack or a full meal with music and art to make your meal filling for the soul too.
Rating: Taste: 7, Ambience: 8, Service: 7, Value for Money: 8, Total: 30
Specialities: Pork sausage and hot dogs
Veg/Non-veg: Non-veg
Contact Details/Timings: Matter Of Taste, Laitumkrah, Opposite Post Office, Shillong. Phone: 0-9436755390.
Prices: Between ₹ 100 and ₹ 150 per person, khasi sandwich ₹ 60, triple-decker vegetable sandwich ₹ 40, cappuccino ₹ 60, frappe ₹ 45, deep-fried sausages and hot dogs ₹ 30

Samosa maker at 'Purani Litty Dukan', Patna, Bihar

Mountains of the famous 'Khaja' at Silao, enroute Bodh Gaya, Bihar

(मुल्य तालिका)

...वल दाल सब्जी भुजिया ---	25.00	23. करेला भुजिया ½ प्लेट ---	10.00	45. रसमलाई ---	14.00
स्पेशल थाली (बासमती)	45.00	24. भिन्डी भुजिया " ---	10.00	46. खीर --- 1 प्लेट	15.00
...टी 4 पीस दाल सब्जी भुजिया	22.00	25. गोभी भुजिया " ---	10.00	47. घी 2 चमच	04.00
...टी घी लगा 4 पीस	30.00	26. पनीर मशाला ---1 प्लेट	50.00	48. पापड़ ---	03.00
...न्दूरी रोटी 4 पीस	X 00	27. शाही पनीर ---- "	60.00	49. मशाला टोसा ---	25.00
...न्दूरी रोटी घी लगा 4 पीस	X 00	28. पनीर भुजिया --- "	40.00	50. फ्रूट टोसा ---	20.00
...रोटा 1 पीस घी लगा ---	10.00	29. मलाई कोप्ता ---	40.00	51. स्पेशल टोसा ---	35.00
...वा रोटी 1 पीस	3.00	30. पनीर चिल्ली --- "	60.00	52. बटर स्पेशल मशाला	38.00
...न्दूरी रोटी ---	4.00	31. मटर पनीर --- "	30.00	53. ओनियन उत्तपम	20.00
...टरे नान ---	18.00	32. पनीर पकोड़ा --- "	40.00	54. उत्तपम मशाला	25.00
...टवड़ नान ---	25.00	33. मिक्स भेजीटेबुल --- "	30.00	55. पेपर सादा	30.00
...मिसी रोटी ---	10.00	34. चना मशाला --- "	25.00	56. पेपर मशाला टोसा	35.00
...वा रोटी घी लगा 1 पीस ---	5.00	35. आलू दो प्याजा --- "	20.00	57. ओनियन मशाला	28.00
...न्दूरी बटर रोटी ---	6.00	36. पालक पनीर --- "	25.00	58. ओनियत प्लाटा	22.00
...लू पराठा ---	16.00	37. परवल आलू --- "	30.00	59. रावा टोसा	35.00
...नीरे पराठा ---	22.00	38. गोभी आलू "	30.00	60. स्पेशल रावा ---	40.00
...नी पराठा ---	20.00	39. तड़का " "	20.00	61. इडली 1 प्लेट	15.00
...च्चा पराठा ---	18.00	40. दाल फ्राई " "	20.00	62. सांमर बड़ा(2 पीस) ---	20.00
...ल्चा नान ---	25.00	41. दाल फ्राई बटर --- "	25.00	63. दही बड़ा ---	20.00
...प्रोनियत पराठा ---	10.00	42. परवल पनीर --- "	30.00		
...लू भुजिया ½ प्लेट ---	5.00	43. दूध --- 1 गिलास	10.00		
...खल भुजिया " ---	10.00	44. दही --- ½	10.00		

Menu, 63 items no less, Kailash Bhojnalaya, Devghar

Assortment of Khaja, Peda Gali Baidyanath Mandir, Devghar, Bihar

'Ponkh' being beaten loose into a bag at Surat, Gujarat

All India Famous Bhel Raja Bhau, Kolhapur, Maharashtra

'Dads Masala Trout' at Johnson Café, Manali, Himachal Pradesh

Fresh Fish, Tezpur, Assam

Nand Bhature Wala, New Delhi

Fresh Eels at Naga Bazaar, Kohima, Nagaland

Grilled Chicken, Beera Chicken, Amritsar, Punjab

Bhatkali Cuisines, Alibaba Restaurant, Bangalore

Chai at Shantiniketan, West Bengal

Boondi ka Ladoo Maker, Malerkotla, Punjab

Thalis at Andhra Bhawan, Delhi

Foot Span, Horns and Rhino skulls at Kaziranga National
Park, Assam

Kohima

DREAM CAFÉ   This little café with a mighty view is located just opposite the Kohima War Cemetery. The byline of the place is 'Just Believe'. Dream Café is owned and run by Theja Meru, one of the leading musicians of Nagaland, and it has a chilled-out and laid-back feel to it. This is a gentle place and will relax you as soon as you step into it. Music is in the very soul of Kohima, the people just love their music and you can find it everywhere. The café brings musicians from all across Nagaland and tries to get them together. There is a guitar at hand which you can pick up and just sing. If you sing well the crowd will join in.

We loved it because this is the only place where we found Naga king chilli pickle, which is the bhoot jalokia or the hottest chilli in the world. The café also serves up snacks and simple noodles and fried rice with pork is recommended. You can grab your momos here as well and they make a mean cup of coffee. We loved this little place for its view and its vibe.

SOMETHING ON THE SIDE   The Hornbill festival is held in December in Kohima and offers a first prize of ₹ 4,00,000. This is a festival of music and art and is a must-see.

Rocky's Verdict: Come here to buy the bhoot jalokia (Naga king chilli) pickle and to unwind and relax. Don't rush—enjoy the music.
Rating: Taste: 7, Ambience: 9, Service: 7, Value for Money: 6, Total: 29
Specialities: Fried rice with pork and bhoot jalokia pickle
Veg/Non-veg: Non-veg
Contact Details/Timings: Dream Café, TCP Gate, Kohima. Phone: 0-9856972762.
Prices: Cost per person ₹ 125

NAGA BAZAAR   The place is famous for having every possible type of meat you can think of and many that you can not even imagine. First piece of advice, be careful here because a lot of the food items on sale will bite you back. We went to a little shack that sold dried preserved meats. The first item was three small snake-like eels called saap maas coiled and dried together and black in colour. Apparently it has amazing recuperative powers and is had when you have an injury. Nullah is a snail or escargot which is popular in soups. Kuchia are large (about two feet long) snake-like eels or eel-like snakes, which can be found in hundreds in big metal containers filled with water. They are brown in colour and are extremely muscular and, strangely, swim backwards. Catfish are popular as are many other varieties. The highlight of the place was little frogs, which are eaten fried whole with masala and are rather tasty. The taste is a little like a fishy chicken. They can also be used to make a thick soup. They are apparently always sold alive (and kicking). Bodol is a hornet grub sold in the nest. There are worms called pukkas that look like caterpillars which are very good for joint pains. Fresh honeycomb is highly prized. There are many vegetables that you would have never seen before and several species of insects which are a great source of protein.

SOMETHING ON THE SIDE   The Nagas are traditionally a fierce and proud people. Great warriors, they have lived off the land for generations and will eat almost anything. We found evenings in Kohima to be surprisingly silent, not a cheep from the birds (we did not see any) nor a woof from a dog (we did not see any of those either).

Rocky's Verdict: Bring a camera and take a walk here. Try the frogs if nothing else, they are pretty good.
Specialities: All kinds of meat
Veg/Non-veg: Non-veg
Contact Details/Timings: Opens about 11 am

> **Prices:** Little frogs (a packet-full of about thirty of them)
> ₹ 25 per three, dried snake-like eels ₹ 10, a 'Lala Pukka' (red
> worm) ₹ 2 per piece

Medziphema

PRIYA MANIPURI RICE HOTEL   It is one small dhaba on this
stretch of NH39 amongst a bunch of dhabas all of which claim
to be 'Manipuri' hotels. Typically these places are run by whole
families with the wife cooking, the husband taking orders and
collecting cash, and the kids clearing up and chipping in. The
food is well loved and the taste goes well with the tourists and
the locals.

The kitchen is made up entirely of bamboo and cane with
large gaps and is therefore well ventilated. Food is prepared on
clay ovens which are wood fired. The choices are few but the
food is delicious and very spicy. Chicken stock is kept separate
and is used to make curry in case a customer prefers it. The
chicken itself is fried with spicy masalas and is ready to be
heated and served. The whole chicken is used and the chicken
claws in particular are a delicacy. There are locally grown beans
called 'sim' which are bitter and taste great when cooked. The
favourite, however, hands down, is pork.

Meals are served thali style along with the staple, rice. The
food is accompanied by a tasty salty fish called 'nga' which
serves as an accompaniment. It is delicate and boneless and
very spicy. The chicken curry is called 'yen' and the pork, 'aow'.
The pork is cooked with lots of fat and lots of oil. The curry is
thick and spicy and is perfect with the rice.

Our host, the owner Mr Anand, was an entertaining character
who was more than a little eccentric. He refused to serve us
food at first, then he refused to let us stop eating and finally he
made us sing for him before he let us leave. A true character, he
never stood still or stopped talking through the whole meal.

Rocky's Verdict: Good, spicy food. A popular stopover for many.
Rating: Taste: 6, Ambience: 7, Service: 10, Value for Money: 6, Total: 29
Specialities: Pork and chicken claws
Veg/Non-veg: Non-veg
Contact Details/Timings: Around 50 km short of Kohima on NH39. Priya Manipuri Rice Hotel, Medziphema, NH39.
Prices: Veg pukham boti ₹ 40 and non-veg pukham boti ₹ 60

ORISSA

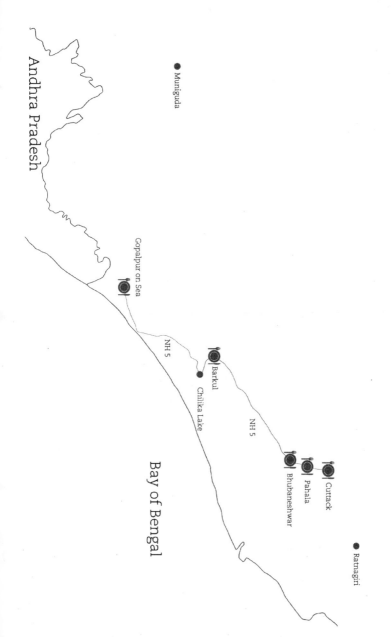

Barkul

CHILIKA DHABA   Chilika Dhaba has the distinction of being Rocky's favourite dhaba in the world. This is a major stop for buses and is large, open, and well lit with massive wooden tables and plastic chairs. You can sit or lie on the manji while waiters rattle off the menu from memory and spoil you with the choice. It's a high energy sort of place serving tasty vegetarian food and prawns, crabs, fish curries, and just about every type of seafood you can think of.

The mighty Chilika Lake is walking distance ensuring that all the food served is fresh. The kitchen is a three-way counter manned by four to five chefs at any given point, whipping up terrific seafood and all sorts of other yummy things. Each preparation is made dhaba style which means plenty of spices, plenty of colour, and a lot of deep frying. Ready within minutes, it is served to you piping hot.

A two kg giant crab for ₹ 300 and the chilli prawns, about ten of them, medium sized and deep fried for ₹ 140, make this supremely affordable seafood. The service is super fast and you can follow up your meal with delicious dhaba chai.

SOMETHING ON THE SIDE   Orissa has a great variety in its cuisines. People here love their recipes and food is a very important and much discussed part of an average day. Don't just stick to the seafood, even non-vegetarians here will love the vegetarian food. A mighty cuisine.

Rocky's Verdict: STOP!! EAT!! Do not miss this place if you love seafood!
Rating: Taste: 9, Ambience: 9, Service: 9, Value for Money: 10, Total: 37
Certified: Rocky and Mayur rating of excellence
Specialities: Chilli prawns
Veg/Non-veg: Non-veg

Contact Details/Timings: Near Chilika Lake, past the railway line towards Behrampur. Chilika Dhaba, Barkul, NH5.
Phone: 0-9861264714
Prices: Cost per person ₹ 200

Bhubaneshwar

DALMA   This restaurant is well known for its authentic Oriya food and is named after the most popular vegetarian dish in the state's cuisine. Dalma, an all-vegetable food made with brinjal, tomato, white pumpkin, papaya, cauliflower, and several other vegetables chopped fine and cooked in arhar dal with a tadka of spices and red chillies, is the speciality of the house and is simply delicious. If you want non-vegetarian options there are many such as mutton or chicken kassa (fry) for around ₹ 45 and mutton or chicken curry for ₹ 30. Seafood is plentiful with spicy curries of crabs, prawns, and fish. Dalma also serves a delicious mustard-based fish curry and a wild mushroom curry which are a must-try.

The vegetarian thali costs ₹ 40 and has servings of dalma, plain rice, special rice, smashed potato fry, spinach, fried vegetable, vegetable curry, and papad. The menu does not change except in the choice of the fried vegetable and vegetable curry. You can add items to a thali for an extra charge.

SOMETHING ON THE SIDE   This eatery is part of a main market so after a justifiably filling meal go for a long walk and digest your food while doing some window shopping.

Mayur's Verdict: A big thumbs-up to Dalma for its authentic food, its wide range of offerings, and its very reasonable prices. A great place to enjoy Oriya food in clean, cool, and quiet surroundings.
Rating: Taste: 10, Ambience: 7, Service: 9, Value for Money: 9, Total: 35
Certified: Rocky and Mayur rating of excellence

Specialities: Dalma, mustard-based fish curry, and wild mushroom curry
Veg/Non-veg: Non-veg
Contact Details/Timings: On Janpath just short of the Master Canteen Circle, in Bhubaneshwar surrounded by shops selling electronics, clothing, silverware, coffee, etc. is Dalma. Unit III, Bhubaneshwar. Phone: 0-9437013461.
Prices: Mutton or chicken kassa ₹ 45, mutton or chicken curry ₹ 30, and vegetarian thali ₹ 40

Cuttack

BARABATI STADIUM AREA   Outside the Barabati Stadium in an open lawn shaded by beautiful, old, gnarled peepal trees are a row of wheeled carts selling all types of street food from large aluminium vessels. Some carts provide makeshift tables and plastic chairs for customers to eat at.

The full name of the traditional breakfast dish is 'dahi vada dum aloo gugni'. Yes, this elaborate dish has dum aloos or potatoes fried in spice and boiled chickpeas added to it. Garnished with sliced raw onions, coriander, and chiwda, and sprinkled with masala and finally some sweet chutney, this is a delicious way to start any day. Going at an average of ₹ 12 a plate it's very good value for money too.

SOMETHING ON THE SIDE   This area is very popular with families and young people so you will always find a lot of activity and lots of smiling, well-fed faces.

Mayur's Verdict: A good place to get a real taste of what Cuttack likes to wake up to in the morning.
Rating: Taste: 8, Ambience: 7, Service: 9, Value for Money: 10, Total: 34
Specialities: Dahi vada dum aloo gugni
Veg/Non-veg: Veg
Contact Details/Timings: Outside the Barabati Stadium.
Prices: Average of ₹ 12 a plate

GAURANG SAHU SWEET STALL   Right on the main road of the crowded and busy Bakshi Bazaar is this basic yet obviously popular eatery. The traditional breakfast in Cuttack is the dahi vada aldam and chenna pod. While you can get your standard dahi vada here at ₹ 8 a piece, the thing to try is the chenna pod. Soft, moist, and sweet, this cross between caramel custard and milk cake seems to be India's answer to cheesecake. At ₹ 120 per kg this is light neither on your wallet nor on your stomach but is well worth it.

This sweet stall also serves other dishes like chola bhaturas, dosa-sambar, and samosas besides selling mithai by the box or by weight from a counter.

SOMETHING ON THE SIDE   We found many young people enjoying a decidedly non-traditional (in Cuttack) breakfast of chola bhaturas before heading off to work.

Mayur's Verdict: If you are in the area and hungry then stroll down here and satisfy your craving for a milky sweet start to the day.
Rating: Taste: 7, Ambience: 7, Service: 7, Value for Money: 8, Total: 29
Specialities: Chenna pod
Veg/Non-veg: Veg
Contact Details/Timings: Gaurang Sahu Sweet Stall, Bakshi Bazaar, Cuttack. Phone: 0-9437673111
Prices: Chenna pod ₹ 120 per kg, vada aldam ₹ 8, masala dosa ₹ 15

Gopalpur on Sea

THE BEACH   The standard Indian snack of chana (chickpea) has a different avatar here. Boiled and served with shredded onions and radish, this is a sort of bhelpuri type of concoction which really hits the spot as you laze in the clean blue waters. Don't come here expecting anything more than strong sun and clean waters.

SOMETHING ON THE SIDE Gopalpur on Sea has one of the cleanest beaches in the country; the water is blue and the waves are powerful. This small village was once a hub of Indo-Burmese trade and home to many wealthy merchants. Many of the rich and famous who made their holiday homes here left after Independence, never to return. Giant crumbling mansions and once-grand English-style dance halls are all that remain. Gopalpur on Sea has gone back to being a fishing village.

Rocky's Verdict: Blue water and soft sand. A great beach but almost nothing else.
Rating: Taste: 7, Ambience: 8, Service: 7, Value for Money: 10, Total: 32
Specialities: Boiled spicy chana
Veg/Non-veg: Veg
Contact Details/Timings: By the waters.
Prices: Cost per person: Bhelpuri ₹ 6 a plate and channa ₹ 5

Pahal

ROSOGOLLAS BY THE ROAD The small village of Pahal is famous for its halwais who make chenna pod, chennagaja, and the rosogolla, which many Oriyas claim originated in Orissa. All are based on chenna—fresh, unripened curd cheese.

More than fifty open shacks with thatched walls and roofs line the highway selling hundreds of rosogollas and giant wheels of chenna pod, and they all seem to do well! The sweets lie invitingly in giant tubs of sugar water or are laid out in the open on shelves in the stalls. You can stop before any halwai and make your purchase.

The rosogollas here are a creamier and softer version of the spongier Bengali rasgullas and they taste different too thanks to the cardamom used for flavouring. The rosogollas come in three or four sizes and according to the jaggery added, have different flavours. The chennagaja is dried chenna deep fried in sugar, while the chenna pod gets its unique flavour from being wrapped in sal leaves and baked in a charcoal oven.

It is baked in large wheels from which slices can be cut out as desired.

SOMETHING ON THE SIDE The story goes that originally there were only two or three families selling from little shops outside their homes and after a fire in the area the government gave aid enabling a lot of shops to crop up by the road.

Mayur's Verdict: A highly recommended sweetstop, which will leave you with a smiling face for the road ahead.
Rating: Taste: 8, Ambience: 6, Service: 7, Value for Money: 9, Total: 30
Specialities: Chenna pod, chennagaja, and rosogolla
Veg/Non-veg: Veg
Contact Details/Timings: On NH 5 just a few kilometres outside of Cuttack.
Prices: Rosgolla and chennagaja Re 1 to ₹ 5 and chenna pod ₹ 80 to ₹ 100 per kg

---

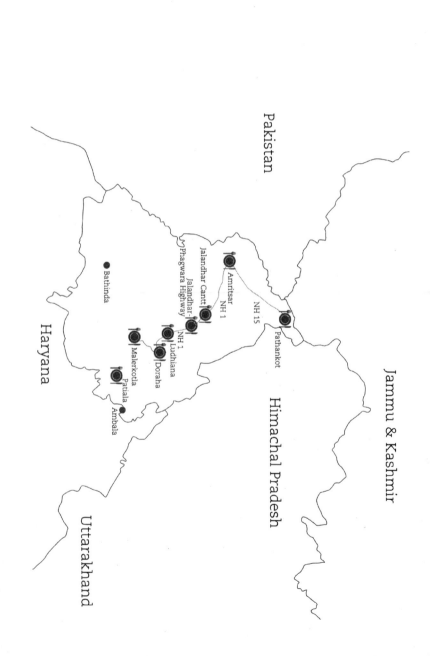

Amritsar

AHUJA LASSI The shop located near Hindu Mahasabha College serves what we think is the best lassi in the country. This refreshing summer drink made with yogurt, milk, and water relies heavily on the quality of the milk and yogurt. Mr Ahuja started this in 1955 and since then all comers are treated to the best lassi money can buy. If you know of any better lassi in India for god's sake stop reading and go and drink it.

SOMETHING ON THE SIDE Mr Ahuja attributes it to 'God's grace' and 'kwaaltee' but we seriously think it is the high quality and purity of the milk. In addition he is supplied fresh milk twice a day and that makes for a wicked glass of lassi.

Rocky's Verdict: Must have!!
Rating: Taste: 10, Ambience: 5, Service: 8, Value for Money: 10, Total: 33
Certified: Rocky and Mayur rating of excellence
Specialities: Lassi
Veg/Non-veg: Veg
Contact Details/Timings: Near Hindu Mahasabha College, Amritsar. Opens at 7 am and the lassi usually finishes by lunch. Starts again at 5 pm.
Prices: ₹ 20 per glass

ALL INDIA FAMOUS AMRITSARI KULCHA The kulcha made by the young, smiling owner has a filling of potatoes mixed with sliced onions, red and green chillies, coriander, and pomegranate seeds and is famous nationwide.

The secret of its rich flavour is the layer of ghee inside thanks to which the kulcha cooks from the inside out too. The crisp, browned kulcha is divine tasting. It can be eaten by itself or a meal can be made of it along with dark, imli-flavoured chana, and a piquant salad of finely chopped green chillies and onions.

SOMETHING ON THE SIDE   It's situated right opposite the chungi (police post) on Maqbool Road and has an amusingly large sign informing people that they have no branches.

Mayur's Verdict: By far and away the tastiest kulcha ever tasted on or off the show so make sure you visit and eat a kulcha or few.
Rating: Taste: 10, Ambience: 5, Service: 10, Value for Money: 10, Total: 35
Certified: Rocky and Mayur rating of excellence
Specialities: Kulchas
Veg/Non-veg: Veg
Contact Details/Timings: All India Famous Amritsari Kulcha, Purani Chungi, Amritsar. Phone: 0-9815672759. 8:30 am to 4:30 pm
Prices: Amritsari kulcha ₹ 20 per plate

BEERA CHICKEN   As evening sets in, a horde of restaurant and roadside eateries all over Amritsar line up trays of marinated meat and fire up their tandoor. The courtly Balbir Singh aka Beera started Beera Chicken in 1972 and has been serving tandoori chicken since then. A dedication to quality and personal attention has seen his business grow from a single stall to a row of four adjoining restaurants doing brisk business every evening. There is an indoor seating area or you can have your food packed to take away and eat at leisure. Even standing on the road outside you can enjoy the aroma of meat frying, grilling, or roasting a stone's throw away.

Tandoori chicken is prepared by grilling the chicken over a bed of glowing coals after it has been lightly seasoned. The resultant meat is extremely succulent and tender.

SOMETHING ON THE SIDE   It gets really busy during the peak hours from 7 pm until 10 pm so come early to avoid the rush especially if you are with your family.

Mayur's Verdict: If you like chicken then you will love the unique taste of chicken at Beera.
Rating: Taste: 10, Ambience: 6, Service: 10, Value for Money: 9, Total: 35
Certified: Rocky and Mayur rating of excellence
Specialities: Tandoori chicken
Veg/Non-veg: Non-veg
Contact Details/Timings: Beera Chicken House, Majhita Road, Amritsar.
Prices: Grilled chicken ₹ 200 per plate

GOLDEN TEMPLE The Golden Temple, Harmandar Sahib Gurdwara, began construction in 1604 and the foundation stone was laid by Mian Mir. Guru Arjan Dev decreed that none of the people of this city should ever have to go to bed hungry and thus began the tradition of 'langar' (free food) at the gurdwaras for all comers. The money is provided by the devotees and most cooks are volunteers. The kitchens, of which there are many, serve between 70,000 and 1,00,000 people every day. Ranjit Singhji, the cook, will be happy to chat any time you are there and is proud of his recipes and the high quality of the food he puts out for the 'sangat'. It is strongly recommended that you stop here for your langar. It is somehow the most satisfying meal you can have.

SOMETHING ON THE SIDE The giant roti maker is worth a dekko.

Rocky's Verdict: God bless you, who are we to pass verdict on this one.
Specialities: The kara prasad and everything else they serve.
Veg/Non-Veg: Veg
Contact Details/Timings: Phone: 0183-2553951
Prices: Langar free. You can make a donation if you wish. You can also pay for the prasad in the main hall. Any payment is sufficient, none will do just as well.

KANHA SWEETS   Kanha is one of the best places for breakfast in the country. The shop was started eighty years ago by the present owner's grandfather with 'love and desi ghee' as he tells us. The halwas (jaggery and carrot) are amazing and float in ghee. They are overly sweet and terrible for your health but so good to taste! They are made of caramelized jaggery prepared by cooking for hours. This is a part of the popular Amritsari breakfast. The main breakfast though is the puri launji thali served with two regular puris or one giant puri, a generous helping of the spicy and sweet launji (potatoes cooked with tamarind chutney), lots of Amritsari choley cooked Punjabi style, a salad of onions, and a pickled beetroot. The sweetness of the launji is balanced well by the spice of the choley. Puris are hot and fresh. Be prepared to overeat!

SOMETHING ON THE SIDE   They have an air-conditioned seating area in the back that seats about fifty customers so that they may enjoy the goodies.

Rocky's Verdict: Need I say more? Go there and eat!
Rating: Taste: 10, Ambience: 9, Service: 10, Value for Money: 10, Total: 39
Certified: Rocky and Mayur rating of excellence
Specialities: Puri launji thali and halwas of all types
Veg/Non-veg: Veg
Contact Details/Timings: Kanha Sweets, Lawrence Road, Amritsar. Phone: 91-183-2222855, 2211518
Prices: Launji ₹ 200 per kilo, gur gajar ka halwa ₹ 30 per plate

---

KESAR DA DHABA   Kesar is now run by the fourth generation of the family and many of the recipes have been passed down in the family since 1916. The open-fronted kitchen of the dhaba looks ancient, with crumbling paint and smoke-darkened walls. An army of cooks and helpers prepare hot food at various stations and waiters flit in and out with orders and stacked plates of food. The glow of a tandoor is softened by the smoke of a dozen burbling kadahis and pots, which give off heavenly aromas, while sunbeams escaping in through holes in the roof light up patches of soot-stained walls. The small, extremely neat and clean eating area adjoining the kitchen is loud and busy as groups of diners enjoy their meals. A couple of family sections give some privacy behind chest-high walls but you can still overhear many comments about the delicious food.

The baingan bharta with mattar has a delicate smoky flavour and is hand ground to a smooth seedy paste while the dal fry cooked in ghee and spices is hot, creamy, and spicy. The ghee-laden palak paneer has soft, fresh paneer cubes and little chunks of garlic in a creamy spinach puree. We highly recommend the scrumptious lachcha paratha, which is crisp, flaky, layered and fried in ghee.

SOMETHING ON THE SIDE   As you twist and turn your way down the crowded and seemingly endless lanes and bylanes of the old city near Chowk Passion directions are offered without even asking. Everyone seems to know where you are going and will helpfully point the way. Cars cannot make it here so be prepared to walk or take a cycle rickshaw.

Mayur's Verdict: This is a pure vegetarian eatery and yet it has a huge fan base even among meat lovers. Do not miss eating here if in Amritsar and since there are many seasonal items on the menu, every visit can be an invitation to try new delicacies.

Rating: Taste: 9, Ambience: 8, Service: 10, Value for Money: 10, Total: 37

Certified: Rocky and Mayur rating of excellence

Specialities: Baingan bharta, lachcha paratha

Veg/Non-veg: Veg

Contact Details/Timings: Passe waala Chowk, Bombay waala Kher, Amritsar.

Prices: Dal fry ₹ 30, palak paneer ₹ 90, and baingan bharta ₹ 60

MAKHAN FISH Makhan Fish on Lawrence Road in Amritsar is a bit of a legend. It has been around for as long as most care to remember and is run by the large, portly, good- natured Mahinder Singh. He is quite the character and is proud of his fish for good reason. It is eminently edible and always fresh. He uses some great tricks to get his singhara fish tikkas looking as good as they do, such as using cumin water and egg white water to add flavouring. His marinade is a secret and sticks to the fish all through the cooking process.

The tandoori chicken is pretty good too and is a favourite with people who want to pick up some hot tikkas to go with their cold pegs in the evening. It is largely a takeaway and cars can be seen parked down Lawrence Road for a long way. There are multiple other famous places like Chajju da Dhaba, famous for mutton and the Janta Vaishno Dhaba for its vegetarian goodies in the same row which makes for plenty of variety. Do what the Amritsarias do in the evening, and head for Lawrence Road.

SOMETHING ON THE SIDE Restaurants are in Mahinder Singh's blood. His father ran a restaurant as well. Amritsari fish is world famous and is considered a speciality in an otherwise predominantly chicken loving state.

Rocky's Verdict: Make the pilgrimage, eat a little at all the places, have a few drinks and as the Punjabis put it 'Khao, piyo te aish karo' (eat drink and be merry).
Rating: Taste: 8, Ambience: 6, Service: 9, Value for Money: 8, Total: 31
Specialities: Amritsari 'Machhi' (fish)
Veg/Non-veg: Non-veg
Contact Details/Timings: On the road.
Prices: Unavailable

Doraha

NEW BABA NEEMWALA ZAMINDARA DHABA Dal, hot tandoori rotis, and delicious paneer, washed down with cool, fresh chaachh, an authentic Punjabi dhaba experience. The food here is always fresh and served piping hot. The desi tomatoes served to us had been plucked the same day and were organic and delicious. They have switched over to commercial packet masalas in recent years but the ingredients remain the finest you will get anywhere in Punjab.

SOMETHING ON THE SIDE All visitors to this dhaba are met with jugs of free chaachh or buttermilk, continuing the local zamindari tradition of hospitality. Make sure you are thirsty for they will never grudge you your fill of chaachh. Doraha is home to at least three of these 'Zamindara' dhabas and they are all owned by imperious-looking, large Sikh gentlemen. The hosts are gracious, enforce discipline, and are obviously well respected by the locals.

Rocky's Verdict: Great for the dhaba meal and experience. Enjoy the chaachh.
Rating: Taste: 7, Ambience: 6, Service: 9, Value for Money: 9, Total: 31
Specialities: The paneer
Veg/Non-Veg: Veg
Contact Details/Timings: Doraha, 30 kms before Ludhiana on NH 1.
Prices: ₹ 75–₹ 100 per head, paneer bhurji ₹ 60, dal ₹ 25, butter milk free

---

Jalandhar Cantt

JAWALI DI HATTI Jawali di Hatti was established in 1852 and claims to be serving the same dal ke pakore since then. Jwala Prasad started this humble little shop and served pakoras primarily to the British Army's sepoys who were stationed here. His descendants remember his stories of British ladies pulling up in their carriages to nibble on some hot pakoras in the nineteenth century. That's a long legacy of pakoras and obviously they have become quite good at making them. Made with masoor dal and a whole bunch of secret ingredients, the pakoras are served hot with a sweet tamarind chutney and shredded radish. There is something about them which will make you eat more than you think you can.

SOMETHING ON THE SIDE   Grab a masala lemon 'banta' to go with the pakoras. Banta is local lemonade and tastes best with extra lemon and rock salt. The patrons at Jawali include visitors from England and Canada, who keep coming back for a taste of childhood.

Rocky's Verdict: The pakoras are special and you will know it as soon as you bite into one.
Rating: Taste: 7, Ambience: 7, Service: 8, Value for Money: 8, Total: 30
Specialities: Dal ke pakore
Veg/Non-veg. Veg
Contact Details/Timings: Sadar Bazaar, Jalandhar Cantt. Phone: Rajesh: 0-9815797888
Prices: ₹ 120 per kg

Jalandhar–Phagwara Highway

HAVELI   This is a plush place, air conditioned and well run. We recommend the thali at Haveli which has makki ki roti (corn bread Indian style), sarson ka saag (a rich paste of well cooked mustard leaves), chilled lassi, and jaggery and ghee. This is a winter speciality and will not be available in the summer. The other option is the thali with dal, seasonal vegetable, dahi bhalla, shahi paneer, rice, and some delicious kheer with rotis and a pungent mint and chilli chutney.

SOMETHING ON THE SIDE   Right next to it is Rangila Punjab, a part of the Haveli complex which is also a small museum on how traditional village life used to be in Punjab. The museum has typical scenes from a Punjabi village, from the village baniya doing his accounts down to women combing each other's hair in one of the huts and a whole lot of others. It's a pleasant ten-minute walk and shows you how people live in Punjabi villages.

Rocky's Verdict: Food is painstakingly prepared making this a good dining experience.
Rating: Taste: 9, Ambience: 8, Service: 8, Value for Money: 7 Total: 32
Specialities: Thalis (makka in winter, the standard one in summer)
Veg/Non-veg: Veg
Contact Details/Timings: Jalandhar–Phagwara Highway, NH 1. Phone: D.K. Umesh, 0-9814250000
Prices: Both thalis are for ₹ 100

LUCKY VAISHNO DHABA Lucky Dhaba is one of those places that make people love dhabas. Food here is always served hot and it is always delicious. The recommended breakfast at this Vaishno Dhaba is the Amritsari kulcha, along with yogurt, and dal. The parathas are popular too. All of this is topped with large lumps of white home-made butter. The pickles are a standard accompaniment and are all made in house. The chunky mango pickle is delicious as is the lime pickle. Seasonal chutneys and murabbas (preserves) are always present and vary depending on the time of year you are there. The juices are fresh and available all day. Breads range from missi roti, lachha paratha, naan, tandoori roti to methi roti. Dal makhni and chana masala are also very good. The shahi paneer is excellent as well and accompaniments are served generously.

SOMETHING ON THE SIDE Everybody who is anybody in Punjab has visited Lucky's. From Dara Singh, the famed wrestler, to all chief ministers, this place has pictures of them all up on the wall. Worth a walk to see the rich and famous up on the walls.

Rocky's Verdict: Possibly the best dhaba in the district and a must-stop for the Punjabi dhaba experience.
Certified: Rocky and Mayur rating of excellence
Rating: Taste: 9, Ambience: 8, Service: 9, Value for Money: 9, Total: 35
Specialities: Kulchas and parathas
Veg/Non-veg: Veg
Contact Details/Timings: Jalandhar–Phagwara Highway, NH 1. Phone: Jasbir Singh, 0-9815241915.
Prices: Dal makhni ₹ 30, shahi paneer ₹ 50, chana masala ₹ 40, missi roti ₹ 8, lachha paratha ₹ 10

Ludhiana

BASANT ICE CREAM Basant Ice Cream is popular for its pista kulfi. This traditional Indian ice cream can be enjoyed on a stick or sliced up in a bowl with sweet falooda strings and rose water. If this is not enough for you, Basant also offers the usual ice cream in cones along with a mouth-watering array of traditional sweets like hot gulab jamuns dripping with syrup, piping hot gajar halwa dripping with ghee, and aromatic panjeeri sprinkled liberally with cashews. The kulfi is creamy and rich in taste with the delicate flavour of pistachio and cardamom urging you on to ask for more.

SOMETHING ON THE SIDE You can eat standing on the street but given the huge amount of traffic and noise we recommend you opt for the inside. It not quieter but at least no one jostles you.

Mayur's Verdict: One bite of any sweet at Basant will explain why in fifty years it has grown from a single stand to a position where its kulfi is sold in thirty-five outlets and over 150 dealerships all over Ludhiana.
Rating: Taste: 10, Ambience: 6, Service: 8, Value for Money: 10, Total: 34

Certified: Rocky and Mayur rating of excellence
Specialities: Pista kulfi
Veg/Non-veg: Veg
Contact Details/Timings: Field Ganj, Ludhiana.
Phone: Rajinder Singh: 0-9814166000.
Prices: ₹ 15 per stick of pista kulfi, gajrela ₹ 180 per kg

CHAWLAS2 Chawlas2 is a restaurant-cum-takeaway that earlier served only chicken dishes but now has a mind-boggling variety of fish and chicken preparations as well as a good vegetarian mix including dishes like paneer tikka, creamy mushroom, dal makhani, rice, and naan.

The cream chicken gravy is made with only milk and cream, with pepper, cardamom, and the secret spice mix added (this mix is prepared centrally and sent to all franchisees to ensure uniform taste). The chicken is served with mint chutney and white bread. The tandoori chicken is heavily spiced and crisp on the outside and succulent and flavourful on the inside. The quaintly named '50-50' dish containing portions of spiced and grilled paneer and mushrooms is served with a ring of sliced tomatoes and is quite flavourful. The best item on the menu though is the creamy paneer cooked and served in the same delicious signature pepper sauce and best enjoyed with a hot naan.

SOMETHING ON THE SIDE The name was changed from Chawla Chicken to Chawlas2 to communicate that they now offered more than chicken. A nod at the huge vegetarian population we think.

Mayur's Verdict: Though they do offer pretty decent vegetarian food Chawlas2 is mainly a meat eater's paradise. The focus is on hot, tasty food prepared with care and served with enthusiasm by people who proudly claim to be '100 percent non-vegetarian'. Look out for a franchise near you.

Rating: Taste: 8, Ambience: 7, Service: 8, Value for Money: 7, Total: 30
Specialities: Cream chicken and creamy paneer
Veg/Non-veg: Non-veg
Contact Details/Timings: Bahadur House, Ludhiana.
Phone: Divjyot 0-9872727222
Prices: Cream chicken ₹ 120, creamy paneer ₹ 90

PUNNU KE PAKORE   At Punnu's you can see the pakoras being prepared in giant kadahis right in front of the shop. The paneer pakoras are truly spectacular and prepared by wrapping chickpea flour around a double layer of fresh paneer cubes with a secret masala mix stuffed in between. Mixed pakoras, filled with crunchy mouthfuls of different vegetables wrapped in besan, are equally satisfying. All pakoras are served with the usual green chilli and mint chutney along with an unusual sweet apple chutney.

SOMETHING ON THE SIDE   Come early, in fact come very early, as the pakoras fly off the kadahi almost faster than they are being fried.

Mayur's Verdict: Located in an industrial area with lots of traffic, dirt, and crowd, this may not be your idea of a food heaven. Make the leap though and your belly will thank your spirit of adventure.
Rating: Taste: 9, Ambience: 4, Service: 7, Value for Money: 9, Total: 29
Specialities: Paneer and mixed pakoras
Veg/Non-veg: Veg
Contact Details/Timings: Gill Road, Ludhiana. Phone: Baldev Raj 0-9888880199
Prices: Paneer pakoras ₹ 160 per kg and mixed pakoras ₹ 100 per kg

Malerkotla

MAQBOOL DHABA   This place specializes in chicken dishes. We went with the chilli chicken, butter chicken, and chicken stew. The stew has almonds but tastes mostly of onions and lots of chilli, since it is deep fried and then cooked in strong spices. The chilli chicken is fried Chinese style with capsicum, ajinomoto, and green chillies.

SOMETHING ON THE SIDE   This is a place for drinkers to gather in the evenings. The strong flavours go well with the local alcohol. The single room is dingy and uncomfortable—you're better off eating outside in the evenings.

Rocky's Verdict: Don't look for unique flavours here.
Rating: Taste: 8, Ambience: 4, Service: 9, Value for Money: 8, Total: 29
Specialities: Chicken dishes
Veg/Non-veg: Non-veg
Contact Details/Timings: Maqbool Dhaba, Nautarani Chowk, Malerkotla.
Prices: Chicken stew ₹ 170 per kg, chilli chicken ₹ 170 per kg, butter chicken ₹ 170 per kg

---

Pathankot

BANARSI DI HATTI   This place has a reputation for inventing the deliciously naughty 'palang tod' or bed breaker—a sweet that has captured the imagination of all Punjabis and is famous throughout the country. The palang tod is a heavy, ghee-laden, sweet, sort of like a firm brown cake that has to be eaten in small quantities or else you will not be able to move. At ₹ 150 per kg we were impressed with the amount of ghee it had. Very sweet and very tasty, it is a must-have. The panjeeri is expensive at ₹ 350 per kg but made with pure ghee and with lots of dry fruits in it.

The restaurant also serves choley bhature, and many types of Indian fast food snacks. The snacks are moderately priced—the famous choley bhature will set you back by only ₹ 20.

SOMETHING ON THE SIDE   Started in Gujranwala in Pakistan the shop moved here during the partition. The palang tod was invented at this very location by Banarsi Das, the owner of Banarsi di Hatti, and his Rajasthani chef in the 1950s. The rival to the title of the best palang tod in the world is a little place called Akhnoor in Pakistan along the Indian border, but the Banarsi palang tod is better. There are old photographs of the establishment hanging on the walls and four generations of the family still sit here together to serve customers.

Rocky's Verdict: Come here for a meal and some palang tod. It has to be tried at least once. If you've had it before then the Banarsi palang tod is as good a palang tod as anywhere else.
Rating: Taste: 6, Ambience: 7, Service: 5, Value for Money: 8, Total: 26
Specialities: Palang tod
Veg/Non-veg: Veg
Contact Details/Timings: Banarsi di Hatti, Banarsi Sweets Pvt. Ltd, Main Bazaar, Pathankot. Phone: 09855241301
Prices: Palang tod ₹ 150 per kg, panjeeri ₹ 350 per kg, choley bhature ₹ 20

Patiala

AMBALA CHAAT HOUSE   Look out for the bright yellow board advertising 'Special Satrangi Gol Gappe'. The name derives from the colours of five different flavours of water and two sauces that you can choose from. Heaps of crisp, golden golgappas compete for space with containers of tamarind, chilli, chaat masala, finely chopped potatoes and onions, chickpeas, and fresh dahi on the cart in the front of the chaat shop. The vendor deftly adds the ingredients into each golgappa, ladles in the sauces (tamarind or dahi), and serves it to customers.

SOMETHING ON THE SIDE The water inside each golgappa also offers health benefits: the zesty jeera (cumin) water aids in digestion as does the hing (asafoetida) water. The pudina (mint) has a cooling effect, the pungent kali mirch (black pepper) water helps clear blocked sinuses.

Mayur's Verdict: In the spirit of the true foodie, see how many golgappas you can put away and 10 is barely average if you judge by the crowds around the cart.
Rating: Taste: 9, Ambience: 7, Service: 9, Value for Money: 9, Total: 34
Certified: Rocky and Mayur rating of excellence
Specialities: Golgappas
Veg/Non-veg: Veg
Contact Details/Timings: Ambala Chaat House, Modi College Road, Patiala.
Prices: Satrangi gol gappa ₹ 20 per plate

ACHAAR WALI GALI True to its name this lane is lined on both sides with achaar stores displaying their wares in large plastic containers of all shapes and sizes. Take your pick from a vast range of pickles, which range from the familiar mango pickle to the exotic cherry murabba pickle.

SOMETHING ON THE SIDE The lane is very narrow so be prepared for the sounds of horns, bells, and yelling people all trying to squeeze pass. The pickles in the jars look more comfortable.

Mayur's Verdict: You can try samples at the shops before you buy the pickles.
Specialities: Cherry murabba
Veg/Non-veg: Veg

Contact Details/Timings: A lane
Prices: ₹ 90 to ₹ 350 per kilo

DEEPA MUTTON AND CHICKEN CORNER This little hole-in-the-wall eatery lies just off the main market street and tempts shoppers with the tantalizing aroma of roasting meat. Started fifteen years ago, this small shop is run by two gentle and smiling Sikh gentlemen who instantly make you feel at home. They offer a range of tandoori items such as fish tikkas, chicken malai tikkas, and seekh kebabs but their speciality is the tandoori mutton. Extremely tender and juicy mutton pieces seasoned only with salt-and garlic-infused water are roasted in the tandoor and served with raw onions and lime. The meat is succulent and the light seasoning lets you really enjoy the flavour of the mutton.

SOMETHING ON THE SIDE They do have other items on the menu but stick with the mutton and you will be content.

Mayur's Verdict: A must-visit. The food is top notch.
Rating: Taste: 9, Ambience: 6, Service: 10, Value for Money: 9, Total: 34
Certified: Rocky and Mayur rating of excellence
Specialities: Tandoori mutton
Veg/Non-veg: Non-veg
Contact Details/Timings: Behera Road, near Anardana Chowk. Phone: 0-9888312123.
Prices: Tandoori mutton ₹ 340 per kg

PATIALA SHAHI LASSI This small, clean, air-conditioned shop takes great pride in the quality of its dahi and lassi. The owner Mr Mehta tells us that their dahi is of such good quality that it stays fresh for three days. The front of the shop has a couple of high stool tables and a marble-top counter inviting the description 'lassi bar'. The cold lassi, made on the premises, comes with a frothy head in which a dollop of cream floats. It's a sweet and fresh taste thanks to the excellent quality of the milk and cools you down instantly. The place also has a range of traditional sweets on offer if your sweet tooth is not satisfied by the lassi.

SOMETHING ON THE SIDE   Try crumbling a piece of soft plain burfi into the lassi if you feel like being experimental.

Mayur's Verdict: The perfect antidote for a hot summer day, the lassi at Shahi Lassi is a must-try.
Rating: Taste: 8, Ambience: 8, Service: 8, Value for Money: 8, Total: 32
Specialities: Lassi
Veg/Non-veg: Veg
Contact Details/Timings: Sherawala Gate, Patiala.
Prices: Lassi ₹ 20 per glass, plain burfi ₹ 200 per kg

SADHU RAM KACHORI WALA   Started about eighty years ago, Sadhu Kachori is now run by the third generation of the family. Hot, thick, crisp kachoris are served with hot aloo subzi ladled out from a large pateela. The entire process happens before your eyes as dough is kneaded, rolled into balls and prepared for frying. You have to eat standing by the side of the road so watch out that you don't get run over by motorists.

SOMETHING ON THE SIDE   Everyone seems to know the location of this street food specialist but it's still a long walk through a narrow winding lane dodging manic traffic to get there.

Mayur's Verdict: Visit this place if you are in the area and need a filling snack but consider having the aloo subzi with fresh, fluffy puris instead of the kachoris.
Rating: Taste: 5, Ambience: 4, Service: 6, Value for Money: 7, Total: 22
Specialities: Aloo subzi and kachori or puri
Veg/Non-veg: Veg

Contact Details/Timings: Sadhu Ram Kachori Wala, Chowk Kacha, Patiala.
Prices: Aloo subzi and kachori ₹ 12 per plate, puri sabzi ₹ 12 per plate.

SAMRAT FISH AND CHICKEN SHOP   Samrat claims to be the oldest shop on this street and conducts its business right out on the pavement. A metal and glass grill, a glowing tandoor, and a large kadhai burbling with boiling oil are at the centre of the action. Once prepared, your choice of meat or fish is sprinkled with masalas, garnished with coriander, and served with raw onions, lime, and fresh mint and green chilli chutney.

Chunks of freshwater sole fish smeared lightly with masala paste before frying are extremely succulent, with a subtle flavour enhanced by the lime. The tandoori chicken is a delightfully tender and juicy treat. There is not too much masala and this allows the natural flavour of the roasted chicken to come through.

SOMETHING ON THE SIDE   Just ask for 'baee' or 22 in Punjabi and anyone will direct you to the area so named, as it is the 22nd underpass of the main highway.

Mayur's Verdict: Most customers seem to prefer having their food packed to take away but you can enjoy it hot while standing on the pavement too. The food is fresh with careful attention paid to the quality of ingredients and the preparation.
Rating: Taste: 8, Ambience: 6, Service: 8, Value for Money: 8, Total: 30
Specialities: Tandoori chicken and sole fish
Veg/Non-veg: Non-veg
Contact Details/Timings: Samrat Fish and Chicken Shop, No. 22 Phatak, Patiala.
Prices: Sole fish ₹ 360 per kg and tandoori chicken ₹ 140 per kg

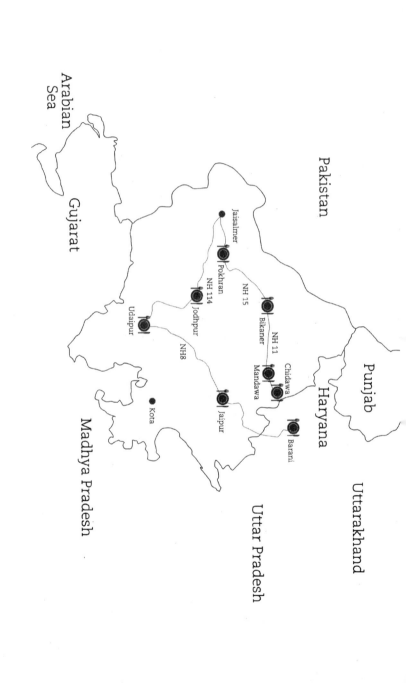

Barani

HOTEL YASH DHABA   The setting of the dhaba is idyllic. It is surrounded by fields and it's situated at a distance from the highway, which reduces the noise and dust from the vehicles passing by. However, the company of stray dogs, birds, insects, and rats tends to interfere with the enjoyment of the meal. Stick with mineral water (carry your own since the dhabas usually don't have any) since the water drawn from the hand pump is brackish. The fare includes dal, chana masala, bhindi, and roti. The flavours are strong and very spicy. The Rajasthani palate is attuned to chillies and most dhabas deliver. The fare is tasty and the people are quick to smile and happy-go-lucky. So eat well and then rest on the manjis they have laid out in the shade.

SOMETHING ON THE SIDE   Dhabas are few and far between in this area. Grab the first one you find else be prepared to wait for a long time till the next one.

Rocky's Verdict: Great place to sleep off the afternoon heat and get going once it gets cool towards the evening. The food is unremarkable. Keep an eye open for chinkaras and other possible wildlife that is frequently seen here.
Rating: Taste: 6, Ambience: 9, Service: 8, Value for Money: 8, Total: 31
Specialities: None
Veg/Non-veg: Veg
Contact Details/Timings: Hotel Yash, Barani, NH 89.
Prices: Dal ₹ 25, chana masala ₹ 35 and bhindi ₹ 35

Bikaner

CHOTU MOTU SWEET SHOP   The Chotu Motu Sweet Shop was set up by two brothers, Chotu Lal and Motu Lal, a hundred years ago. The retail area of the shop has rows of display cabinets stacked with namkeens, sweets, and savouries of every shape and size. There are even cans of rasgullas which they claim are so good that they are exported to Bengal, the home of this sweet. Namkeen is sold by the packet while sweets are sold by weight. Some of the more popular items are the Bikaneri bhujia, panchmal, kaju katli, and chidwa. There is also a dining area for those who want to sit down and enjoy a full meal. The methidana subzi and aloo subzi are rich with ghee and spices and best enjoyed with hot, crisp puris and a side of fresh yogurt or chilled lassi. Do as the locals do and tuck into the sweets first to really get your appetite going.

SOMETHING ON THE SIDE The owner, a very interesting and dapper elderly gentleman, takes great pride in the fact that he pays a higher tax than the chief minister.

> **Mayur's Verdict:** The namkeen is fresh, crisp, and extremely tasty while the rasgullas, raj bhog, and burfi are sweet enough to satisfy the soul. The shop is in the middle of a crowded marketplace so both driving and finding parking can be challenging though the food is definitely worth it.
> **Rating:** Taste: 9, Ambience: 7, Service: 8, Value for Money: 8, Total: 31
> **Certified:** Rocky and Mayur rating of excellence
> **Specialities:** Bikaneri bhujia and rasgulla
> **Veg/Non-veg:** Veg
> **Contact Details/Timings:** Station Road, Bikaner. 10 am to 9:30 pm.
> **Prices:** Puri subzi ₹ 20, methidana ₹ 8, sponge rasgulla ₹ 4.50, bhujiya ₹ 96 per kg, kaju katli ₹ 320 per kg

NATIONAL RESEARCH CENTRE ON CAMEL Besides learning all sorts of interesting things about camels the more experimental amongst you can visit the little retail shop near the entrance to sample the taste of exotic camel milk products including tea and coffee, flavoured milk, and even kulfi.

SOMETHING ON THE SIDE The hump of the camel is a fatty tissue and not a storage area for water as is commonly believed. Camels from the Bikaner Camel corps were used in World War I and II.

Mayur's Verdict: If you like the strong, slightly metallic taste of the camel milk you can buy raw camel milk to accompany your Bikaneri bhujia snack.
Rating: Taste: 4, Ambience: 6, Service: 6, Value for Money: 8, Total: 24
Specialities: Camel milk products
Veg/Non-veg: Veg
Contact Details/Timings: Post Box-07, Jorbeer, Bikaner. Phone: 91-151-2230183, Fax: 91-151-2231213. 2.30 pm to 6 pm
Prices: Ask the camel because I don't know

SANKHLA BHUJIYA BHANDAR This store is popular for its kulfi. Wrapped in printed paper and rich with the taste of saffron, almonds, cashews, and pistachios, these mouth-watering kulfis are served without the usual falooda and rose water.

SOMETHING ON THE SIDE You might want to take the kulfi home as the loud traffic on the road outside can be a serious distraction, and something this tasty does deserve your full attention.

Mayur's Verdict: A few bites of the kulfi and you can almost believe the owner's claim of a man eating forty-eight kulfis at one sitting!
Rating: Taste: 10, Ambience: 5, Service: 6, Value for Money: 10, Total: 31
Specialities: Kulfi
Veg/Non-veg: Veg
Contact Details/Timings: Sankhla Bhujiya Bhandar, Station Road, Bikaner 334001. Phone: 0151-2521555
Prices: Kulfi ₹ 15

Chidawa

RAHUL DEV MASHOOR PEDA WALA   There are two types of pedas available here, the plain khoya, and the kesar peda, both of which are light and chewy. They are both made from sweetened reduced milk.

The Mathura peda is made by adding powdered sugar to the mawa and then stirring it till cooked, the Chidawa peda on the other hand is made by adding the mawa to sugar syrup which is then cooked till the extra liquid disappears.

SOMETHING ON THE SIDE   The best way to eat the pedas is to go around to the back where they are being cooked and eat them from the kadhai in which they are being cooked.

***

Rocky's Verdict: Eat the hot peda from the kadhai in which it is being cooked before it cools.
Rating: Taste: 7, Ambience: 5, Service: 8, Value for Money: 8, Total: 28
Specialities: Peda
Veg/Non-veg: Veg
Contact Details/Timings: Rahul Dev Peda Wala, Khetri Road, Railway Crossing, Chidawa, Jhunjhunu.
Prices: Kesar peda ₹ 200 per kg and plain khoya peda ₹ 140 per kg

***

Jaisalmer

BHANG SHOP   Just outside Jaisalmer Fort is a shop which legally allows you to buy products made of bhang (freshly ground leaves of the cannabis plant) like cookies, fruit milkshakes, and, on advance notice, even chocolates. The shop is very popular with both the locals, and the tourists who often carry a few cookies or some chocolate for consumption during their desert camel safaris. Bhang is supposed to have medicinal value too and is said to be good for the digestion, easing arthritic pain, and also enhancing virility!

SOMETHING ON THE SIDE You can sit on the steps outside the shop or in a little room adjoining the shop as you munch on the cookies and wash them down with some bhang banana lassi.

Mayur's Verdict: Start small and be warned that bhang products will leave you feeling very hungry. If you are feeling adventurous and not too worried about being a bit dazed for a while then give the bhang lassi a try.
Rating: Taste: 6, Ambience: 10, Service: 7, Value for Money: 10, Total: 33
Specialities: Bhang lassi and bhang cookies
Veg/Non-veg: Veg
Contact Details/Timings: Outside the Jaisalmer fort.
Prices: Cookies ₹ 50 to ₹ 70 each and lassi ₹ 70 upwards

CHANDAN SHREE RESTAURANT Situated in a busy part of town this restaurant offers thalis and non-alcoholic drinks of all kinds. They are open throughout the day for meals as well as snacks.

The Rajasthani thali has the usual ker-sangri, besan ke gatte, kadhi, dal, ghotwa, chapatti, and rice. The Gujarati thali is sweet since every item has added sugar. Other options include the Bengali thali. The thalis are good for multiple refills and you can also order stand-alone dishes such as dal bati churma, pav bhaji, kadhi-chawal, and chowmein as well!

SOMETHING ON THE SIDE The outside area is very busy and the sound of traffic and the huge crowds lead us to suggest that you eat inside.

Mayur's Verdict: The food is served hot, freshly cooked and makes for a well-balanced, reasonably priced meal. Follow the old adage of 'when in Rome...' and order the Rajasthani thali, which is the tastiest option by far.

Rating: Taste: 8, Ambience: 7, Service: 9, Value for Money: 9, Total: 33
Specialities: Rajasthani thali
Veg/Non-veg: Veg
Contact Details/Timings: Hanuman Chauraha, Jaisalmer 345001. Phone: 2992-253965
Prices: Rajasthani and Gujarati thali ₹ 70 and Bengali thali ₹ 45

8 JULY RESTAURANT The restaurant is remembered fondly by all visitors for not just the food but the love and attention that the owners Jagmohan and Rama Bhatia lavish on everyone. This quaintly named eatery is in a prime location overlooking the central square right outside Jaisalmer Palace, and has a menu so extensive it would put most big city restaurants to shame. The all-day breakfast menu consists of muesli, porridge, sandwiches, omelettes, cheese toasts, fruit salads, smoothies, pancakes, and apple pie. There are pizzas, burgers, Chinese dishes, and really well-cooked Indian food too.

The skewed waffles (Australian slang for closed toasties) are delicious as is the home-made Swiss muesli which is served with fruit, curd, and honey. If you are feeling adventurous you can try toast smeared with the strange tasting vegemite, a dark, yeasty paste of herbs and vegetables imported from Australia.

SOMETHING ON THE SIDE The couple who own and run the place are a delight to chat with and have a lot of stories, so sit back and enjoy the mango lassi and the tales.

Mayur's Verdict: A must-visit if you are in Jaisalmer. The food is fresh, tasty, and served with a lot of love and care though it is a bit pricey. The view is amazing with a choice of looking down to watch the milling hordes of tourists and assorted livestock, or looking upwards to see the gorgeous Jaisalmer Palace.

Rating: Taste: 9, Ambience: 10, Service: 10, Value for
Money: 7, Total: 36
Certified: Rocky and Mayur rating of excellence
Specialities: Apple pie, omelettes, and skewed waffles
Veg/Non-veg: Non-veg
Contact Details/Timings: On Fort Deshera Chowk,
Jaisalmer-345001
Prices: Special swiss muesli curd, fruit salad, and honey ₹ 80,
apple pie ₹ 75, special omlette ₹ 70, garlic toast buttered ₹ 50,
juice ₹ 45

Jaipur

BAJWA DHABA   Wander here not oh ye faint of heart. Bajwa
Dhaba is a no-frills, hard-core Punjabi dhaba and a well-kept
Punjabi truck drivers' secret. The food caters to the taste of
the truck drivers and is surprisingly delicious. One can expect
robust and wholesome vegetables, spicy, well-made dal and
fresh chapattis from the tawa. The tandoori roti is especially
good. This is the quintessential dhaba dining experience. The
post-meal tea, strong enough to make a spoon stand in is a
must. Beware of the tendency to stir in six spoons of sugar. The
waiters are referred to as 'order master' or 'abe oye' depending
on the mood of the driver.

The dhaba is run by Bajwa, a quiet, hard-working man
with a shy smile. His food, he says, speaks for itself and he is
always around to ensure that things don't get out of control. He
manages to get his hands on some terrific onions and chillies
to go with your food that are surprisingly better than those
served at Highway King across the road.

SOMETHING ON THE SIDE   At the foot of a small hill, Bajwa Dhaba
has a cement tank where truck drivers may wash and bathe in
full view of the dhaba, so do not go there if semi-nudity offends
you while you eat. You can do your laundry there as there is
even a dhobi to iron your clothes after they are washed. Other
facilities include manjis or khats to sleep on, plenty of parking
space for trucks, and above all a trustworthy owner. Many

drivers will leave money and letters with the owner for their friends or family to pick up in a couple of days.

Rocky's Verdict: A truck drivers' stop. Go there for good food and to see how the truck drivers live. Ladies, I would recommend that you skip this one. You may make the bathing truck drivers a little shy.
Rating: Taste: 8, Ambience: 4, Service: 6, Value for Money: 8, Total: 26
Specialities: Dal
Veg/Non-veg: Veg
Contact Details/Timings: Opposite Hotel Highway King towards Jaipur
Prices: ₹ 50–₹ 75 per head

HIGHWAY KING   Highway King is one of the most visible among the midways, restaurants, and dhabas that dot the Delhi–Jaipur stretch. The food is clean but singularly unremarkable. The place serves dosa, idli, vada, and sambar (with a distinct north Indian touch), the regular 'dal aur subzi', tandoori rotis, and a decent kulfi to top up your meal. Breakfast is eggs, parathas, and pakoras. They have some decent cold coffee but make it very sweet so ask for less sugar. The attractions are the clean bathrooms and pleasant gardens.

Usually taxi drivers will bring you here as they get a free meal for driving in clients. There are clean bathrooms, a small garden for children to run around in, and plenty of parking space. The structure is set well back from the highway and it's better to stop here in the winter when you can sit in the garden and enjoy the sun without getting the smoke and dust from the highway. When it comes to the food, you're much better off going to the RTDC Midway, Behror, which has a greater choice of dishes and will serve you chilled local draught beer.

SOMETHING ON THE SIDE   True Indian eateries are slowly giving way to places such as this one. The food is different and the emphasis is on cleanliness and comfort. Local flavour creeps into even the fast foods. The food is very unremarkable.

Rocky's Verdict: It's clean and has good bathrooms. There's plenty of parking. Stop in the winter to get some sun.
Rating: Taste: 5, Ambience: 7, Service: 7, Value for Money: 6, Total: 25
Specialities: King ki kulfi
Veg/Non veg: Non-veg
Contact Details/Timings: On the Delhi–Jaipur highway (NH 8), approximately 12-15 km before Shahpura.
Phone: 0141-2811527
Prices: ₹ 150 per head

KISHAN LAL RAM NARAYAN AGGARWAL LASSI WALA The lassi served in clay kulhars is fresh and refreshing but a little too sweet. Nothing really to write home about. Their claim to fame is rather that they have been making and serving lassi since 1944. The shop has become so popular that it has a couple of imitators next to it that do great business when Kishan Lal's lassi runs out.

Rating: Taste: 4, Ambience: 5, Service: 7, Value for Money: 5, Total: 22
Specialities: Lassi
Veg/Non-veg: Veg
Contact Details/Timings: Kishan Lal Ram Narayan Aggarwal Lassi Wala, MI Road (Near Paanch Batti Chowk), Jaipur.
Prices: Unavailable

SANTOSH BHOJANALAYA Once the staple food for the Rajasthanis, the dal bati churma is getting harder and harder to find these days. One of the best places you can still find it served in its traditional way, is at Santosh Bhojanalaya. Step in here to enjoy the delicious 'special thali' for ₹ 40, the highlight of the dhaba menu.

The dal is of course the famous garlic dal of Rajasthan, the batis are roasted wheat dough balls traditionally cooked with cow dung patties, and the churma is the sweet powdered sugar that goes on top. You will also get some awesome lassan (garlic) chutney, kaddu or petha (pumpkin) called 'kola' in Rajasthan, aloo tamatar (potatoes and tomatoes), moong dal, Rajasthani kadhi (cooked with sour yogurt), and to top it all a generous ladle of ghee.

Mash the batis, cover them with powdered sugar, put some ghee on it, and dig in with large helpings of the lassan chutney. Nothing quite matches the taste and the experience. This is truly the flavour of Rajasthan and is well worth the trip to the crowded Station Road.

SOMETHING ON THE SIDE   A place run along the ideals of the 'khatirdari' tradition. Be prepared to be forced to eat more when you finish. A true example of Indian hospitality.

Rocky's Verdict: Make the trip to Station Road. Go in the evening and make sure you are hungry!! This will taste better than you can imagine.
Rating: Taste: 9, Ambience: 6, Service: 9, Value for Money: 10, Total: 34
Certified: Rocky and Mayur rating of excellence
Specialities: Dal, baati, churma
Veg/Non-veg: Veg
Contact Details/Timings: Santosh Bhojanalaya, Station Road, Jaipur. Phone: 0-9829260665
Prices: Special thali ₹ 40

SHARMA DHABA   As you head out of Jaipur towards Sikar you will come to the grand Sharma Dhaba. Starting as a small hole in the wall with a few tables and chairs Sharma Dhaba is now a large, well-lit, smoothly run, efficient, and successful dhaba serving excellent Rajasthani food to families and tourists.

Run by the ever-present and sage-like Puranmal Sharma the place has everything you could want from a dhaba. Above all, his presence ensures that the quality of the food remains consistent. There is an army of waiters and chefs to run this place. They pride themselves on the freshness of their ingredients. The naan is cooked in milk brought fresh from cows owned by them and is their speciality. Mr Sharma can proudly rattle off the names of all the film stars who stop at his place and enjoy the fare. He can tell you many stories, his favourite being about the legendary eating abilities of Bollywood he-man Dharmendra.

The must-have is the mawa naan or mawa roti. This bread is rare to find simply because of the difficulty with which it is made. The sweet mawa is put inside the roti and it is roasted in the tandoor. The mawa tends to melt and gather at the bottom of the roti and then bursts through, ruining the process. After being featured on the show, the mawa roti now has place of pride on the menu and sells for ₹ 100 per piece. If you go there on a cold winter evening, they will give you little pails of coal to keep you warm and you may eat under the stars.

SOMETHING ON THE SIDE   One of those rare true dhabas where you can take foreign guests and not worry about the standards of food or hygiene. Great value for money and a well-run place.

Rocky's Verdict: Another place that has to be visited. A family dining place where the food is always very good.
Rating: Taste: 9, Ambience: 8, Service: 9, Value for Money: 9, Total: 35
Certified: Rocky and Mayur rating of excellence
Specialities: Mawa naan
Veg/Non-veg: Veg
Contact Details/Timings: Sharma Dhaba, Sikar Road, NH11, Jaipur. Phone: 0-9413341753
Prices: ₹ 100–₹ 150 per head

Jodhpur

JANTA SWEET HOUSE Every town has one favourite food place and this one is Jodhpur's. The place is always packed with customers, primarily because every item on the menu is delicious and also very affordable. Start with a mirchi vada, move on to the samosas, pyaaz kachori, mawa kachori, and do not forget to try the ghevar. Made with rabri, the ghevar has a honeycomb sort of structure and is a tasty chewy treat. Try the makhaniya lassi, a thick and sweet yogurt drink with delicate flavouring. The rabri ke laddu are a must-try. End with the sohan papdi.

SOMETHING ON THE SIDE A watering hole for rich and poor alike. You will find royalty here, rubbing shoulders with camel herders. The taste here appeals to all types of eaters.

Rocky's Verdict: The real taste of Jodhpur, a must-visit place when you are here.
Rating: Taste: 9, Ambience: 7, Service: 10, Value for Money: 10, Total: 36
Certified: Rocky and Mayur rating of excellence
Specialities: Mirchi vada, kachori, and ghevar
Veg/Non-veg: Veg
Contact Details/Timings: Branch 1, Janta Sweet House Pvt. Ltd, 3, Nai Sarak, Jodhpur, 342001. Phone: 0291-2636666, 0291-5103997, Fax: 0291 2615255. Branch 2, Janta Sweet Home Pvt, Ltd, Outside Railway Reservation Office, Station Road in front, Minerva Complex, Jodhpur 342001.
Prices: All sweets approximately ₹ 150 per kg, kachoris, and vadas both under ₹ 10

SODAWAS KITCHEN Situated inside Karni Bhawan Hotel, Sodawas Kitchen is run by Vikramaditya and Gayatri Sodawas and owned by their family. It is spotlessly clean and the recipes it boasts of are from their grandfather's era. The food here is royal fare and has the little extra that intricate recipes offer. The sekhyodi murgi (skewered chicken) is marinated with spices and yogurt and then cooked in ghee over an open coal fire. The Sodawas cuisine has fifty-seven recipes and they are mostly non-vegetarian. The achaari aloo is prepared with all the ingredients used typically in making pickle.

SOMETHING ON THE SIDE Try and get Vikramaditya or Gayatri to cook for you for a truly special treat. Make sure you eat the food hot, it's too good to allow it to cool. Traditional and innovative Rajasthani cuisine served with care.

Rocky's Verdict: Delicious food and terrific value for money.
Rating: Taste: 9, Ambience: 8, Service: 8, Value for Money: 8, Total: 33
Specialities: Sekhyodi murgi
Veg/Non-veg: Non-veg
Contact Details/Timings: Sodawas Kitchen, Hotel Karni Bhawan.
Prices: ₹ 300–50 per head

Mandawa

JODHPUR SWEET HOME Opening at about 6 am, the place is run by Bajrang Singh, a friendly man who is rightly proud of his amazing kachori. The lassan and pyaaz kachori is a deep-fried bread filled with pre-cooked onions and garlic. It is served with a tasty mint and chilli chutney. You can also try the popular mawa kachori which is delicious.

SOMETHING ON THE SIDE Watch out for the giant hornets that abound in the town of Mandawa—they usually don't bite but it's quite painful just in case they do. They are attracted to sweets so pack a few and run right out.

Rocky's Verdict: A little rich for breakfast but great kachori all the same.
Rating: Taste: 8, Ambience: 4, Service: 8, Value for Money: 8, Total: 28
Specialities: Kachoris of all kinds
Veg/Non-veg: Veg
Contact Details/Timings: Jodhpur Sweet Home, Subhash Chowk, Mandawa. Phone: 0-9352627142.
Prices: Lassan aur pyaaz ki kachori ₹ 6 per piece and mawa kachori ₹ 10 per piece

Pokhran

SHRI ANNAPURNA RESTAURANT The exorbitant prices at this restaurant reflect the fact that most customers are tourists. The menu consists of typical, though badly cooked, Rajasthani dishes like ker-sangri, besan ka gatta, and pyaaz paneer. Plain rice, jeera rice, and pulao along with different types of rotis and parathas are also available.

SOMETHING ON THE SIDE It's a great place for people watching on this busy section of the highway as you dip some biscuits into your masala tea and enjoy the view.

Mayur's Verdict: Unremarkable food and very high prices make this a place to be eaten at only if you have no other choice.
Rating: Taste: 5, Ambience: 5, Service: 6, Value for Money: 4, Total: 20
Specialities: Rajasthani dishes
Veg/Non-veg: Veg
Contact Details/Timings: Shri Annapurna Restaurant, Pokhran, NH 15. Phone: 0-9414470150.
Prices: Ker-sangri ₹ 100 and other items under ₹ 50 per portion

Udaipur

AMBRAI RESTAURANT This restaurant has the best view in all of Udaipur. Even though it is only ten years old it is housed in a 300-year-old building and it has a shady seating area on the bank of the lake and an astounding view of the Grand Palace across the water. It also affords a great view of the Lake Pichola Hotel in the middle of the lake. You can see many of the wonderful temples and ghats of Udaipur from this location.

The food and snacks are unremarkable, though not bad and service is a bit slow but the view will take your breath away so make sure you come here.

SOMETHING ON THE SIDE The lake was expanded at the cost of submerging an entire village by Maharaja Udai Singh II and is now massive and gives the whole city an ethereal look towards sunset. There are a surprisingly large number of water-birds here in the winters. Try and get across to the Lake Pichola Hotel where the James Bond movie *Octopussy* was shot.

Rocky's Verdict: Come here for the view. It is a must-visit place. Remember to bring the camera or you will regret it.
Certified: Rocky and Mayur rating of excellence (for the view)
Rating: Taste: 6, Ambience: 10, Service: 7, Value for Money: 7, Total: 30
Specialities: None
Veg/Non-veg: Non veg
Contact Details/Timings: Near Chandpol, close to Lake Pichola Hotel, across the water from the Grand Palace.
Prices: ₹ 100–₹ 150 per person

JMB (JAYESH MISHTHAN BHANDAR) This looks like a humble small-town sweet shop but hidden behind that façade is an awesome array of delicious food. Owned by the Gujral family this is one of two shops, both of which are called JMB. The new generation has six brothers and so there is scope for four more shops by the same name in Udaipur. The original opened its doors in 1970 and the one at Chetak Circle started in 1999. They do a mighty pyaaz kachori. The sweet one is a mawa kachori which is a little too sweet. The phapadas (deep-fried chickpea pieces) are served with fried green tomatoes and green chilli pieces. The mirchi vada (whole chilli deep fried with a chickpea batter coating) is always present in Rajasthan. The sweets are pretty good but the savoury snacks are what make this place special. The inside is bright and well lit and all items are made fresh at a kitchen close by and best eaten hot.

SOMETHING ON THE SIDE   The shop has a counter out on the road that does brisk business and the inside is dedicated to bulk buyers and for all mithais (sweets).

Rocky's Verdict: They make a mighty pyaaz kachori—it's worth the drive to get here. It's by far the best we have ever had.
Rating: Taste: 8, Ambience: 6, Service: 6, Value for Money: 9, Total: 29
Specialities: Pyaaz kachori, mawa kachori, mirchi vada
Veg/Non-veg: Veg
Contact Details/Timings: 124, Parmatma Plaza, Udaipur 313001. 7am to late night.
Prices: Kachori ₹ 10, mirchi pakora ₹ 10, and jalebis ₹ 160 per kg

---

NATRAJ DINING HALL   It is owned by the family of young Jayant Srimali and the place was started fifty years ago by his grandfather. They have grown from their humble origins into a huge establishment on the strength of the great food. On most days you will have to wait a bit to get in as it is almost always full. Their byline is 'Ghar se door, ghar jaise khane ka swaad' (the taste of home food away from home) and in this rare case it is true.

Their Gujarati thali is superb and is justly famous. They serve a huge thali with seven katoris (bowls) which are filled with delicious food within seconds of you sitting down. It's 'All you can eat' so don't hesitate to ask for seconds. Start with dhokla, imli chutney, yogurt, and the incredible lassun chutney. There is spinach thepla, khichdi, sweet dal, seasonal vegetables, and lots of pure ghee.

The place is only open at mealtimes and they are rather strict about their timings. It opens for dinner at 6:30 pm and is usually filled up by 6:45 pm. We were early and were not the first in line so be prepared to wait a little.

SOMETHING ON THE SIDE There is an unspoken language of signals here to ask to be served or seconds. For example, a raised index finger will get you rice, raising your hand with fingers spread widely and twisting it left and right will fetch you a hot roti. The place has air conditioning and is a very comfortable dining experience. Sit down, eat a giant unlimited meal and learn the language over seconds and thirds. The more you eat the happier your waiters are. They are trained to serve you despite your refusal in true Indian style and do not be surprised if you eat too much. A trip to Udaipur would be incomplete without this experience.

Rocky's Verdict: Delicious, wholesome, spotlessly clean and very reasonably priced. This is the best value-for-money dining experience you will have on all fronts. If you want to eat one meal in Udaipur, this is the one you should eat. Essential!!
Rating: Taste: 9, Ambience: 9, Service: 10, Value for Money: 9, Total: 37
Certified: Rocky and Mayur rating of excellence
Specialities: Gujarati thali
Veg/Non-veg: Veg
Contact Details/Timings: Near Railway Station, City Station Road, Udaipur.
Prices: Gujarati thali ₹ 90

SAVAGE GARDEN   This gem is tucked away in some narrow lane, away from the chaotic traffic of Udaipur. It may take you a while to find but once you are there the effort is instantly rewarded as you walk in. The place is coloured a deep Mediterranean blue and soothes your eyes when you enter. There is a little tinkling marble fountain at the entrance which calms your ears and a heavenly smell from the kitchen which tells you that you have made a good choice. Decorated with some lovely little pieces it has several large bougainvillea plants and banana trees that transport you instantly to heaven.

The modern kitchen is clean and on the ground floor of the traditional haveli-like building. Seating is in the cool and shady courtyard as well as up on the first floor and on a cold winter's day you can go all the way up to the roof to get some sun while you eat.

They serve mainly continental food and the highlight was the salmon fillet with pearl potatoes and Tagliatelle al pesto. They have a choice of home-made pastas and do a mean bruschetta as well. The recipes are simple and the dishes are well turned out with creative presentation. You can get a chilled beer as well, which is refreshing for a small place like this. A lot of effort has gone into getting the place to look like it does and getting the food just right.

SOMETHING ON THE SIDE   A magical ambience, an oasis of tranquillity in the noisy and hectic old part of Udaipur.

Rocky's Verdict: A delightful little place which we highly recommend even though it was a little too expensive for our taste.
Rating: Taste: 8, Ambience: 10, Service: 9, Value for Money: 7, Total: 34
Specialities: Salmon fillet with pearl potatoes and Tagliatelle al pesto
Veg/Non-veg: Non-veg
Contact Details/Timings: Near Chandpol
Prices: Salmon fillet with pearl potatoes ₹ 470, bruschetta ₹ 145, and tagliatelle al pesto ₹ 210, cost per person ₹ 300–₹ 400

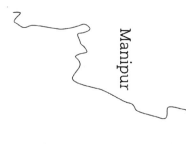

Bhutan

Arunachal Pradesh

Gangtok

Assam

Nagaland

Manipur

Gangtok

ROLL HOUSE In a little alley just off the KG Marg market is Roll House, which claims to make better rolls than Nizam's in Kolkata (the originators of the roll). A giant sign across the whole width of the alley entrance ensures you will not miss the little hole-in-the-wall shop. The shop itself is painted a deep blue with bright yellow tiles providing a colourful contrast. This is a vegetarian eatery and you can choose from a range of paneer, vegetarian, and cheese rolls cooked fresh on giant tawas and served to the constant flow of customers.

The paneer roll is a tasty treat and adds to the fun of eating a roll without letting it unroll and spill out the ingredients. The vegetarian momos are light, fresh, served hot, and accompanied by a decent spicy sauce for dipping.

SOMETHING ON THE SIDE The paved, clean, and completely litter free MG Marg with pockets of pots with brightly coloured flowers and row of benches almost makes you believe that you are in Switzerland. Even if you are not hungry just sit there and feed your soul.

Mayur's Verdict: Extremely clean surroundings, a bright environment, and staff that pays great attention to hygiene are only some of the reasons for the popularity of this eatery. A pretty good roll offering the opportunity for a quick and tasty snack is what brings the customers back for more.
Rating: Taste: 6, Ambience: 7, Service: 8, Value for Money: 9, Total: 30
Specialities: Rolls
Veg/Non-veg: Veg
Contact Details/Timings: Roll House, KG Marg, Gangtok.
Prices: Paneer roll ₹ 20 and vegetarian momos ₹ 15

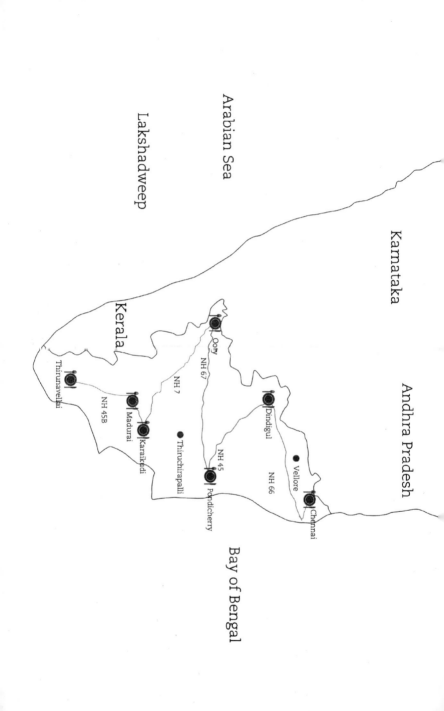

Chennai

ANJAPPAR   Anjappar is possibly the most successful Chettinad restaurant in the world. The place is focused on the food and efficient waiters will take your orders on electric pads. The menu is attractive and extensive and the place is clean, bright and smells great. We went with the vegetarian set meal which offers sambar, rasam, kara kolumbu (mixed vegetables), kuttu (cabbage), and many other delicious preparations. The variety of seafood is mind-boggling and is a speciality of the house. The nethili fry (anchovies) is delightful; the huge nand (crab) roast is extraordinary value for money. Make sure you try the kadai (quail).

SOMETHING ON THE SIDE   Anjappar is now an international chain with restaurants in places like Dubai. A good representation of the wonderful non-vegetarian cuisine of Tamil Nadu.

Rocky's Verdict: Recommended for its seafood, which is outstanding.
Rating: Taste: 8, Ambience: 7, Service: 9, Value for Money: 8, Total: 32
Specialities: Seafood
Veg/Non-veg: Non-veg
Contact Details/Timings: J.P. Tower, 7/2 Nungambakkam High Road, Chennai. Phone: 28217200/ 28256662/ 42144573. 12 noon to 11 pm.
Prices: Crab ₹ 95 per portion, anchovies ₹ 79 per portion, cost per person ₹ 150

MURUGAN IDLI SHOP   What can one say about a place that claims to have the best idlis in the world? In addition to the idlis you can also get dosai, vada, pongal, and a variety of rice. The idlis are the spongiest, fluffiest, tenderest, whitest, and lightest that you'll ever taste and they will be served with all kinds of tasty chutneys: tomato and garlic chutney, coconut chutney, chilli garlic chutney, and gun powder. This is an old favourite with tourists and locals alike. Expect a crowd any time you go and be prepared to wait on weekends. There are several branches all over Chennai and, of late, one even in Singapore. Ask the customers about the best idlis in the world and the prompt answer will be 'Murugan idli'.

SOMETHING ON THE SIDE   The cooking and preparation of food at Murugan Indli is done with great pride by every staff member of the place. This results in nothing but the best reaching the customers. It also means that this place would offer the cleanest and the most hygienic food experience.

Rocky's Verdict: Service is immaculate and it would be surprising if you are not served within 2 to 3 minutes of entering the place. As for the food, need I say more? Eat it!
Rating. Taste. 10, Ambience. 8, Service: 9, Value for Money: 10, Total: 37
Certified: Rocky and Mayur rating of excellence
Specialities: Idlis
Veg/Non Veg: Veg
Contact Details/Timings: 7th Avenue, Besant Nagar, Chennai—044 42018181
Prices: Idlis ₹ 4 per plate, vadas ₹ 10 per plate, pongal ₹ 23 per plate.

PONNUSAMY HOTEL   This place dispels the myth that most Tamilians are vegetarian. It started about fifty years ago and has been serving the most delightful, predominantly non vegetarian food since then. The shell less crab is a specialty, the quail a must try as is the chicken kozhambu. The mutton pepper fry is made with a whole bunch of curry leaves and lots of pepper. Most dishes are prepared in the chettinad style and extra chillies and spices have been added to make them even more fiery. The place is hugely popular and a Chennai institution. Be prepared to wait for lunch and dinner and believe me, the wait will be worth it. Seating is much more comfortable on the first floor where there is passable air conditioning. The place is crowded and you will probably have to share your table with strangers if even one seat is empty. For some reason everyone here speaks loudly and it is abuzz with loud conversation.

SOMETHINGONTHESIDE Remembertofoldyourbananaleaf(which serves as the plate here) towards yourself if you have enjoyed the meal, folding it away from yourself means that you did not like the food, which is not a possibility in this place. Vegetarians, you may not have much variety but your food is cooked safely away from the influence of meat of any kind so feel free to go with your meat eating friends.

Rocky's Verdict: Try as many dishes as you can, each dish has a unique and different taste. This is one culinary adventure you will not forget in a hurry. Go wild in here, that's the rule.
Rating: Taste: 9, Ambience: 8, Service: 9, Value for Money: 10, Total: 36
Certified: Rocky and Mayur rating of excellence
Specialities: Mutton pepper fry, crab masala, and chicken kozhambu.
Veg/Non Veg: Primarily Non Veg
Contact Details/Timings: 55/1, Gowdiya Mutt Road, Royapettah, Chennai—044 28133067
Prices: Mutton pepper fry ₹ 60, crab masala ₹ 90, chicken kozhambu ₹ 66.

SRI KALPAGAMBAL MESS You can experience traditional Brahmin cuisine here. The entrance is made of nicely carved solid wood and covered with fresh flowers. A rangoli will welcome you on most days. The walls inside are lined with pictures and paintings of gods and deities and a strong scent of incense is omnipresent as is traditional Tamil prayer music. Young Prabhudas, the owner, makes sure all goes smoothly. The recipes belong to his grandmother and are unchanged. As soon as you enter you are served badam halwa, gajar halwa, and suji appam (this is a wonderful sweet dish made especially for sons-in-law in Brahmin homes in Thanjavur). The pongal vada is served with a choice of chutneys. Eat the vada with the pongal. The podi (chilli powder dosa) is supremely good. The kal dosa is a thick dosa traditionally eaten for breakfast.

SOMETHING ON THE SIDE   This little restaurant stays true to the 'Brahmin cuisine' of Chennai. Great pains are taken to ensure that all dishes are authentic and extraordinary care and attention is given to every item on the menu.

Rocky's Verdict: A unique taste and a must-visit place for all foodies. If you're going to eat one meal in Chennai, make it the breakfast here.
Certified: Rocky and Mayur rating of excellence
Rates: Taste: 9, Ambience: 9, Service: 10, Value for Money: 9, Total: 37
Specialities: Traditional Tamil Brahmin cuisine
Veg/Non-veg: Veg
Contact Details/Timings: Mylai Sri Kalpagambal Mess, East Meda Station, Sankarpuram, Mylapore, Chennai.
7 am to 10 pm. Phone: 91-44-24642902.
Prices: Badam halwa ₹ 30 per plate, dosa ₹ 30, and filter coffee ₹ 12

Dindigul

PONRAM BIRYANI HOTEL   As you enter the restaurant, the brightly painted walls telling you the story of how biryani reached Dindigul from Iran, via Afghanistan greet you.

Ponram Hotel makes the biryani with short-grained local rice, cinnamon and other spices that make the biryani taste sweet and give it a rich aroma. They also serve the local pukki biryani in which the meat is cooked first then added to raw rice in a container which is then sealed with charcoal and mud. The container is then heated from the top to make an unusual and tasty biryani.

Another must-try is the mutta curry which is egg whipped together with mince and then scrambled. There is also the dalcha which is dal cooked with mutton bones.

SOMETHING ON THE SIDE   Biryani comes from the word 'birian' meaning fried before cooking. A meal of choice for the Mughal armies, it was said to have been perfected by Mumtaz Mahal for the troops. Hyder Ali brought biryani to Tamil Nadu and today it is prepared using local ingredients.

Rocky's Verdict: A must-visit not just for its tasty food, but also quirky facts on biryani.
Rating: Taste: 7, Ambience: 5, Service: 7, Value for Money: 6, Total: 25
Specialities: Dalcha, mutta curry, and biryani
Veg/Non-veg: Non-veg
Contact Details/Timings: 91-451-2401964
Prices: Cost per person ₹ 150, biryani ₹ 135, mutta curry ₹ 30, dalcha is served complimentary, for 10 percent extra, you can eat in an air-conditioned dining area

---

Karaikudi

SOUNDARAM'S   Soundaram's serves traditional Chettinad sweets and snacks. You will have to take off your shoes before you can enter as is the custom with most homes here. You enter into a garishly lit room with a television, a few sofas, and a slow moving ceiling fan and wait till your snack is prepared. Everything is done by hand at Soundaram's, including powdering the rice and urad dal, the base for all the snacks prepared here. Traditional tools are used to make the shapes and textures for the batters from which the snacks are made. Murukkus, mamurundai (sweet flour balls), and laddus are all worth a try.

SOMETHING ON THE SIDE   Karaikudi is a living tribute to the Chettys of this region. The suffix 'ar' denotes respect and the

Chettiars were a progressive and forward-looking people. Our home minister in the year 2010, P. Chidambaram, too hails from this region.

Rocky's Verdict: Fresh and edible. Make sure you get lots to eat on your journeys.
Rating: Taste: 7, Ambience: 6, Service: 7, Value for Money: 8, Total: 28
Specialities: Murukkus, mamurundai, and laddus
Veg/Non-veg: Veg
Contact Details/Timings: Soundaram's, Soodamanipuram, Karaikudi. Phone: 04565-650733
Prices: Murukkus and laddus ₹ 5 a piece

THE BANGALA   The Bangala is an old Chettiar home that has been converted into a well-maintained heritage hotel. There are old paintings on the walls depicting the wealth and culture of this region. The chef here is R. Kharpaiah, who has been the family chef since 1970. He promised to prepare some traditional Chettinad food for us. He started with the vendekai mandi (ladyfinger). This is cooked using fenugreek seeds, mustard seeds, whole onions, whole garlic, and whole green chillies. Tamarind is another popular ingredient and rice water is used to make the gravies. The end result is a hugely spicy and flavourful dish. We also tried the kodi malaga masala, made with malaga (pepper), coriander seeds, dried red chilli, garlic, and onions. The spicy chicken Chettinad gets its flavour from green chillies and pepper.

Rocky's Verdict: Expensive but worth it for a truly authentic Chettinad flavour.
Certified: Rocky and Mayur rating of excellence
Rating: Taste: 9, Ambience: 10, Service: 10, Value for Money: 7,

Total: 36
Specialities: Chettinad food
Veg/Non-veg: Non-veg
Contact Details/Timings: The Bangala, Devakottai Road,
Karaikudi. Phone: 91-44-24934851, 91-45-6220221
Prices: ₹ 450 per head

Madurai

AMMA MESS   Delicious aromas waft in from the little kitchen
at the back where in keeping with the tradition (serving home-
cooked food to migrant workers) the owner's wife supervises a
range of dishes cooking in giant kadhais. Food is served on fresh
green banana leaves and the first item ladled on is chutney
made of pickled and spiced vegetables. The delectable bone
marrow omelette is a light, fluffy dish with a rich taste thanks
to the filling of marrow cooked with a secret mix of spices. The
oily and extremely spicy chicken kallikattu is also a speciality
of the house and is best enjoyed mixed with steaming hot rice.
The dark, spicy rabbit roast has a strong flavour, and there is
surprisingly little meat on the bone. The spicy, light, deep-fried
mutton balls are a great side and disappear into your mouth
faster than you can count them.

SOMETHING ON THE SIDE   Have a wander around this eatery
and check out the photoboards on the walls for pictures of all
the politicians, film stars, and other notables who have eaten
here.

Mayur's Verdict: Non-vegetarians will love the food here, but
there is nothing vegetarian available.
Rating: Taste: 9, Ambience: 6, Service: 9, Value for Money: 10,
Total: 34
Certified: Rocky and Mayur rating of excellence
Specialities: Chicken kallikattu
Veg/Non-veg: Non-veg

Contact Details/Timings: 125 Algr Road, Tallakulam, Madurai 625002. Phone: 0452-2534544, 2533502
Prices: Kallikattu chicken gravy ₹ 75, special bone marrow omelette ₹ 100, rabbit roast ₹ 90,mutton balls ₹ 10, Meals ₹ 50

HOTEL SREE SABAREES Legendary for its pure vegetarian recipes, inviting smells, and quick service, Sree Sabarees is also innovative with food. The traditional dosa is transformed here into the rocket dosa, shaped like a rocket or the family dosa with its giant proportions. Idlis are converted to mini-bite- sized idlis floating in sambar. A wide range of tasty chutneys accompany the meal: black pepper mint chutney, garlic chutney, red chilli and garlic with coconut, tomato chutney with spices, and the ever-tasty gunpowder. You can share your meal with drivers, policemen, and rich businessmen. The owner M. Sayambur himself supervises the cooking and personally tastes everything to see that it is perfect.

SOMETHING ON THE SIDE Just outside Sree Sabarees is a moustached gentleman who makes frothier and tastier coffee than any machine, which makes for the prefect end to a great meal.

Rocky's Verdict: This place is a must-visit if you are in Madurai.
Rating: Taste: 8, Ambience: 8, Service: 10, Value for Money: 9, Total: 35
Specialities: Ragi dosa, seven taste platter, mini idli. Also, the wide variety of chutneys.
Veg/ Non-Veg: Veg
Contact Details/ Timings: Hotel Sree Sabarees, 56, West Perumal Maistry Street, Opposite New College House, Town Hall Road, Madurai.
Prices: Seven taste platter ₹ 27, rocket dosa ₹ 12, and coffee ₹ 7. Average cost per person ₹ 50

MODERN RESTAURANT Rice, rasam, sambar, kootu (made of vegetables and lentils), pitla (made from brinjal and gram), intriguingly spiced spinach subzi cooked to the consistency of a chutney, yogurt, and mouth wateringly delicious kesari bhath all compete for attention on a bright green banana leaf. You can ask for multiple refills and once you taste the food rest assured that you will ask for more. The vegetable items on offer change every day but make sure you end your meal with aromatic, hot, frothy filter coffee.

SOMETHING ON THE SIDE Modern Restaurant has fed dignitaries like Jawaharlal Nehru, C.V. Raman, and Abdul Kalam and yet they take pride in their ability to offer great value for money meals to the common man on the street.

Mayur's Verdict: Anyone who eats here is having a meal worthy of a king.
Rating: Taste: 9, Ambience: 7, Service: 9, Value for Money: 9, Total: 34
Certified: Rocky and Mayur rating of excellence
Specialities: Thali
Veg/Non-veg: Veg
Contact Details/Timings: No. 160, Netaji Road, Madurai, 625001. Phone: 0452-2344487, 0452-2345798
Prices: ₹ 42 or ₹ 62 depending on whether you eat in the air-conditioned dining room or outside

---

Thirunavellai

THE HALWA SHOP WITH NO NAME Driving down this section of NH7, you come across a small poorly lit sweet shop with only one item on the menu: a delightful, chewy, thick, and sweet halwa. The owner of the shop is Mr Singh, whose family migrated here from Rajasthan many years ago. Although his family now retains very little of their north Indian heritage, their classic Karachi halwa brings to mind the best north Indian hospitality. Although the shop is open from 6 pm to 9 pm every day, they are usually sold out by 7:30 pm, so reach well in time.

SOMETHING ON THE SIDE The halwa tastes just like Karachi halwa and unites the north and the south.

Rocky's Verdict: Classic Karachi halwa. Chewy and tasty!
Rating: Taste: 7, Ambience: 5, Service: 7, Value for Money: 7, Total: 26
Specialities: Karachi halwa
Veg/Non-Veg: Veg
Contact Details/Timings: On NH7 between Kanyakumari and Dindigul is the town of Thirunavellai. The halwa shop is near the Nellaiappar temple, Thirunavellai. The shop is open from 6 pm to 9 pm. Phone: 0-9025222224
Prices: ₹ 240 per kilo

Udhagamandalam (Ooty)

OOTY HOT BREADS BAKERY Ooty Hot Breads has a great location in the very heart of the town. The bakery sends aromas down the busy street where it is located, and the smell is enough to drive you crazy, or at least to drive you into the bakery. There is something fun about bakeries in hill stations. They are simply irresistible.

At Hot Breads locals and tourists come in frequently for a snack or some pastries. The fare is tasty and fresh, with them baking twice a day, morning and evening. It is warm and cosy inside and glass shelves display everything from pastries to patties. They do a good chilli chicken soft roll for ₹ 21. The vegetable plait (₹ 22) is interesting and the pastries are fairly good. Don't expect gourmet tastes though, this is just another small hill town bakery. They also make cakes for occasions and birthdays. There's plenty for both vegetarians and non-vegetarians.

SOMETHING ON THE SIDE Strange as it may sound to most big city people, most bakeries here make things to sell out by the end of the day to ensure freshness. On most days they are sold out by closing time. I think it's a wonderful display of sincerity and care for their customers.

Rocky's Verdict: Simple tasty fare.
Rating: Taste: 6, Ambience: 6, Service: 7, Value for Money: 6, Total: 25
Specialities: Chilli chicken soft roll
Veg/Non-veg: Non-veg
Contact Details/Timings: Charing Cross
Prices: Chilli chicken soft roll ₹ 21, vegetable plait ₹ 22. Average cost for one ₹ 50

SIDEWALK CAFÉ Sidewalk Café may just be the most famous eatery in Ooty. Brightly lit and cosy, this is a happy sort of eating place where you can almost always count on being served hot food. In a freezing cold hill station this counts for a lot. The entrance is rather grand and has been recently done up, the seating area is basic but clean, and the service is a little laid back and relaxed.

The highlight of the place is their wood-fired oven. You can sit at their 'Pizza Bar' which is a small counter that looks like a standard bar but where they serve you pizzas instead of drinks. The dough is tossed fresh while you look on from the barstools and the ingredients are local, making the Sidewalk Café pizza the best available in Ooty. We tried the fun Chettinad and Nilgiri pizzas, and enjoyed the heat and delicious aromas coming out from their quaint wood-fired oven. Ingredients include cardamom, curry leaves, cloves, capsicum, and mushrooms all from the area around Ooty.

What's also worth trying are the home-made chocolates (₹ 400 to ₹ 800 per kg) available here and at several other places in Ooty. Do note that this place serves only vegetarian food. You must definitely try out the coffee. It's rather pleasant.

The tourist season starts in December and lasts till about

March so the place is buzzing during these months. In the other months it's mostly the locals who make up the clientele.

SOMETHING ON THE SIDE   Shahnawaz, the manager, will greet you with a smile and is a jovial sort of fellow who takes good care of things at the Sidewalk Café but apart from his efforts, the service is indifferent.

Rocky's Verdict: Get into the Sidewalk Café and hang with the 'hip' crowd. Despite being vegetarian the place is recommended for its cleanliness.
Rating: Taste: 7, Ambience: 7, Service: 5, Value for Money: 6, Total: 25
Specialities: Pizza and coffee
Veg/Non-veg: Veg
Contact Details/Timings: Sidewalk Café, Charing Cross, Ooty. Phone: 0423-2442173
Prices: Veg Nilgiri ₹ 125/200, tandoori attack ₹ 140/210, chettinad pizza ₹ 130/200

A Side Dish...

Puducherry

SATSANGA   Puducherry is an old French colony, and nowhere is this more apparent than at the Satsanga which is packed in the evenings but fairly empty in the mornings. The unhurried pace of Puducherry seeps into everything and an order could take anything from twenty minutes to an hour to get there, but who minds? Satsanga is bright and cheerful and uses pastels and Mediterranean influences to put you at ease. Much attention is paid to detail and the cheeses are locally made and are very good. Even the garlic butter is home made. Breakfast is the standard continental one with fresh juices, eggs, cheese, and butter along with thick toasts that make for a satisfying meal.

SOMETHING ON THE SIDE If you're lucky you could catch the owner Pierre who has been here for the past forty years and has a wonderfully simple philosophy of life. Also, ask him to order for you if you can and then sit back and enjoy your meal.

Rocky's Verdict: Elegant and simple place. Good for lunches but best for dinners.
Rating: Taste: 6, Ambience: 9, Service: 5, Value for Money: 6, Total: 26
Specialities: Continental breakfast
Veg/Non Veg: both
Contact Details/Timings: 5 kms from Puducherry to Chennai.
Prices: ₹ 200–300 per head for food, wine is extra.

RENDEZVOUS This restaurant is located in a hundred and twenty two year old building. It is situated in elegant and beautiful surroundings and has a great wine cellar. Rendezvous serves authentic French food and the highlight is the pork chops. The clams are fresh and seafood is one of the specialties of the house. Old time favourites like the French onion soup and the Coq Au Vin (Chicken in wine and mushrooms) are typical French dishes.

You can choose to sit indoors but we recommend the first floor verandah to get a real old style feel of Pondicherry. They also have an extensive wine list which the waiters will proudly inform you about.

The lively and jovial owner Vincent used to sit here everyday and now that he does not, standards have fallen due to his absence.

SOMETHING ON THE SIDE The chef Johnny comes out to talk to customers and then uses his experience to alter the dishes subtly so that customers get dishes suited to their tastes.

Rocky's Verdict: Possibly the most pleasant place to dine in while you are in Puducherry. They've got most things just right.

Rating: Taste: 8, Ambience: 8, Service: 8, Value for Money: 7, Total: 31

Specialities: Coq au vin, seafood of all kinds for the non vegetarians and vegetable gratin for the vegetarians. The wines are great.

Veg/Non Veg: Primarily non veg but with great veg options

Contact Details/Timings: Romain Roland Street, Puducherry

Prices: Soup ₹ 50, Vegetables ₹ 100, Coq Au Vin ₹ 210 per portion.

UTTAR PRADESH

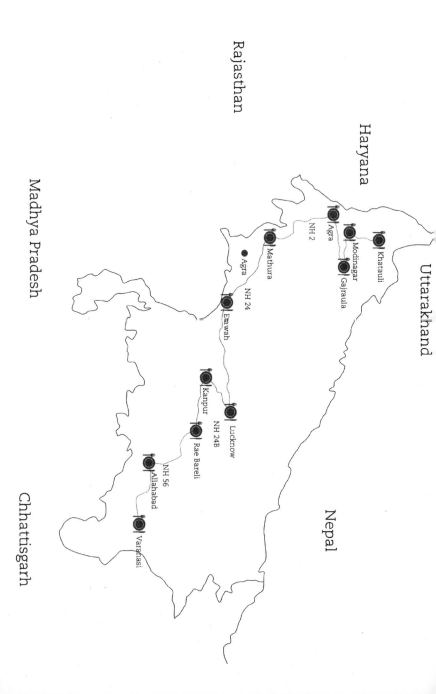

Agra

AGRA CHAAT HOUSE In a happy little alley in Sadar Bazaar you will find a lot of street food vendors catering to a crowd of people out enjoying the food of Agra by night. Agra Chaat House serves up a range of hot, delicious snacks, each one tastier than the other. They serve chola-bhaturas, fried potato chaat, golgappas or puchkas, and dosas with sambar. The piping hot fried aloo tikkis that are covered with spicy and sweet chutneys and yogurt, and then garnished with ginger slices are mouth wateringly good and along with besan (gram flour) chillas, are the street food specialities of Agra.

SOMETHING ON THE SIDE In Agra aloo tikki is called bhalla and dahi bhalla is called dahi vada or gujiya. It really doesn't matter what they are called because they are all super tasty and the crowds that flock here every night are proof of this.

Mayur's Verdict: You like the tasty street snacks? If you are in Agra then there are sights that look just as good as the Taj Mahal in the moonlight. The advantage is that they smell and taste a lot better. Do it!

Rating: Taste: 8, Ambience: 8, Service: 8, Value of Money: 9, Total: 33

Certified: Rocky and Mayur rating of excellence

Specialities: Aloo tikkis, besan chillas

Veg/Non-veg: Veg

Contact Details/Timings: Agra Chaat House, Sadar Bazaar, Agra. Phone: 0-9719011167

Prices: Bhalla ₹ 15, dahi gujiya ₹ 15, aloo chaat ₹ 10

PANCHHI PETHA   Agra has a plethora of shops selling all shapes, sizes, and flavours of its most famous mithai, the sweet petha. The best known of these is the Panchhi Petha shop. Pethas are made from (get this!) white pumpkin or kaddu, to which different flavours such as vanilla, orange, pineapple, rose, and pistachio are added.

SOMETHINGONTHESIDE   The success of Panchhi Petha has resulted in a number of imitators freeloading on the name. This seems like good business sense as the petha industry is estimated at ₹ 600 crore, and even a slice of that pie has to be sweet!

Mayur's Verdict: Start your time in Agra on a sweet note and grab some pethas to munch on and take home as a memory of your visit. The ones to try first are those of the original flavour which are ivory white in colour, and the 'angoori' which are soaked in sugar syrup.
Rating: Taste: 8, Ambience: 6, Service: 6, Value for Money: 7, Total: 27
Specialities: Petha, especially the angoori petha
Veg/Non-veg: Veg
Contact Details/Timings: Panchhi Petha Stores, Sadar Bazaar, Agra. Phone: 91-562-3253478
Prices: Plain petha ₹ 40 per kg, kesari petha ₹ 70 per kg, honey petha ₹ 100 per kg, rasbhari petha ₹ 120 per kg

---

PRAHLAD DHABA   Prahlad Dhaba is a cramped little place with only seven tables between two floors. Dishes that must be tried here are the chicken which is well cooked and tender, and the chana subzi which is delicious. Hot tandoori rotis dripping with butter are a great accompaniment to the food.

SOMETHING ON THE SIDE   Prahlad Dhaba has had the same cook for the past forty years. Even though this eighty-year-old gentleman is a vegetarian, he turns out a nice menu of vegetarian and meat dishes which old customers swear taste exactly the same each time you eat here!

Mayur's Verdict: If you like to eat at places where attention is paid to hygiene, do not eat here. The walls carry the accumulated grease of decades of cooking, and food is being cooked right by the tables where you eat. The food is tasty, fresh, and filling though for those who do end up choosing to eat here.
Rating: Taste: 7, Ambience: 4, Service: 7, Value for Money: 7, Total: 25
Specialities: Chicken and chana subzi
Veg/Non-veg: Non-veg
Contact Details/Timings: Sadar Bazaar, on the Naulakha crossing, Prahlad Dhaba, Sadar Bazaar, Agra Cantt.
Phone: 0-9319115364
Prices: Chicken curry ₹ 45, chana masala ₹ 25, sarson ka saag ₹ 25

RAJ DHABA Raj Dhaba has an open kitchen and is a bustle of activity with waiters taking orders and shouting them across to the cook, customers shouting for waiters, and people shouting just for no other reason than that they have obviously had a few drinks before coming to eat. The menu is extensive with many different types of subzis, dals, paneer, stuffed and plain tandoori rotis, and parathas on offer. The food is flash cooked at very high temperatures in large pans and brought out accompanied by fresh salad and rotis hot from the tandoor. The khoya paneer, dal fry, and mixed paratha are acceptable in taste though a bit heavy on the spices and oil.

SOMETHING ON THE SIDE The town of Runakta has a few dhabas all brightly lit up with numerous tube lights and with giant posters of exotica ranging from the Taj Mahal to a Hollywood actress in a mask and a cat suit!

Mayur's Verdict: If you are bypassing Agra on the highway and get hit by pangs of hunger, by all means stop at Raj Dhaba for a bite. Then stroll around the adjoining outdoor market and shop for some shoes, small televisions, or even some hot chai.
Rating: Taste: 6, Ambience: 6, Service: 7, Value for Money: 7, Total: 26
Specialities: Khoya paneer, dal fry, and mixed paratha
Veg/Non-veg: Veg
Contact Details/Timings: By the road on NH2 on the outskirts of Agra. Raj Dhaba, Agra.
Prices: Khoya paneer ₹ 50, dal fry ₹ 25, and mixed paratha ₹ 25

Allahabad

LOK NATH BAZAAR This is the legendary food market of Allahabad. There are many great eateries here and they serve some truly exceptional items. Start at the Nirala Mishthan Bhandar for aloo tikkis. Deep-fried potato patties and crunchy strips of fried potato served with some delicious chutneys, this tikki is arguably the best you can find in Allahabad. In the winter try the black carrot halwa, a little firmer than regular carrot halwa and very pleasant to the palate. The laddu motichoor is also delicious and at ₹ 140 per kg is quite cheap.

The streets are lined with food stalls and the smells are unbelievable. Walk on to Rajaram Lassi Wala a little way off for a refreshing glass of lassi with rabri. This super sweet and fresh drink is a truly mighty lassi. Try as hard as you can to get the sweetness reduced, but be warned, you might just not be able to! All in all it's a great lassi, and at ₹ 10 a glass just cannot be beaten.

Across the road is the world famous Hari Ram and Sons, selling 'UNIQUE DELICIOUS SALTED FOOD PRODUCTS,' all made in pure ghee. The choices will spoil you and everything here is fantastic. The khatta chanas are the highlight of this show and cost ₹ 160 per kg.

SOMETHING ON THE SIDE Established in 1890 this place was the favourite of Indian prime minister Lal Bahadur Shastri.

Rocky's Verdict: A quintessential Indian experience. Unless you have done this walk and eaten the goodies you cannot call yourself an Indian foodie. So get there and qualify.
Rating: Taste: 9, Ambience: 10, Service: 10, Value for Money: 10 Total: 39
Certified: Rocky and Mayur rating of excellence
Specialities: Aloo tikkis, black carrot halwa, laddu motichoor, lassi, khatta chana
Veg/Non-veg: Veg
Contact Details/Timings: Nirala Mishthan Bhandar, Lok Nath Bazaar, Allahabad. Phone: 0532-6452079. Rajaram Lassi Wala, Lok Nath Bazaar, Allahabad. Phone: 0-9336195477. Hari Ram and Sons, 16, Lok Nath Bazaar, Allahabad, Uttar Pradesh, 221011. Phone: 91-532-2651367
Prices: Nirala Mishthan Bhandar: Tikki ₹ 10 per plate, motichoor laddu ₹ 140 per kg, kali gajar ka halwa ₹ 140 per kg. Rajaram Lassi Wala: Lassi ₹ 10. Hari Ram and Sons: Samosa ₹ 160 per kg, dal moth ₹ 160 per kg, Khatta chana ₹ 160 per kg

---

Etawah

BHANG SHOPS Etawah has many authorized bhang shops where bhang is available in powdered form or a ready-to-mix paste, and you can even buy it with thandai, a sweetened milk concoction with cardamom, pistachios, etc. One small pellet is for ₹ 6 and can knock out a 100 kg man for the day. Drinking a little, however, will make you perky and relaxed and keep you going like you're on rocket fuel. The bhang plant is a close relative of the marijuana or cannabis plant and has the same properties. This one is more conducive for drinking though and gives you the appetite of an elephant.

SOMETHING ON THE SIDE Be prepared to wake up the owner who is usually passed out after trying his own bhang.

> **Rocky's Verdict:** A must-have as long as you do not drive afterwards or have kids to take care of. Be warned. It WILL make you giggly and irresponsible.
> **Rating:** Taste: 5, Ambience: NA, Service: NA, Value for Money: 10
> **Specialities:** Bhang in many forms—thandai, for example
> **Veg/Non-veg:** Veg
> **Contact Details/Timings:** Dotted across the city.
> **Prices:** ₹ 6 for a pellet

Gajraula

BHAJAN TADKA Bhajan Tadka is the new face of the dhabas in India. Run by the always smiling brothers Vikram and Prem this takes the best of what traditional dhabas had to offer and combines it with a great location, clean surroundings, and fast service. Started in the late 1960s, this is a vegetarian dhaba. The prices are very reasonable and the favourite items are the chana masala, kadhi pakora, paneer butter masala along with the garlic lachha naan and lassi.

SOMETHING ON THE SIDE Second and third generation of the family are doing a great job of providing restaurant like facilities at dhaba rates.

> **Rocky's Verdict:** A great location, fresh air, and fresh food, what more can a dhaba offer?
> **Rating:** Taste: 7, Ambience: 8, Service: 9, Value for Money: 8, Total: 32
> **Specialities:** Lassi, garlic lachha naan, chana masala, and paneer butter masala
> **Veg/Non-veg:** Veg

Contact Details/Timings: NH 24, Gajraula. Phone: Prem Bedi, 0-9837080188, 0-9837020601
Prices: A meal consisting of one dish, two naans, and a glass of lassi ₹ 85–₹ 105.

Kanpur

DEEPU CHAUHAN KA DHABA The food is nothing special here though it is cleaner than most. The ingredients are fresh and the service is efficient. We tried the butter chicken, tandoori chicken, and pepper chicken which were about ₹ 130 per chicken, so good value for money. The paneer and dal were better than the non-vegetarian food and at ₹ 40 a plate made them even more affordable. The place is more suited to marriage receptions and the large shady trees probably even make lunch a possibility, but the place was empty when we went there.

SOMETHING ON THE SIDE This dhaba was inaugurated by Shri Mulayam Singh Yadav, a fact that means a lot to the owner, Deepu Chauhan. Deepu is a rather large and obviously politically connected man, and claims that once a customer enters his gate he becomes 'Deepu's responsibility'. While this may not seem like a big deal at most places, security and safety while going to a dhaba at night must be considered. So enter fearlessly and take the long walk to the sitting area for some food.

Rocky's Verdict: You can come here to let the kids run around a garden in safety while you eat good, clean food.
Rating: Taste: 6, Ambience: 7, Service: 6, Value for Money: 7, Total: 26
Specialities: Pepper chicken and masala paneer
Veg/Non-veg: Non-veg
Contact Details/Timings: Bhawati, Pratappur, NH2. Deepu Chauhan Dhaba: Bhaunti Pratappur, Kanpur. Phone: 0-9415538949
Prices: ₹ 130 per chicken and ₹ 40 per plate of masala paneer

THAGGU KE LADDU In the bustling and chaotic city of Kanpur amidst thousands of cycles, cars, and constantly blaring horns, you will find this famous Kanpur stalwart. Mr Ramavatar Pandey, a stout Gandhian to this day, once read a piece by the Mahatma which said that by giving people excess sugar you rob them of their health. When he started selling his laddus, about twenty-five years ago, he made his now famous by line 'Aisa koi saga nahi jisko hamne thaga nahi' (there is no relative or person who we have not cheated) to warn people about the ill effects of 'white poison' or sugar. 'Thaggu' comes from thug or cheat, hence the name thaggu ke laddu. Whatever the gimmick may be, the laddu recipe is a closely guarded secret and the laddus are brought from a kitchen where Mr Pandey to this day oversees their preparation.

The other famous item is the badnaam kulfi, or the kulfi with the bad reputation. This name comes from the fact that it is sold every day on the streets and therefore has a maligned character. (If it were sold in big bungalows it would not have been in such disrepute!) It is a hit and at ₹ 200 per kg, a real bargain.

SOMETHING ON THE SIDE Mr Pandey is a great poet and a man of much wisdom and humour. His byline is so popular that Gulzar lifted it directly for his lyrics for the Bollywood movie 'Bunty Aur Babli'. Enjoy the laddus and have a few laughs with him or his son Prakash if you ever go to Kanpur.

Rocky's Verdict: A must-visit place and at ₹ 260 per kg, it is a must-buy laddu.
Rating: Taste: 6, Ambience: 9, Service: 10, Value for Money: 7, Total: 32
Specialities: Thaggu ke laddu, badnaam kulfi
Veg/Non-veg: Veg
Contact Details/Timings: Thaggu ke Laddu, Bada Chauraha, Kanpur. Phone: 0-9839084733
Prices: Badnaam kulfi: ₹ 200 per kg, thaggu laddu ₹ 260 per kg

Khatauli

CHEETAL GRAND   Mr Rana, the owner, claims that the Cheetal Grand is the most popular amongst the more than 200 dhabas on the Delhi–Dehradun highway. The food available here ranges from the typical roti, dal, gobhi, paneer, paratha, etc., to Western-style breakfast food including omelettes, sandwiches, fries, cutlets, etc. and south Indian delicacies like dosas, idlis, and lots more. They do an unusual tubular omelette and a really good cold coffee with or without ice cream. The grilled cheese sandwich, paneer pakoras, and cold coffee are highly recommended. The restaurant is open for breakfast, lunch, and dinner.

SOMETHING ON THE SIDE   Mr Rana tells us the restaurant's success is due to the personal touch that he and his family bring to this enterprise. It may be that, or the hundreds of plants and flowers of all hues and sizes planted on the premises, the giant cages with beautiful, exotic multicoloured birds, the clean bathrooms, the choice of indoor or outdoor seating, and the varied and exhaustive menu. But boy, this place sure does draw customers! They even have a little store where you can stock up on treats such as sweets, imported chocolates, biscuits, chips, and more for the drive ahead.

Mayur's Verdict: Enjoy not just the ambience and the food but also the stern signs with messages such as 'What you bring from home Eat at home', 'No loitering' and our personal favourite, 'Leave the Birds Alone'. Don't be misled though as the tasty food is served hot and fresh by efficient and mostly cheerful waiters. There is always a crowd of people in this highly popular restaurant and it is well deserving of its success.
Rating: Taste: 9, Ambience: 8, Service: 10, Value for Money: 8, Total: 35
Certified: Rocky and Mayur rating of excellence

Specialities: Tubular omelette and cold coffee.
Veg/Non-veg: Non-veg
Contact Details/Timings: Cheetal Grand, Khatauli.
Phone: 01396-272468
Prices: Paneer pakora ₹ 45 per plate, masala omelette
₹ 35, assorted pakoras ₹ 65, grilled sandwich ₹ 80 per plate

Lucknow

GYAN VAISHNAV HOTEL   You better believe it! In the midst
of the city of kebabs, you can find a pure vegetarian hotel. The
brinjal bharta, karela (bitter gourd) subzi, dal, and hot fresh
rotis are all delicious and highly recommended. For dessert the
only dish served is a delicious rice kheer garnished with raisins
and cashews. It tastes just as good whether you have it piping
hot or chilled. Catering to a lot of legislators and politicians
that come to attend the assembly sessions, this hotel has
small private booths besides the tables in the open space. It
is air-conditioned to combat the Lucknow summers, and the
emphasis is on fresh food cooked just like it is at home.

SOMETHING ON THE SIDE   We love the fact that this vegetarian
restaurant is owned and run by two Sikh gentlemen who love
their dal and subzi ☺

Mayur's Verdict: If you are vegetarian and looking for
somewhere to eat that is not all about meat, meat, and more
meat, then this place is highly recommended. The food is
cooked with just the right amount of desi ghee and spices
making for a filling but not too heavy meal.
Rating: Taste: 9, Ambience: 8, Service: 9, Value for Money: 9,
Total: 35
Certified: Rocky and Mayur rating of excellence
Specialities: Brinjal bharta, karela subzi, kheer
Veg/Non-veg: Veg

Contact Details/Timings: On Vidhan Sabha Marg
surrounded by office buildings is the Gyan Vaishnav Hotel,
very cleverly located right next to the state assembly offices
in Lucknow. Gyan Vaishnav Hotel, Vidhan Sabha Marg,
Lucknow. Phone: 0-9415107575
Prices: Bharta ₹ 30, karela ₹ 30, kheer ₹ 20

LUCKY JUICE CENTRE In the stories of the Wild West, the
first place that the hero visits when he rides into town is The
Bar. In keeping with that spirit, on arriving in Lucknow the first
place to visit is the Lucky Juice Bar. In the middle of a busy
market bordering an even busier street is this haven of health
with large colourful signs advertising the different types of
juices and shakes available. The owner Mr Mahindroo is just
as colourful and has advice on what juice to drink for different
situations and ailments. All the juices and shakes are made
on the spot from freshly cut and squeezed fruits. Sugar can
be added or not, depending on how healthy you want your
juice to be. A nice, fresh, and unusual juice to try is the 'lauki'
(bottle gourd) juice, which is cooling, calming, and diuretic. It
also apparently helps to reduce cholesterol in the system. The
house speciality is the quaintly named Aashiqui nimbu masala
cola—the natural, local answer to the fizzy cola challenge.

SOMETHING ON THE SIDE There is a juice made from guavas,
papayas, apples, pineapples, oranges, and some secret
ingredients which strangely help increase your appetite for
meat. Vegetarians beware!

Mayur's Verdict: Fresh, healthy, yummy juices and shakes
which help you get your daily intake of nutrients, vitamins,
minerals, and fibre. Besides this, according to a sign up on
the wall, you get satisfaction and relief. How can you go
wrong? Do it.
Rating: Taste: 9, Ambience: 5, Service: 9, Value for Money: 8,
Total: 31

Specialities: Aashiqui nimbu masala cola, lauki juice
Veg/Non-veg: Veg
Contact Details/Timings: Lucky Juice Bar, Gautam Buddha
Marg, Lucknow. Phone: 0-9839132889
Prices: Mixed juice ₹ 18, lauki juice ₹ 10, aashiqui nimbu
masala cola ₹ 15

TUNDE KABABI   Lucknow is proud of its kebabs. The kakoris, galawatis, shami kebabs, botis, patili-ke-kebabs, ghutwas kebabs, and seekh kebabs are among the best known varieties. You may disagree on which of these is the best, but there is no argument about the best place to eat them...Tunde Kababi.

The famous tunda kebab is so named because it was a speciality of a one-armed chef famous for his deftness and speed while slicing onions, despite using only his good arm. The uniqueness of this kebab is the masala of home-made spices, which is a zealously guarded family secret and is said to incorporate 165 herbs and spices in the mixture. The kebabs can be eaten with wheat rotis and are served with lots of sliced onions with a sprinkling of lime and garnished with fresh coriander. Though not available at Tunde, there are vegetarian versions of the kebab like the dalcha (chana dal with garlic and ginger paste), arbi (taro), zimikand (yam), and rajma (kidney bean). These too are best enjoyed with hot rotis and freshly cut onions. The sheermal at this eatery is just fantastic. These are saffron covered parathas made from dough of flour mixed with milk and ghee and baked in iron tandoors.

SOMETHING ON THE SIDE   Legend has it that a rich Lucknowi nobleman once lost all his teeth, yet couldn't give up his love for kebabs. He ordered his master chef to whip up a kebab that he could eat without his missing teeth, implying that the kebab had to just melt in his mouth. This kebab made without any additives or binding agents, and comprising just minced meat and the spices is galawati kebab. And so successful was the experiment that the recipe lived on!

> **Mayur's Verdict:** This place really deserves its reputation and one bite will explain why there are always hordes of people waiting to eat here. It's so popular that people will hover at your table waiting for you to get up so that they can take your place. If you are a vegetarian among non-vegetarians, go for the sheermal and you may have the joy of watching your meat eating companions experience bliss.
> **Rating:** Taste: 10, Ambience: 7, Service: 8, Value for Money: 10 Total: 35
> **Certified:** Rocky and Mayur rating of excellence
> **Specialities:** Galawati kebab, kakori kebab
> **Veg/Non-veg:** Non-veg
> **Contact Details/Timings:** Tunde Kababi, Ameenabad, Lucknow. Phone: 0-9335911858
> **Prices:** Galawati kebab ₹ 30 per plate, sheermal ₹ 5

Mathura

BRIJWASI MITHAI WALA In Vrindavan, the city famed as the birthplace of Lord Krishna, lies a temple dedicated to the infant god. The city is visited by hundreds of thousands of devotees and there are numerous eateries, especially mithaiwalas, to cater to this rush.

Brijwasi is one of the oldest shops in the city and has been selling the popular Mathura ka peda and khurchan as well as laddus, burfis, halwas, and salted snacks since 1925. It is a clean, brightly lit place and is evidently quite popular.

The famous khurchan is a dish made by boiling milk down to remove all the water content and then scraping off the slightly charred residue. It is always highly in demand given the long time it takes to make, it sells out very quickly.

Pedas are priced in a range with the most expensive being the ones cooked in desi geee and believe us you can taste the difference. Khurchan which is ₹ 140 per kg was all sold out though some regular customers who were there insisted it was the tastiest sweet we would ever try.

SOMETHING ON THE SIDE The young owner who is of the third generation of the family is always experimenting with new items so you must enquire about recent additions to the menu.

Mayur's Verdict: If you love Indian sweets then go down to Brijwasi and enjoy the fresh pedas. If you are very lucky you might get to try some khurchan too.
Rating: Taste: 8, Ambience: 7, Service: 7, Value for Money: 8, Total: 30
Specialities: Khurchan and Mathura ka peda
Veg/Non-veg: Veg
Contact Details/Timings: Brijwasi Mithai Wala, Krishnajanambhoomi, Mathura.
Prices: Pedas ₹ 80 to ₹ 140 per kg, khurchan ₹ 140 per kg

SHANKAR MITHAI WALA In the super crowded and busy area called Holi Gate, this sweet shop does not just depend on its reputation for delicious food. It proves it with its steaming hot moong ki dal ka halwa, and the gajar halwa sitting in containers just off the street. Garnished with lavish helpings of dried fruit the halwas, especially the moong halwa, are the best we have ever tried.

This shop is not just famous for its sweet stuff though. In Vrindavan and beyond it is known for its puri, kachori, chole bhature, and khasta kachori. There is an upstairs area with seating and the food is served piping hot. The mixture of spices offset by the underlying taste of the hiing (asafoetida) proved that a mithaiwala can also serve great food. The dahi bhallas are served with thick creamy dahi and freshly sliced ginger while the chilled lassi served in little kullars (clay pots) is thick, fresh, and deliciously sweet. We rate it as the second best lassi tried across India so far.

With prices ranging from ₹ 14 to ₹ 25 a plate this place gives you amazing value for money.

SOMETHING ON THE SIDE Ask people in the crowded marketplace and as you get close just follow the enticing aromas of the halwas until you arrive at this paradise.

Mayur's Verdict: By far the most delicious meal of this sort eaten on the show. This comes as highly recommended as is possible without shouting it from the rooftops.
Rating: Taste: 10, Ambience: 7, Service: 9, Value for Money: 9, Total: 35
Certified: Rocky and Mayur rating of excellence
Specialities: Puri kachori, chole bhature, and moong ki dal ka halwa
Veg/Non-veg: Veg
Contact Details/Timings: Shankar Mithai Wala, Holi Gate, Mathura. Phone: 0565-2500955
Prices: Prices range from ₹ 14 to ₹ 25 a plate

Modinagar

JAIN SHIKANJI Along this busy section of NH58 in Modinagar you will find a row of shops that serve shikanji to thirsty travellers. Shikanji is a delicious concoction with lemon juice, ice, soda and/or water, sugar, and salt combined together in a perfect blend to beat the heat. There are quite a few shops selling the same product and the most famous of these is Jain Shikanji.

Started in 1932, this shop claims its product is the most popular thanks to the masala they add to the drink. The recipe of course is a secret. You can have it with water or with soda, and if you're feeling healthy you can always ask them to hold off on the sugar syrup. Have it right there in a glass or carry it away in a disposable plastic glass. Just don't dispose of the glass by chucking it on the road please!

SOMETHING ON THE SIDE If you like a snack with your drink then look no further than the front of the shop where an enterprising chap has set up a cart selling all manner of street food including golgappas or puchkas, fried vadas, fried potato tikkis, and fried aloo chat. Ah! Clogged artery heaven. At least the soda in the shikanji will help with the acidity.

Mayur's Verdict: A must-stop if you are on this highway. Watching multiple glasses of the shikanji being made at high speed is almost as much fun as drinking it. As the shops are right on the highway you will have to deal with the noise and the fumes from passing traffic.
Rating: Taste: 9, Ambience: 4, Service: 8, Value for Money: 7, Total: 28
Specialities: Shikanji
Veg/Non-veg: Veg
Contact Details/Timings: The advertisements for Jain Shikanji start around 20 km short of Modinagar. If you are driving with your eyes shut and miss the place you will be informed by signs on the highway past Modinagar that you have missed it. Jain Shikanji, Modinagar.
Prices: Shikanji ₹ 15 per glass, ₹ 18 for a disposable glass

Rae Bareli

NEW NARESH SWEETS The quality of the sweets in Uttar Pradesh is usually measured by how sweet they are and how much ghee there is in them. The rule seems to be the more, the better. Since this place prides itself on being one of the best along the stretch of road between Lucknow and Allahabad, you can only imagine the richness of their sweets. The sweet and savoury snacks are the things to be had. Try the gajar halwa. It's delicious. The other yummies are the kaju paan, badam burfi, and pista burfi. (The badam burfi is the most expensive at ₹ 500 per kg). The samosas and the chola bhaturas are a little too oily but good if you like them that way.

SOMETHING ON THE SIDE This famous sweet shop is a favourite stopover for judges, politician, IAS, and IPS officer types who travel between the Vidhan Sabha in Lucknow and the high court in Allahabad for their court cases. (Ever wonder why they have so many court cases against them...?)

Rocky's Verdict: Unless you have a sweet tooth and love items cooked in desi ghee, keep driving.
Rating: Taste: 7, Ambience: 7, Service: 5, Value for Money: 6, Total: 25
Specialities: Gajar halwa, kaju paan, badam burfi, and pista burfi
Veg/Non-veg: Veg
Contact Details/Timings: New Naresh Sweets, Ratapur Chauraha, Rae Bareli. Phone: 0535-2217318
Prices: Pista burfi ₹ 700 per kg, badam burfi ₹ 500 per kg, kaju paan ₹ 350 per kg

SOMU DA DHABA   Somu da Dhaba is a peaceful and quiet place where families can sit and enjoy their meals in privacy. One can eat in a covered courtyard, centred around an artificial tree, or alternatively in the indoor family rooms. The food is nondescript and nothing worth writing about. At best it is edible and satisfactory.

SOMETHING ON THE SIDE   Uttar Pradesh is a major political state and with the violence connected with politics, safety must always be a consideration when choosing a dhaba. The rooms are an important attraction when you take into account the many 'antisocial' types that you find in dhabas in Uttar Pradesh.

Rocky's Verdict: Eat here only if you must. Very unremarkable.
Rating: Taste: 5, Ambience: 5, Service: 5, Value for Money: 6, Total: 21
Specialities: Stick to the basics like dal and roti.
Veg/Non-veg: Veg
Contact Details/Timings: Somu da Dhaba, Ratapur Chauraha, Rae Bareli.
Prices: ₹ 150 per head

Varanasi

BABU LAL KACHORI WALA   The shop is not even a shop, just a little ledge outside a small temple with a large wok for frying and some large thalis for the prepared food. Piping hot kachoris are served in peepal leaf bowls along with a sweet, fried jalebi and a clay pot full of thick vegetable stew called bhaji.

SOMETHING ON THE SIDE   This place is located in a street called Kachori Wali Gali since at one time all the shops on this street sold kachoris, the name given to the deep-fried wheat flour puris in Benares.

***

Mayur's Verdict: This is an excellent place not just for breakfast but also for people watching. Get your food, sit on a wooden bench, and enjoy a great meal as you watch the teeming hordes go by on their day's work. The food is hot, fresh, and delicious, so go for it!
Rating: Taste: 8, Ambience: 7, Service: 8, Value for Money: 10, Total: 33
Specialities: Kachoris
Veg/Non-veg: Veg
Contact Details/Timings: Babu Lal Kachori Wala, Mandir Chowk, Kachori Wali Gali, Varanasi.
Prices: Kachori ₹ 10 per plate, jalebi ₹ 6 per plate

***

HAIFA RESTAURANT   The American writer Mark Twain wrote, 'Benares is older than history, older than tradition, older even than legend, and looks twice as old as all of them put together.' Benares or Varanasi is said to be one of the oldest continuously inhabited cities in the world, competing with the likes of Middle Eastern cities like Damascus (Syria) and Jericho (Left Bank). What better way to honour this legacy but by going to Benares and eating Middle Eastern cuisine?

Haifa Restaurant located at Assi Ghat specializes in this delicious and nourishing cuisine. Catering mostly to foreign customers visiting Benares, it offers labneh (sour strained yogurt), babaghanoush (mashed aubergine, lemon juice, garlic, olive oil, and various seasonings), hummus (a paste of chickpeas, sesame seeds, lime juice, garlic, and olive oil) and falafel (fried balls made from ground chickpeas and sesame seeds) served with pita bread (wheat bread similar to rotis). The owner takes great pride in his unique offerings and the restaurant caters to those travellers who want a break from the temple food and feel like meeting others of their travelling ilk.

SOMETHING ON THE SIDE The restaurant is situated on the ground floor of a hotel of the same name so you can rent a room and enjoy piping hot and fresh food in your room or go down to eat and chat with other travellers.

Mayur's Verdict: The food was given a thumbs-up by a bunch of visiting Israelis who were eating there so it's not just tasty, it's authentic. If you need a break from Indian food then this is the place to go.
Rating: Taste: 9, Ambience: 7, Service: 8, Value for Money: 8, Total: 32
Specialities: Labneh, babaghanoush, falafel
Veg/Non-veg: Veg
Contact Details/Timings: Haifa Restaurant, Assi Ghat, Varanasi. Phone: 0542-2312960
Prices: Middle Eastern thali ₹ 70, fatoosh ₹ 50, falafel sandwich ₹ 40

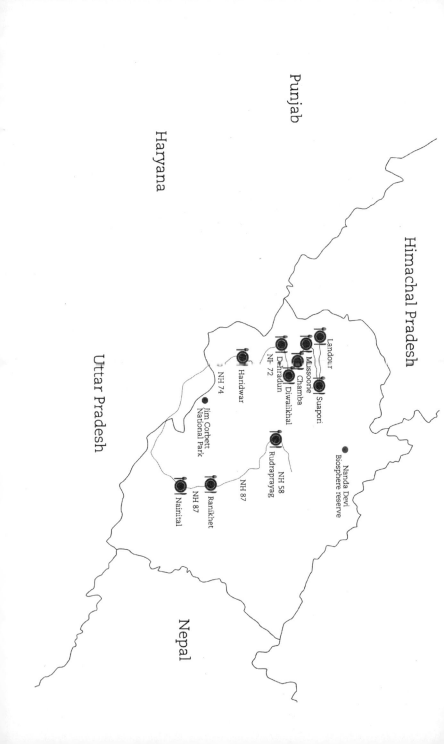

Chamba

SATKAR RESTAURANT The highlights on the Satkar menu are the pakoras, chola bhaturas, and hot parathas. Add to this fresh sweetened and boiled buffalo milk and you have a healthy mountain meal. The parathas are loaded with ajwain (carom seeds) typical to a lot of hill eateries in the north. Everything is served with a lot of butter or ghee. This is not 'light' food. It sits like a stone in your stomach for a few hours after you have eaten, so be a little frugal.

SOMETHING ON THE SIDE There are quite a few little hotels and camps in Chamba where you could spend a few days enjoying the fresh air and watching the rich birdlife. There are plenty of little treks around Chamba and the mighty Tehri dam is close by and worth a visit. You will be astounded by the amount of water it holds. Make sure you try the salads, the fruits, and vegetables in Chamba as they are fresh and organically grown.

Rocky's Verdict: Tasty snacks and the hot sweetened milk is a must-try, especially if you are here in the morning.
Rating: Taste: 5, Ambience: 6, Service: 8, Value for Money: 8, Total: 27
Specialities: Buffalo milk and ajwain parathas
Veg/Non-veg: Veg
Contact Details/Timings: Satkar Restaurant, College Road, Chamba.
Prices: Paratha with choley ₹ 15 and a glass of milk ₹ 8

Dehradun

ELLORA'S BAKERS & CONFECTIONERS Since 1953 this bakery has been a landmark on Rajpur Road and a favourite among generations of locals and the hordes of students studying in the many schools in and around Dehradun. The specialities are the freshly baked cakes and pastries, especially the lemon tarts and rum balls. The choice of biscuits and cookies both sweet and namkeen, and the packets of oily, super salty, super addictive chips are also key attractions.

SOMETHING ON THE SIDE Dehradun was declared the state capital of the new state of Uttarakhand. The resulting growth has been rapid and the city's eateries too have evolved to match the ever- increasing number of customers. The quaint laid-back feel of the town's bakeries has been replaced by the efficient hustle and bustle seen more often in modern Indian metros. The bakeries are still preferred places for a quick snack for the ever-growing populace.

Mayur's Verdict: If you like your sweets to be of the baked, non-mithai kind then this is your spot in Dehradun. If you lived or studied here—hey! You really don't need a recommendation! You know where it is and what it's good for.
Rating: Taste: 8, Ambience: 7, Service: 8, Value for Money: 8, Total: 31
Specialities: Lemon tarts, rum balls, and chips
Veg/Non-veg: Veg/Non-veg. Eggs are used in preparation.
Contact Details/Timings: Ellora's, Rajpur Road, Dehradun.
Prices: Plum cake 160/600 gm, butter pista biscuit ₹ 160 per kg, milk rusk ₹ 34

KUMAR SWEETS Right by the clock tower in what is pretty much the city centre of Dehradun is Kumar Sweets. Thanks to the prime location and the quality and range of its mithais, this is a very popular stop. Mr Kumar, the owner, informed us that of the huge range of sweets they sell the most popular ones are their baal mithai, milk cake, and milk chocolate. They also make an unusual green laddu from lauki (bottle gourd), which is very filling and delicious too. Besides the sweets, the famous 'Kumar ki Kulfi' served with warm rabri and falooda makes for a really sweet and tasty treat.

SOMETHING ON THE SIDE You can also get milkshakes made from whatever fruits are in season.

Mayur's Verdict: If you have a sweet tooth for Indian mithai and you are in Dehradun then Kumar Sweets is well worth a visit. The sweets are all fresh and of excellent quality.
Rating: Taste: 8, Ambience: 5, Service: 7, Value for Money: 7, Total: 27
Specialities: Baal mithai, lauki mithai, and Kumar ki kulfi
Veg/Non-veg: Veg
Contact Details/Timings: Kumar Sweets, Clock Tower, Dehradun. Phone: 0135-2657272/6547272
Prices: Hara laddu ₹ 180 per kg, baal mithai ₹ 180 per kg, milk cake ₹ 190 per kg, milk chocolate ₹ 180 per kg

---

Diwalikhal

JAI MATA DI HOTEL Dhabas and restaurants are few and far in between in the Garhwal hills so you often arrive at an eatery famished and ready to devour whatever is set down in front of you. The food at this hotel is served from behind a waist-high white-tiled counter, which has stacks of shiny bowls and plates on it, and looks quite out of place in these surroundings.

There is no menu and you eat whatever dishes have been cooked for the day. The highlight of the meal is the raiee subzi, which is mildly bitter with a strange and yet pleasing bite that lingers in your mouth especially if you eat the giant leaves raw. Once cooked, every item served has a slightly smoked taste thanks to the wood fires used in cooking and this only adds to the flavour. The food is wholesome and hearty.

SOMETHING ON THE SIDE The rare mountain air always ends up making you feel hungry and yet eating too much is not recommended if you are prone to travel-sickness on winding roads.

> **Mayur's Verdict:** If you are driving down this highway and
> are hungry be sure to stop here because the food is great
> and the next meal might be a long way off.
> **Rating:** Taste: 7, Ambience: 6, Service: 7, Value for Money: 9,
> Total: 29
> **Specialities:** Raiee subzi
> **Veg/Non-veg:** Veg
> **Contact Details/Timings:** Post Marora, Chamoli.
> **Prices:** Mixed dal ₹ 5, garhwali kadi ₹ 5, raiee ki sabzi ₹ 5,
> roti ₹ 3

Haridwar

MATHURA WALON KI PRAACHIN DUKAN This place can
only be accessed by a long walk through an ancient market
full of the colours, smells, and sounds of India. This city's old
quarters are as they might have been a thousand years ago
(barring electricity) and with all its charming distractions it is a
delightful approach to the eatery. At Mathura Walon Ki Praachin
Dukan one can taste the piping hot kaddu ki subzi (pumpkin)
along with a host of other tasty preparations. The family who
owns the shop, cook the food themselves and pay meticulous
attention to each and every item. The taste is spectacular. Puris
in desi ghee, the chandrakala, kachori, samosa, suji halwa, and
the ever-popular puri-subzi (just for ₹ 20!)—this is the place to
get the real taste of holy India.

SOMETHING ON THE SIDE The shop has no shutters and is left
open all night but surprisingly not a single thing ever goes
missing!

> **Rocky's Verdict:** Take the long walk to this place, smell the
> smells, and taste the tastes. The walk will take you to the
> heart of India and the food is incredible.
> **Rating:** Taste: 8, Ambience: 10, Service: 9, Value for
> Money: 10, Total: 37

Specialities: Kaddu ki subzi
Veg/Non-veg: Veg
Contact Details/Timings: Thanda Kuan, Haridwar.
Prices: Puri and kaddu ₹ 20, suji halwa ₹ 100 per kg,
chandrakala ₹ 140 per kg

Landour

TIP TOP TEA SHOP   The menu at Tip Top is geared towards its
primary customers: schoolchildren. Hence everything is sweet,
butter laden and/or fried. The bun omelette is a heavy meal
with fried buns smeared with butter, and even the eggs are
cooked in butter. The French fries are oily and salty as are the
closed cheese and butter toasted sandwiches. A good way to
enjoy a meal here is to wash it down with some hot honey
lemon ginger tea.

SOMETHING ON THE SIDE   The kind owner runs a tab letting
school children buy food on credit and says most are good at
returning the money.

Mayur's Verdict: Enjoy a filling meal sitting at little wooden
benches outside the shop or bask in the sun sitting on
benches in the little gravel park right in front of the shops.
Rating: Taste: 7, Ambience: 8, Service: 7, Value for Money: 7,
Total: 29
Specialities: Bun omelette with honey lemon ginger tea
Veg/Non-veg: Non-veg
Contact Details/Timings: Landour, near St Paul's Church.
Prices: Bun 'n' omlette ₹ 35, cheese butter toast ₹ 30, french
fries ₹ 40, honey lemon ginger tea ₹ 15

Mussoorie

CHICK CHOCOLATE   One step into this shop and a look at the goodies on display at the glass-fronted counter takes you back to your schooldays especially if you studied in one of the numerous schools in Dehradun and Mussoorie. This is a snack food destination, supplying schoolkids and visitors with a range of tinned foods like jams, peanut butter, condensed milk, along with their famous home-made chocolates, ice creams, imported chocolates, chewing gum, candy, and so on. If you are looking for something more filling you will also find grilled sandwiches, sausages, chicken nuggets, pizzas, pastas, eggs, juices, and more.

The pizzas, both vegetarian and chicken, are served hot with generous amounts of toppings of vegetables and meat and have a great, cheesy, home-made taste to them. The hot dog is great with fresh buns and a sizzling hot sausage best eaten with lots of mustard smeared on. No matter what you eat make sure it's accompanied by creamy, sweet cold coffee served in vintage stout glass bottles. The garlic bread is served hot with the cheese still bubbling. The vegetarian salad is very creamy and is served in a cabbage leaf so it looks as well as tastes good.

The signature dish is the Chick Chocolate developed by the owner Naresh and his wife Neelam. It is a dark chocolate brownie topped with vanilla ice cream, chocolate ice cream, chocolate syrup, and chocolate chips.

SOMETHING ON THE SIDE   Ask any student or school going kid for immediate directions to this iconic place. Enjoy the film posters that line the wall especially of the James Bond movies series.

Mayur's Verdict: Chick Chocolate is a must-visit if you are walking the Mall in Mussoorie. The softy ice cream and the Belgian-style chocolates are a must-try and you can always pack a few to carry home some memories.

Rating: Taste: 8, Ambience: 8, Service: 8, Value for Money: 7, Total: 31
Specialities: Chick chocolate
Veg/Non-veg: Non-veg
Contact Details/Timings: Mall Road, Kulri, Mussoorie.
Phone: 91-135-2632887, 10 am to 11 pm
Prices: Non-veg pizza (medium) ₹ 160, veg pizza (medium) ₹ 130, cold coffee ₹ 35, chick chocolate ₹ 95, veg salad ₹ 110.

Nainital

MAMU'S NAINI SWEETS A large shop by hill standards this is a popular breakfast joint for desi breakfasts in Nainital. Mr Bisht, the owner, will declare to you how people have been referring to him as 'Mamu' ever since the popular Bollywood film *Munna Bhai MBBS* was released. The place is famous for its best-selling item—baal mithai. The other famous items are the sweet samosas and the laddu made with fenugreek. The laddu has pepper, cardamom, clove, and a whole lot of other spices and is rumoured to heat you up.

SOMETHING ON THE SIDE Away from the crowds on the Mall, Nainital still retains that old, small hill town feel. It's a pleasure to walk these lanes early in the morning. Grab a hot cup of tea or a freshly baked bread.

Rocky's Verdict: You must try the baal mithai, sweet samosa, and methi ka laddu—it's a part of your quintessential hill holiday.
Rating: Taste: 7, Ambience: 6, Service: 7, Value for Money: 8, Total: 28
Specialities: Baal mithai, methi ka laddu, and sweet samosa
Veg/Non-veg: Veg
Contact Details/Timings: Mamu's Naini Sweets, Bara Bazar, Mallital, Nanital.
Prices: Baal mithai ₹ 160 per kg, methi laddu ₹ 180 per kg, and desi ghee ki jalebi ₹ 185 per kg

Ranikhet

BABA SWEETS & CHAAT Famous all over Ranikhet for its mouth-watering samosas, Baba Sweets is now run by the grandson of the original owner and samosa expert Dhol Singh. The shop also sells a whole range of traditional sweets including the local baal mithai along with other hot ready-to-go snacks like aloo tikki, papri chaat, and dahi bhallas.

The star of the show though is the hot samosa prepared right in front of you. As you watch with keen anticipation the flattened dough is moulded into triangular samosa shapes, filled with hot masala consisting of potatoes, green peas, onions and a lot of spices, and then dropped straight into a wok of boiling oil resulting in a delicious aroma that permeates the whole restaurant.

Samosas are served on a plate filled with masala chole and side dishes of green chutney, imli chutney, and fresh yogurt. The samosas are soft, tender and the blend of spices in the masala explodes in your mouth with every bite.

SOMETHING ON THE SIDE A morning visit to Baba Sweets is highly recommended for a great start to the day. Enjoy the view both inside—with mounds of samosas piled up in enticing heaps—and outside with a great panorama of snow-clad mountains in the distance.

Mayur's Verdict: Freshly fried samosas fly off the counter, so a morning visit to Baba Sweets is highly recommended for a great start to the day.
Ratings: Taste: 8, Ambience: 8, Service: 8, Value for Money: 10 ,Total: 34
Certified: Rocky and Mayur rating of excellence
Specialities: Samosa chole
Veg/Non-veg: Veg
Contact Details/Timings: Baba Sweets, Sadar Bazar, Ranikhet.
Prices: Samosa chole ₹ 12, tikki chole ₹ 12 , baal mithai ₹ 120 per kg

---

BHAGAT CHAAT BHANDAR Bhagat Chaat serves hot samosas and tikkis with the obligatory sides of chole, green and imli chutneys, and fresh dahi. The dishes are all served piping hot along with hot, milky chai served in colourful ceramic mugs. The tastiest dish served here is the chole accompanying the samosa or tikki, which makes your eyes water with its spiciness and your mouth water with its taste.

SOMETHING ON THE SIDE This chaat shop is a favourite judging by the number of customers hanging around the shop passing the time of day and teasing the owner who is referred to as 'Panditji' by everyone .

Mayur's Verdict: Visit Bhagat Chaat Bhandar to enjoy some hot snacks and tea chats with the friendly locals about local legends.
Rating: Taste: 7, Ambience: 8, Service: 7, Value for Money: 8, Total: 30
Specialities: Samosa and tikki with chole
Veg/Non-veg: Veg
Contact Details/Timings: Bhagat Chaat, Sadar Bazar, Ranikhet.
Prices: Both samosa and tikki chole ₹ 12 per dish

CHOTIWALA As you cross the Ram Jhula over the holy Ganges you start getting caught up by the magic of this holy land. Temples, incense, and holy men abound. The air itself is full of history, but sadly good food at Chotiwala is history too.

This place is possibly the most famous eatery in the state and boasts of having served 50,00,000 customers since it started in 1958. The food served today, however, does not live up to the reputation. The two brothers who started it put in their best, and a legend was born. Now the new generation has divided the place into two different Chotiwalas, and they both serve terrible food. Indifferent thalis, cold food, and poor preparations are all we got. There are air-conditioned rooms to eat in, fancy menus, and items from different cuisines to be had, but sadly the food does not live up to the hype.

SOMETHING ON THE SIDE As you walk up the first thing you see are the two pink painted 'Chotiwala' babas. These two pink coloured gentlemen bless people, and serve as living advertisements for the restaurants.

Rocky's Verdict: Avoid eating here. Take your pictures with the Chotiwala babas at the entrance and move on.
Rating: Taste: 3, Ambience: 6, Service: 6, Value for Money: 3, Total: 18
Specialities: Thalis and puri chole
Veg/Non-veg: Veg
Contact Details/Timings: Chotiwala Restaurant, Swargashram, Near Ram Jhula, Rishikesh, Uttarakhand.
Prices: Gujarati thali ₹ 85, south Indian and bengali thalis ₹ 55

Rudraprayag

SETHI'S PANJABI RESTAURANT In a largely vegetarian town, Sethi's with its delicious mutton and chicken dishes has garnered quite a reputation. Apart from the mutton curry and chicken curry which are both very good there is also the raiee ki subzi, a dish made with the local leaf, and usually accompanied with potatoes. Try the local kulaat ki kadhi made with yogurt, spices, and urad dal.

Old favourites like rajma and baingan ka bharta are also delicious and the best part is that they are served piping hot with fresh rotis or rice. The flavours are bold and strong and this is great for a good lunch or dinner.

SOMETHING ON THE SIDE The holy town of Rudraprayag is named after Lord Shiva (Rudra) and is the site where the Alaknanda river meets the Mandakini. This is also the area where the famous man eater of Rudraprayag operated for ten years. The leopard, possibly the most famous man-eating leopard in history was reputed to have killed 125 people before it was shot dead by Jim Corbett.

Rocky's Verdict: The food is tasty and piping hot and when you're cold, nothing is better. Eat it on the spot though.
Rating: Taste: 8, Ambience: 6, Service: 10, Value for Money: 6, Total: 30
Specialities: Raiee ki subzi, mutton curry, and chicken curry
Veg/Non-veg: Non-veg
Contact Details/Timings: Sethi Restaurant, NH 58, Rudraprayag.
Prices: Mutton and chicken curry ₹ 80 each and raiee ki subzi ₹ 20

Suapori

FOOD SHOPS   As you drive towards Mussoorie from Dhanaulti, 10 km short of Mussoorie you will come to a small place called Suapori. The most popular dish here is instant noodles but you can also dig your teeth into some tasty and hot pakoras. There are six or seven little food shops here and all are as good or as bad as the other.

SOMETHING ON THE SIDE   You will get a bus or taxi to go to almost any part of the surrounding hills if you stay here long enough. This is mostly a stop to pick up or drop off passengers for hill vehicles.

Rocky's Verdict: Stop only if you're dying of hunger.
Rating: Taste: 5, Ambience: 6, Service: 6, Value for Money: 8, Total: 25.
Specialities: Pakoras and maggi noodles
Veg/Non-veg: Veg
Contact Details/Timings: All over Suapori
Prices: Pakoras ₹ 20 per plate, maggi ₹ 20

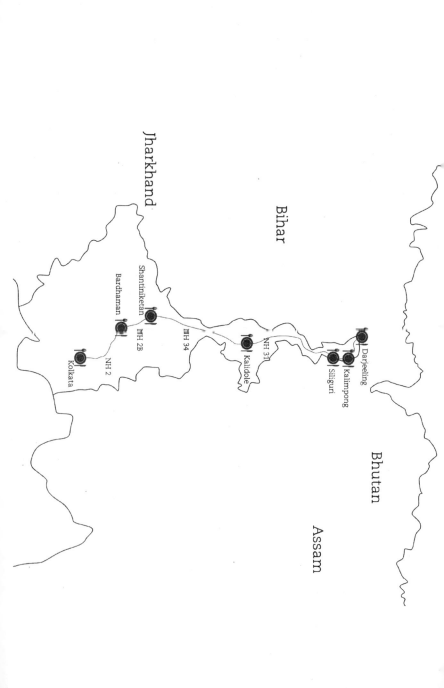

Bardhaman

HOTEL BURDWAN   Stop by the highway at this small thatch-roofed hotel and ask for the dish of the day. The dark, smoky kitchen with a barred window almost brings to mind a prison but the eating area with thatched walls and comfortable, brightly coloured metal charpais informs you of its true nature. Dishes once ordered are prepared fresh in giant kadhais over a jet flame and served piping hot.

The cardamom-flavoured mutton curry here is extremely spicy and yet sweet thanks to lots of sugar, which makes for an interesting dish. The rui macher jhol with chunks of fish including the fish heads is nothing special and the gravy is a mishmash of flavours. The jhada puna fish is cooked for a long time and is succulent with the flavour of freshly ground mustard paste which is also the base for the paneer butter masala, which is golden in colour and precious in taste. The tasty egg tadka is a curious dish made from scrambled egg mixed with dal and then pan-fried.

SOMETHING ON THE SIDE   Enjoy a game or two of carom with the local lads playing on a board placed right outside the dhaba. Make sure you understand the local rules or get a pasting like we did ☺

Mayur's Verdict: Stop at this little eatery if you are very hungry and enjoy the feel of a dhaba in West Bengal.
Rating: Taste: 7, Ambience: 6, Service: 5, Value for Money: 5, Total: 23
Specialities: Jhada puna fish and the egg tadka
Veg/Non-veg: Non-veg
Contact Details/Timings: Hotel Burdwan and Restaurant, Rasoolpur, NH 2.
Prices: Mutton curry ₹ 125, rui macher jhol ₹ 30, jhada puna fish ₹ 50, paneer butter masala ₹ 90, and egg tadka ₹ 25

Darjeeling

GLENARY'S The place is owned and run by the charming Boney Edwards. Glenary's was started in 1915 by an Italian gentleman and was called Wado's. It then took on a German partner and became Wado and Brieva's. In about the 1940s it became Glenary's. As you enter you are greeted by that incredible bakery aroma and a well-lit and tastefully decorated interior. The bakery counter is the centre focus, and on one side there are a few tables in case you wish to sit and eat your goodies there or have a cup of coffee while looking at a view of the mountains.

Walk in and choose from muffins and cakes from a range of cherry, banana, walnut, etc. There are breads, sausage rolls, and even liquor chocolates and spicy pickles. There are brownies and pastries as well. The coconut cookies are great and the rum balls are fun and fresh. There is artwork up on the wall and even a small Internet café counter for patrons. The place has a laid-back and old-world charm and will relax you on those cold Darjeeling evenings. There is an old English-style red telephone booth in one corner adding to the feel of the place. There is a pub and a restaurant here as well.

SOMETHING ON THE SIDE Right opposite it are small stalls selling everything from handkerchiefs to smuggled Chinese electronics and seem to be the favourite 'time pass' for people in Darjeeling. You can find some unique little trinkets here, so take the walk.

Rocky's Verdict: Get in here and eat all you can for a taste of that old-time goodness left in very few places in this country. The meat pies and coconut cookies are recommended.
Rating: Taste: 8, Ambience: 8, Service: 9, Value for Money: 9, Total: 34
Specialities: Meat pie and cookies
Veg/Non-veg: Non-veg

Contact Details/Timings: Open from 7 am to 9 pm every day. Glenary's, Nehru Road, Darjeeling.
Prices: Lemon tarts ₹ 14, jam toast ₹ 14, meat pies ₹ 15, pastries ₹ 8 to ₹ 20

HOT STIMULATING CAFÉ This café serves burgers, noodles, fries, and momos, all of which are vegetarian because he feels it is easy to digest and healthier too. Sit down on wooden benches at square tables and wonder why the wooden walls are painted purple or relax at a table in the little balcony with amazing views of the valley and Darjeeling town as a cool breeze washes over you.

Thick pancakes cooked till brown and served with honey smeared over them are a treat and best had both before and after the meal. Steaming hot thukpa and steamed momos full of fresh vegetables leave you feeling filled, healthy, and full of beans. The chilli momo sauce is thick, red, and fiery so those of you with mild tastes beware. Enjoy the local wheat and millet beer called tumba, which is served in funky long bamboo mugs. The boiling water poured on top of the fermented grains is sipped through bamboo straws and the experience is as much fun as the taste. The tumba is tangy and fizzy with a sweet aftertaste, and leaves a nice fresh feeling in the mouth and a smile on the face. It is also considered to be very good for purifying the blood and for lactating mothers.

SOMETHING ON THE SIDE This cafe has an owner as interesting as his name, Mr Rhumba. He is a big fan of reggae musician Bob Marley. An entire wall of the cafe in covered with photographs and posters of the legend besides various signs advocating peace, love, and music.

Mayur's Verdict: Smiling owners, wonderful views, cool breeze, soft reggae music, hot fresh food…need we say more? Don't forget to try the amazing tumba. If you have the time Rhumba's lovely wife will give you momo making lessons too.
Rating: Taste: 7, Ambience: 10, Service: 8, Value for Money: 9, Total: 34
Certified: Rocky and Mayur rating of excellence
Specialities: Tumba
Veg/Non-veg: Veg
Contact Details/Timings: Perched on a hillside on a quiet road just down from the Darjeeling Zoo. Hot Stimulating Café, Hooker Street, Darjeeling.
Prices: Thick pancakes ₹ 34, hot thukpa, and steamed momos both priced at ₹ 25. Cost for one ₹ 100

KEVENTERS This is an old favourite for locals and tourists and an unforgettable part of growing up for all students who have studied in the many good schools around Darjeeling. The place started as a dairy and has grown into one of the best breakfast places in India. Owned and run by the articulate and energetic Mr R.N. Jha the place was started in 1905 by a Swedish gentleman called Mr Edward Keventer. It was then taken over by Indian ownership and is now owned by Mr Jha.

Every tourist that comes here visits Keventers at least once and this is why the breakfast is awesome. The menu is very interesting and has on it a Keventers menu from 1966–7. You can compare how the rates have changed since the items on the menu are mostly still the same. The smoked sausages were for ₹ 8 per kg in 1966 and today they are for ₹ 200 per kg. The rest of the items have gone up accordingly. Interestingly, a few favourites from 1966 like the tongue and the kidney have gone off the menu. Cold coffee is served in tiny bottles that have been the same since the 1970s. Chicken ham, cheese, bacon, fried eggs, baked beans and toast, pork salami, pork sausage, and the Chinese sausage are all incredibly good. All the meats and the cold cuts are of the finest quality and taste and make for a hearty English breakfast. There are also veggie burgers, sandwiches, and all the yummy stuff that you would associate with a self-respecting hill place.

We recommend that you sit out in the veranda on the first floor and enjoy the view of the Kanchenjunga. The shop itself is kept spick and span by a knowledgeable and committed staff and they will also cook up and heat items for you to eat. It is now also a bakery, provision store, snack shop, and stops just short of being a restaurant.

SOMETHING ON THE SIDE Once a quiet little town, Darjeeling has become a tourist hub for this region. The narrow streets are not prepared for the traffic they see and even in the off season it is hard to find parking in most areas. The townspeople are trying hard to sort out the huge mess Darjeeling turns into come tourist season. Be ready for major jams and loud horns when you get here in season.

Rocky's Verdict: Keventers is legendary. Go there any time of the day but one of my favourite meals ever has been the breakfast on the balcony of Keventers. It was delicious and is a must-visit spot for everyone.
Rating: Taste: 9, Ambience: 8, Service: 9, Value for Money: 10, Total: 36
Certified: Rocky and Mayur rating of excellence
Specialities: Hearty breakfast and cold coffee
Veg/Non-veg: Non-veg
Contact Details/Timings: Keventers, Nehru Road, Darjeeling.
Prices: Cold coffee ₹ 16, Chinese sausages ₹ 70, cheese toast ₹ 22, smoked sausages ₹ 200 per kg

---

TEA ESTATES The little town of Darjeeling is known around the world for its most famous produce, tea. The climate and gentle undulating hills of Darjeeling are ideally suited for growing this bush. Some of the tea plants here are over 100 years old. They remain about waist high as the top three leaves are plucked and used for tea thus restricting the growth of the plant. There are many types of tea and one of the best is the 'silver tip' tea. So called because to gather this, only the tip of the central bud is plucked from the plant, the bud has a soft silvery hue around it and hence it is called the silver tip.

A visit to these tea estates will allow you to buy even as little as 50 gm of tea at a time allowing you to taste the best. Head out in any direction in Darjeeling and you will find tea gardens, go into any tourist travel agency and they will set up a visit and tasting for you close by. It's an experience of a lifetime so try and do this at least once.

SOMETHING ON THE SIDE The Makaibari Tea Estate in Darjeeling has what is possibly the most expensive tea in the world called the 'Silver Tips Imperial' and sells for US$400 per kg which is almost ₹ 20,000 per kg! We cannot tell you what it tastes like as we cannot afford it but reputedly it is one of the finest teas in the world.

Rocky's Verdict: I like tea. Would I pat ₹ 20,000 for a kilo. NO. Do I understand it when people do that? I TRY.
Specialities: Silver tip tea
Veg/Non-veg: Veg
Contact Details/Timings: All over Darjeeling.
Prices: ₹ 20 per kg and up to ₹ 20,000 per kg

Kalidole

DURGA DHABA Straw walls and a thatched roof, two feet wide small clear stream flowing in front of it, and a table for four is all this dhaba is made up of. Durga Dhaba sits in the gentle shade of trees that grow all along the highways. Muri and ghugni was what we had for breakfast. That was all that was available. We also managed to dig out some biscuits and bread to go with our breakfast. Fish heads (₹ 40) are popular and some were left over from the day before but we gave those a miss. Muri is puffed rice heated with mustard oil along with onions, some tomato and coriander, and a generous amount of spicy chilli powder. Ghugni is made with white peas and spiced up with onions, tomatoes, ginger, garlic, and cumin. Served hot after cooking, it is a great snack to have along with some pav. The standard of it remains high across Bengal. Eat it anywhere and it should be pretty good.

SOMETHING ON THE SIDE Bengalis love their snacks and ghugni is usually served as a late breakfast or evening snack.

Rocky's Verdict: Cleanliness is an issue as are insects and small animals in these dhabas along this stretch. We recommend packed food unless you are brave enough to eat this. It is quite tasty if you are so inclined.
Rating: Taste: 7, Ambience: 9, Service: 5, Value for Money: 10, Total: 31
Specialities: Muri and ghugni
Veg/Non-veg: Non-veg
Contact Details/Timings: Durga Dhaba, Kalidole, Shantiniketan Maldah Road.
Prices: Muri ₹ 12, ghugni ₹ 5, and fish heads ₹ 40

Kalimpong

LARK'S PROVISION This popular store has been a mainstay in the Kalimpong market for over thirty-five years and is one of the better known vendors of the famous Kalimpong chocolate lollipops and cheese. There are only three to four places left around in the area that are still producing the cheese and the chocolate lollipops. These are former employees of the dairy though many imitators have come into the market especially for the chocolate lollipops where they now use Dalda (refined oil) and milk powder instead of ghee and fresh milk.

SOMETHING ON THE SIDE Cheese and chocolate lollipops were first produced at the Swiss Welfare Dairy set up in the 1950s by a Swiss priest who presented cows to locals and then bought milk from them to produce his products.

Mayur's Verdict: Neither the lollipops nor the cheese are remarkable in taste and if you do shop it will be more for the novelty than for the taste.
Rating: Taste: 6, Ambience: 6, Service: 8, Value for Money: 8, Total: 28
Specialities: Kalimpong chocolate lollipops and cheese
Veg/Non-veg: Veg
Contact Details/Timings: Lark's Provision, Sahid DB Giri Road, Kalimpong.
Prices: Chocolate lollipops ₹ 40 a packet

Kolkata

BEIJING BAR AND RESTAURANT   This is one of many swank newly done up Chinese food places in Tangra. The owner Monica, a second-generation Chinese, is a focused business lady and usually mills around the restaurant taking care of the customers.

Start with the soups, we went with the hot 'n' sour and the lung fung soup. Typically 'Indian Chinese' in their taste this is a taste that has evolved and is not quite Chinese (although it comes close) and far from Indian but it now lies at a very tasty place somewhere in between. The favourites are the mixed vegetable with bok choy, chicken in black bean sauce, golden fried prawns, the sweet vegetarian delight, the ever popular chilli chicken, and fried tofu with chilli garlic.

SOMETHING ON THE SIDE   There was a large Chinese population here who worked mainly at the leather tanning industry. Places that started as small shacks serving Chinese snacks to the workers evolved and grew and soon turned into these quaint Chinese restaurants.

Rocky's Verdict: A little bit of history can be had when you come to Tangra. The Chinese food places and the narrow streets lit up by Chinese lanterns are a great way to spend

an evening. It is not very exciting at lunch, night is definitely better.
Rating: Taste: 8, Ambience: 8, Service: 9, Value for Money: 8, Total: 33
Specialities: An evolved version of Chinese food.
Veg/Non-veg: Non-veg
Contact Details/Timings: Beijing Bar and Restaurant, New Tangra, Christopher Road, Kolkata.
Prices: ₹ 250 per head, golden fried prawns ₹ 510, and fried tofu with chilli garlic ₹ 180

KC DAS This is the home of the rasgulla (or rosogolla as it is pronounced in Kolkata) and it was here that it was first made in 1868 by a twenty-two-year-old Navin Chandra Das. Fifty years later his son Krishna Chandra Das made the rasmalai. You will rarely find a sweet shop that has got so many brilliantly made sweets down to pat. This place is always teeming with customers who come in to buy and stand around to taste before they leave. Brightly lit and with a few tables in a corner you can stand and try the goodies. They also have a rather plain and basic art collection up on the walls which can be purchased if you are so inclined.

The mishtidoi or sweetened yogurt is an old stalwart and is an 'eat it any time' kind of item. The prices belong to another era and are unbeatable in today's day and age. They even have a range for diabetics, the raitakti. The khir kadam here is spectacular and a must-buy. It is a mini rosogolla covered with a sweetened khoya layer and it is delightful at KC Das. The best we ever had. This place is a must-visit and you need to come in here, sit and eat as many of the treats as you can in lieu of a meal. That is the only way to do it justice and to hell with the sugar rush that will follow. The sugar content though, is fairly low as compared to most other sweet shops as sugar is added to all mithai so that they may have a longer shelf life. The items at KC Das though move fast and therefore are delicately made with less sugar. There is a lot of history and many stories around KC Das. Most patrons will be happy to share some with you.

SOMETHING ON THE SIDE One of the more interesting items is 'lady kenny' developed to honour Lady Canning, wife of India's Governor General Charles Canning.

Rocky's Verdict: A stalwart, one of those rare places that have maintained standards for decades. A place of innovation and quality and a must-visit.
Certified: Rocky and Mayur rating of excellence
Rating: Taste: 9, Ambience: 8, Service: 8, Value for Money: 10, Total: 35
Specialities: Rosogolla and multiple other sweets
Veg/Non-veg: Veg
Contact Details/Timings: KC Das, Esplanade (E) Road, Kolkata.
Prices: Rosogolla ₹ 3 a piece, lady kenny ₹ 6 a piece, kesar rasmalai ₹ 8 a piece, and raitakti ₹ 10 a piece

---

NIZAMS RESTAURANT The restaurant opened in 1932 and started serving the hugely popular kathi kebabs, which most will claim were invented right here. The place itself is right next to a speaker's corner where loud and fiery speeches continue late into the night on blaring loudspeakers. It is a simple basic place, has a few tables packed in and has brightly lit yellow walls. The emphasis is on the kathi kebabs. These are prepared in the other half of the restaurant and you can see them getting done through a glass window. It is mostly for takeaway orders though some foodies will sit and eat the kathis on the spot.

The kathi is a maida roti shallow fried, usually with an egg which is used to wrap some chicken, paneer, or mutton tikkas and is then served with onions and spicy mint chutney. Simple as it may sound this is a powerhouse snack and easily substitutes for a meal. Cooked in Dalda the mutton kathi is a heavy and filling snack and can be made heavier by opting for a double mutton option in which you will get twice the filling. It is eminently edible and order more than you think you can eat or you will regret it later. This is a hearty and cheap snack and in case you have not tried it, you are missing out so get here if you are ever in Kolkata.

SOMETHING ON THE SIDE Enjoy your roll on the street while watching someone air their views from a podium to anyone who cares to listen during a public speaking demonstration that happen spontaneously in Kolkata.

Rocky's Verdict: Since this is where kathis were invented, it is a must-visit place. The kathi is as good as any you can think of.
Rating: Taste: 8, Ambience: 5, Service: 8, Value for Money: 9, Total: 30
Specialities: Kathi rolls
Veg/Non-veg: Non-veg
Contact Details/Timings: Nizams Restaurant, Hogs Street, Kolkata.
Prices: ₹ 20 for a paneer roll, ₹ 26 for a mutton roll, double mutton double egg ₹ 58.

SURUCHI The menu at this famous eatery changes every day and both vegetarian and non-vegetarian dishes are served here. The interior of the restaurant is tastefully decorated and the seating is very simple with rows of tables lining the walls and food served in simple and spotlessly clean stainless steel utensils.

The emphasis here is on the various fish and seafood delicacies though there are some interesting vegetarian items. The chingdi patodi or prawns, marinated in coconut and khus khus paste and then steamed in mustard oil while wrapped in a banana leaf, is a delectable dish with the sweet flavours complementing the delicate flesh of the prawns. The banana leaf gives the dish a faint musky, smoky scent that adds to the taste. The pabda, a freshwater fish, cooked whole in spicy pabda jhal (mustard gravy) after smearing with turmeric and salt is luscious tasting. The hilsa bhapa or steamed hilsa fish though prized for its taste has to be eaten carefully because of the multitude of spines/bones. The trick is to learn to put a whole piece into your mouth and then separate the flesh from the fish. The delicate flavour of the fish seeps into the shorsher (mustard) gravy and one bite will be sufficient to understand why this fish is legendary in Bengal and beyond. The manshor jhol (mutton curry) is extremely spicy and tantalizingly flavourful, cooked and served with a whole potato sliced in half. The flavour of note in most dishes is mustard thanks to the freshly ground mustard paste used in most gravies.

The vegetarian thali has mashoor daal, aloo bhaja, bandha gobhi (cabbage), phool gobhi, and thod, which is the core of the banana tree stem, cooked as a subzi. These are eaten with rice or with hot, crisp, and fluffy lucchis (puris) that release clouds of aromatic steam as you break into them. The karaishutir kochuri, with pea paste stuffed into a puri, is a meal by itself and a delicious one at that. Every item is tantalizingly spiced and each bite is a warm invitation to the next.

SOMETHING ON THE SIDE Starting as a small shop named Misthano Bhandar in 1969, Suruchi, which means 'good taste', is now a full-fledged restaurant serving authentic Bengali cuisine. It provides a livelihood and earns revenue for the destitute women and orphaned girls that live and study here.

Mayur's Verdict: A fantastic eatery where you can enjoy truly authentic, traditional, mouth-watering, finger-licking food. You can also take satisfaction in the fact that your custom is helping provide funds for the rehabilitation of the women and girls that live here. Do not leave Kolkata without eating at Suruchi is our strongest possible recommendation.
Rating: Taste: 9, Ambience: 10, Service: 9, Value for Money: 10, Total: 38
Certified: Rocky and Mayur rating of excellence
Specialities: Traditional Bengali cuisine
Veg/Non-veg: Non-veg
Contact Details/Timings: Suruchi, All Bengal Women's Union, Elliot Road, Kolkata.

> **Prices:** Vegetarian thali ₹ 60, pabda ₹ 95 per piece, and hilsa bhapa ₹ 86 per piece

Shantiniketan

KALA BHAWAN This is a college canteen with a difference. It is open for all comers as long as it does not run out of food. The place is legendary as it once served the likes of Rabindranath Tagore and Amartya Sen amongst others. It is basic in the extreme. There are rows of simple wooden benches, sit on one and eat off another is the norm. The walls are whitewashed with lime and a few paintings are etched on them. The overall impression is of a place that must once have been grand but is now just going through the motions.

Buy a ticket at the entrance which entitles you to a thali-style meal. The meal is tasty, the dal though is a little watery; it also has fresh beans cooked in mustard oil and a tasty potato curry. The thali comes with rice and for non-vegetarians there is usually egg curry and the ever-present macher jhol or fish curry and rice. At the end of the meal make sure to have the incredible tea. It was truly outstanding and we had about five cups each. It is a sweetened ginger tea without milk and it is good. Be warned the cups are tiny and not regular sized.

SOMETHING ON THE SIDE Once you are done with the meal step out of the university complex and cross the road to Kalo Dokan, a meeting place or an adda where students once sat and discussed important things like freedom from British rule, the type of government that was needed once the British left and then followed through with their plans. This place serves as an ideal for those who want to make a difference in the world. It is a little shack with a thatched wooden roof that is almost always closed. Sit here and have a cup of tea and think back to how much history and what discussions this humble shack must have witnessed.

Rocky's Verdict: Baul singers are everywhere and the Vishwa Bharati University is a must-visit if you are ever in Shantiniketan. Not so much for the food, more for the history.
Rating: Taste: 5, Ambience: 5, Service: 3, Value for Money: 10, Total: 23
Specialities: The thali changes daily. Students say the fish is always good.
Veg/Non-veg: Non-Veg
Contact Details/Timings: Kala Bhawan, Vishwa Bharati University, Shantiniketan.
Prices: Vegetarian ₹ 20, non-vegetarian ₹ 30, and tea ₹ 2

Siliguri

KALPANA PICE HOTEL Situated in a narrow street with a grille front and a curtained doorway this eatery proudly displays photographs of its famous visitors including Lata Mangeshkar, Mithun Chakraborty, Sourav Ganguly, and other Bengali celebrities. Started forty years ago Kalpana is famous for its fish preparations and even has a specialist for cooking their signature dish of chital fish. The walls are decorated with framed images of religious deities and the seating is arranged in rows to maximize space in the small area. The kitchen is in another room at the back and sends out tempting aromas to accompany the noise of busy cooks.

The chital patty, cooked to a soft, fleshy texture, and floating in a bed of oil tinted red by the chillies, has a very strong taste that permeates even into the gravy. If you are not a fan of fishy tastes then you might want to focus on the chingdi malai. This is a delectable, creamy dish with whole prawns deep fried before cooking in gravy that has a hint of coconut. The dal and gobhi mattar masala eaten along with the rice are mediocre at best and proof that this hotel caters to lovers of all things fish. The mishtidoi, served in clay pots, is a real winner though and a must-try.

SOMETHING ON THE SIDE We discovered that the 'pice' in the name comes from the fact that dishes costed a 'pice (paisa) or two' when the eatery had first started.

Mayur's Verdict: The fish and prawn dishes make this hotel a worthwhile visit though vegetarians should not expect a life-changing experience. The people are very friendly so take some time out to chat and learn. We discovered that fish from Bihar is prized for its great quality and that the head of the prawn is an unusually tasty morsel.
Rating: Taste: 8, Ambience: 6, Service: 7, Value for Money: 6, Total: 27
Specialities: Fish and mishtidoi
Veg/Non-veg: Non-veg
Contact Details/Timings: Kalpana Pice Hotel, Bidhan Market, Siliguri.
Prices: Chital patty ₹ 300, chingdi malai ₹ 150, and mishtidoi ₹ 20

NETAJI'S CABIN Welcome to the 'adda' or chat central. This legendary hangout is famous for its chai, bread, and omelettes. It's small, it's old, it's smoky with stained walls, and it's very popular. People of all ages, sex, and sizes gather in groups at tables to enjoy thick slices of lavishly buttered bread (sweet or salted) dipped in hot chai. The bread is toasted over a bed of glowing coals, on what looks like a piece of the window grille, giving it a yummy smoky, almost charred flavour. Its also great fun to watch the tea being prepared with foamed milk poured at great speed into rows of white chai cups.

SOMETHING ON THE SIDE We never did figure out the reason for the name but it is a great feeling to think that you are sipping chai where Netaji Subhash Chandra Bose might have sat while discussing freedom for India.

Mayur's Verdict: A must-visit if you ask us. Sit at one of the few tables that stand on the street and enjoy a snack, a chat and a relaxed cuppa as you watch the world go by.
Rating: Taste: 8, Ambience: 8, Service: 8, Value for Money: 8, Total: 32
Specialities: Tea and buttered bread
Veg/Non-veg: Serves eggs
Contact Details/Timings: Opposite Kalpana Pice Hotel, Netaji's Cabin, Bidhan Market, Siliguri.
Prices: Average meal ₹ 20 per person

TRIVENI POINT/CONFLUENCE POINT Stop at the high viewpoint on the way to Kalimpong with magnificent views of a meeting point called Triveni. Here the Teesta River (the name means 'wait for me') and Rangeet River (meaning 'the colourful song') come together in a beautiful medley of colours surrounded by stretches of pebble beaches. Vendors sit here selling packaged namkeen, roasted chana (gram), chocolates, fizzy soft drinks, and bottled water to tourists that invariably stop by for a look-see.

Mayur's Verdict: Surprise surprise! It is not always about the food (almost always but not always). Stop here and feast your eyes and soothe your soul as you listen to birdsong and enjoy the cool air and the amazing eagle's eye view.
Rating: Taste: 6, Ambience: 10, Service: 6, Value for Money: 8, Total: 30
Specialities: Roasted chanas.
Veg/Non-veg: Veg
Contact Details/Timings: Triveni Point, NH 31A, Near Kalimpong.
Prices: MRP

Note on Authors

Mayur believes that life is about finding your special gift and sharing it with the world. He has played, worked, and travelled across sixty-five countries in five continents and is always looking for new adventures at home, work, and in the fridge ☺ Mayur is based in Delhi where he loves playing happy home with his wife Michelle and daughter Amaya. He loves red wine, paneer, ice cream, and gaajar halwa all of which taste best when shared with someone. An avid bookworm, wildlife enthusiast, passionate rock climber, and mountain trekker, Mayur is always ready to dive into anything for a laugh.

'Make food not war' is the mantra that drives Rocky Singh. His passion for Indian street food has taken him across the country and the world. He spent five years travelling through India's amazing foodscape for pleasure and another four for *Highway on my Plate*. A junior national hockey player, state level boxer, and footballer he now scuba dives across the globe and indulges in his passion for street food and travel. He lives in Delhi with his wife, daughter, and son. He believes that life, like food is best when it's shared. So pass around some love and joy! He always comes back for seconds ☺